THE
ECONOMICS
OF
GLOBAL
CLIMATIC
CHANGE

THE
ECONOMICS
OF
GLOBAL
CLIMATIC
CHANGE

P. K. RAO

M.E. Sharpe
Armonk, New York
London, England

Library of Congress Cataloging-in-Publication Data

Rao, P. K.
  The economics of global climatic change / P.K. Rao.
    p. cm.
  Includes bibliographical references and index.
  ISBN 0-7656-0460-4 (hc : alk. paper)   ISBN 0-7656-0461-2 (pbk : alk. paper)
  1. Climatic changes—Economic aspects. 2. Climatic changes—International cooperation.
I. Title.
QC981.8.C5R36 2000   99-41507
363.738′74–dc21   CIP

Printed in the United States of America

The paper used in this publication meets the minimum requirements of
American National Standard for Information Sciences
Permanence of Paper for Printed Library Materials.
ANSI Z 39.48-1984.

BM (c) 10 9 8 7 6 5 4 3 2 1
BM (p) 10 9 8 7 6 5 4 3 2 1

To my family

Table of Contents

Preface   xi
List of Abbreviations   xiii
List of Chemical Symbols   xv

Chapter 1: Introduction   **3**
1.1   Historical Perspectives   3
1.2   Svante Arrhenius and Later   7
1.3   About This Book   13
      References   19

Chapter 2: Scientific Background   **21**
2.1   Introduction   21
2.2   Climatic Renewal and Change   22
2.3   The Science of Global Warming   34
2.4   Greenhouse Gases and Global Warming Potential 37
2.5   The Ozone Factor   41
2.6   The Aerosols Factor   48
2.7   Scientific Uncertainty and Decision Making   49
2.8   Concluding Observations   52
      References   52

Chapter 3: Economic Approaches   **56**
3.1   Introduction   56
3.2   Sustainability and Sustainable Development   57
3.3   Externalities and Transaction Costs   66
3.4   Valuation of Resources and the Environment   67
3.5   Discounting Over Time   73
3.6   The New Green Golden Rule   84

3.7 Economics of Ecotaxes   87
3.8 Economic Policies: Multilevel Approaches   91
3.9 Concluding Observations   94
    References   95
Appendix 3A: Analytics of Low Discount Rates for
             Stochastic Costs   99
Appendix 3B: Optimal Incentives and Disincentives   101

Chapter 4: Economics of the Greenhouse Effect   103
4.1 Introduction   103
4.2 Ecological Economic Aspects   104
4.3 Economics of the Global Warming Potential   106
4.4 Biogeophysical and Public Health Economics   110
4.5 Economic Damage Assessment   113
4.6 Mitigating the Greenhouse Effect and Climatic Changes   118
4.7 Concluding Observations   120
    References   121

Chapter 5: Greenhouse Gas Regimes and Climate Change   124
5.1 Introduction   124
5.2 Climate Stabilization   125
5.3 Greenhouse Gas Reduction and Target Fixation   126
5.4 Market and Nonmarket Policy Instruments   128
5.5 Tradable Permits and Carbon Trade   128
5.6 Carbon Sequestration and Forestry   131
5.7 Cost Effectiveness of Alternatives   133
5.8 Cost Sharing and North–South Issues   134
5.9 Concluding Observations   140
    References   140
Appendix 5A: UN Framework Convention on
             Climate Change Articles   142
Appendix 5B: Kyoto Protocol to the UNFCCC   145

Chapter 6: International Institutional Mechanisms   155
6.1 Introduction   155
6.2 Multilateral Institutions   155
6.3 Joint Implementation and Clean Development
    Mechanisms   157
6.4 Political Economy of Global Environmental Policies   162

6.5 Concluding Observations   163
     References   164

Chapter 7: The Road (or Air) Ahead   **165**
7.1 The Kyoto Protocol and After   165
7.2 New Initiatives and Institutional Mechanisms   166
7.3 Improved Effectiveness of Global Initiatives   168
     References   172

Glossary   173
Web Site Addresses   189
Index   197

List of Tables and Boxes

Tables

2.1 Sources and Sinks Affected by Human Influences   30
2.2 Time Trend of CO_2 Emissions   36

Boxes

2.1 Important Scientific Concepts   25
3.1 Economic Concepts and Definitions   74
4.1 Environment and Health   114
5.1 UNFCCC Article 4 Commitments   136
7.1 Global Climatic Change—Policy Instruments   167

Preface

The state of the science and economics of global climate change has been undergoing rapid transformation, with ever increasing attention to the understanding of the critical issues. Moreover, the theme of global climate change has become a subject for presentation in diverse ways of interpretation, sometimes at odds with each other. Only a few such variations in interpretation have their origins and motivations in self-serving interests; most of the others constitute genuine professional disagreements. This lack of consensus is not to be construed as a sign of weakness or irrelevance within the field of inquiry, especially when it involves continued human survival on planet Earth. In a complex system that governs the global climatic change phenomena, it is feasible that the more we seem to understand, the more we realize what we do not know. This calls to mind the old adage "ignorance is bliss." As such a "bliss" can be full of unwelcome surprises and can also be extremely expensive, we continue to reflect on the imperatives of ever changing earthly factors for sustained survival and quality of life.

This book examines the economic aspects of the dynamics of global climatic changes, with due recognition of the underlying scientific phenomena. The analysis deviates from most studies on the theme in its focus on a comprehensive framework as well as the relative robustness of interpretations. It is not proposed to come up with a single number such as the cost-benefit ratio of avoidance of one degree (on any scale) of temperature change, with little regard to the explicit and implicit assumptions that lead to a real or a fictitious number. It is believed that as long as the quality of input is right, the output is likely to be relevant; if the former is of dubious standing, the latter will have little chance of being relevant.

The text is aimed at a wide readership. Senior policymakers, researchers, graduate and senior undergraduate students will find this text readable and relevant. Given the provisions of scientific foundations, it is also expected that an interdisciplinary focus remains useful for readers who are not entirely grounded in economic studies. A course in economics is generally a useful prerequisite for using this book in advanced courses. Most of the mathematical aspects have been presented in a subdued style so as to enable a larger number of readers to access the contents.

My list of acknowledgments is rather limited. Mr. Sean M. Culhane, economics editor at M.E. Sharpe, has been very enthusiastic in launching and developing this project. Production editor Eileen Maass and copy editor James Tully have made important improvements in the presentation of the contents. My daughter, Uma, has spared considerable time and attention to edit and enhance the quality of the text in many sections of the book. Finally, my wife, Prema, remains an important contributor by supporting my time commitments to this book and to a series of book-related activities.

Abbreviations

AIJ	activities implemented jointly
CBA	cost-benefit analysis
CC	carrying capacity
CDM	clean development mechanism
CE	carbon equivalent
COP	Conference of Parties (to the UNFCCC)
FAO	Food and Agriculture Organization
GE	greenhouse effect
GEF	Global Environmental Facility
GEMs	general equilibrium models
GHG(s)	greenhouse gas(es)
GWP	global warming potential
IBRD	International Bank for Reconstruction and Development
ICSU	International Council of Scientific Unions
IFC	International Finance Corporation
ILO	International Labour Office
IMO	International Maritime Organization
IOC	International Oceanographic Commission
IPCC	Intergovernmental Panel on Climate Change
IUCN	The World Conservation Union
JI	joint implementation
LUCF	land-use change and forestry sector
NGO	nongovernmental organization
NNP	net national product
NPV	net present value
ODA	Official Development Assistance
OECD	Organization for Economic Cooperation and Development

PCSD	President's Council on Sustainable Development
QELROs	Quantified Emissions Limitation and Reduction Objectives
SBCA	social benefit cost analysis
SD	sustainable development
SRTP	social rate of time preference
TEP	tradable emission permit
UN	United Nations
UNCED	UN Conference on Environment and Development
UNDP	United Nations Development Programme
UNEP	United Nations Environment Programme
UNESCO	United Nations Educational Scientific and Cultural Organization
UNFCCC	United Nations Framework Convention on Climate Change
UNICEF	United Nations Children's Fund
USEPA	U.S. Environmental Protection Agency
USGS	U.S. Geological Survey
WCED	World Commission on Environment and Development
WFP	World Food Programme
WHO	World Health Organization
WMO	World Meteorological Organization

Chemical Symbols

CFC	chlorofluorocarbon
CH_4	methane
C_{l2}	molecular chlorine
CO	carbon monoxide
CO_2	carbon dioxide
H_2	molecular hydrogen
HCFC	hydrochlorofluorocarbon
H_2O	water
N_2	molecular (ordinary) nitrogen
N_2O	nitrous oxide
NO	nitric oxide
NO_2	nitrogen dioxide
O	oxygen
O_2	molecular (ordinary) oxygen
O_3	ozone
OH	hydroxyl radical
PFC	perfluorocarbon
SF_6	sulfur hexafluoride
SO_2	sulfur dioxide

THE
ECONOMICS
OF
GLOBAL
CLIMATIC
CHANGE

Chapter 1

Introduction

1.1 Historical Perspectives

The phenomena of climatic variations observed during the past century can be deemed insignificant if we weigh these on the geological time scales of several hundreds of millions of years in relation to the life of planet Earth. This is because periodic (where the time periods involved are on the order of a few million years or several thousands of years, and the periodicity itself is unknown) changes in the climate were indirectly seen as a recurring phenomenon: ice ages, followed by warming, and back to ice ages, and so on. However, climatic changes have been the most important of the phenomena that have led to drastic changes in the evolution of life on Earth. Even if one knows something about the likely periodicity of natural (distinguished from human-induced) climatic changes, what good will that do to those of us currently on this planet to know that after, say, 5,000 years this planet will return to average climatic conditions (whatever those mean, or those mean conditions are)—after systematic global warming and its disastrous consequences? From the evolutionary biological perspective, if we as humans are not biased in favor of the well-being of ourselves and our descendants, we can be most indifferent to climatic changes (including those influences directly attributable to human activities): Some species of life will emerge as a result of complex biogeophysical and climatic factors, will disturb the relative equilibria of biological species and communities, and will lead to a different relative stationary equilibrium of biological configuration. This could imply replacing the human race with another adapted mutant race or new life forms, just as dinosaurs were replaced. If this is an acceptable premise for some readers, perhaps they may not bother to invest time and resources in a book like this. For the rest of us, the issue of global climatic variations is extremely serious and warrants our urgent attention. This book is generally concerned with a set of issues having consequences during and after the twenty-first century.

There exist some well-meaning people who argue that the emerging trends of the past few decades regarding greenhouse gas concentrations and global warming are simply observations of an instant of time, like a second or less, on the geological time scale and thus do not require our concern at all. Yes, one can even bring down the time scale of two centuries or more to an insignificant fraction of a second and simply ignore it—if only the phenomena would let us ignore them. Unfortunately, emerging trends in the changing global climate and the role of human influences in this context are such as to warrant appropriate response—lest human welfare be greatly compromised in a few decades. The adverse effects of climate change are already felt in specific or random locations, and the damages are iniquitous in their incidence across societies, regions, and time.

The geological time sequence dating back millions of years in the life of planet Earth provides different phases of evolution starting with the Precambrian era at about 570 million years ago (MYA). The current era of the Holocene age (the era of human civilization) is said to have started about 10,000 years ago. It was also noted that the planet did go through cycles of global warming and global cooling during various phases. Some of these inferences are based on the characteristics of select rock formations and the use of such methods as "radioactive and radiocarbon dating" for geological structures that were studied (see Schneider 1997 for greater details). Barring the relative extremities of the ice ages and of global warming, a moderate warming was considered a very desirable phenomenon for enhancement of the richness of life and its sustainability; similarly, a relatively moderate cooling would be welcome in the twenty-first century, considering the trend that has seen increases in the global mean surface temperature during the modern industrial era, which began in the 1860s. Let us note that it took over 5,000 years for natural climatic forces to transform the icy landscape of much of present-day Europe and North America to inhabitable current conditions, following an average warming of the temperature by about 5° C per millennium. If such a long-term historical trend and natural causes were behind the contemporary features in climate change, we might not have to bother very much. The postindustrial era phenomena provide evidence of the tangible role of anthropogenic influences in accelerating global warming to an alarming degree and threatening the stability and sustainability of human life itself, unprecedented in the history of the human race.

The early history of climate and human survival abounds with episodes of catastrophes and dislocation, with partial extinction of human civilizations. The coevolution of climate and different life-forms on Earth warrants some understanding if we want to fathom the effect of climate on human survival and vice versa. The roles of biogeochemical cycles remain very critical in this context. These cycles were first described in the early part of the twentieth century and involved an examination of the interaction of human activities and other forms of life with the biochemical elements (based on organic or other) of land, sea, air, and solar radiation. The ingredients of air combined with the phenomena of transpiration (transmittal into the air of water vapor from the leaves of plants), evapotranspiration (transpiration combined with evaporation from the soil and water), infrared (shortwave) radiation, and the concentrations of various (greenhouse) gases in the air are among the factors affecting the effectiveness of the biogeochemical cycles and their renewal capabilities to replenish the planetary resources that support all life.

Historically, the rise and fall of civilizations was inextricably linked to the vagaries of climate changes and variations in the judicious use of natural resources. These disturbances led to the uprooting of populations, eliminating segments of populations when severe hunger and famine afflicted the habitats and affecting the control of territories and countries. To begin with, the location of human settlements was usually influenced by the existence of natural resources, especially water; many settlements were located largely along riverbanks. Most civilizations flourished as "water civilizations," including those that began in Egypt along the Nile River and in southwestern Asia along the Indus River systems. These were known to have thrived before and around 3000 B.C. Some of these settlements were later abandoned when the territory became a desert over a period of time.

Similarly, the Mayan civilization in the Western Hemisphere began to flourish around the third and fourth centuries A.D. The civilization collapsed rather suddenly during the tenth century when the temperature began to rise and climate changes occurred in the region. Likewise, the collapse of the Mali civilization in Africa in the fourteenth century was attributed to severe changes in climatological factors. Climatic variations and environmental mismanagement contributed to these disasters, separately and jointly. There is no major evidence to suggest that the global climate change was due to human influences in the periods any time prior to the twentieth century. Natural disasters and environmental disregard, especially in respect to natural resources, led partly to local climate changes. These were considered the prime causes leading to major problems in the erstwhile flourishing regions.

The current era is faced with human-induced climatic changes, in addition to environmental problems per se. These combined concerns, which will be discussed in subsequent chapters, tend to lead to much more complex and disastrous consequences than ever experienced before in human history. If inertia and inaction were usually inconsistent with biological survival, somewhat similar reasoning suggests that lack of conscious interventions might pose problems for human survival today.

The following salient characteristics dominate the descriptions of the problems narrated above: (a) irreversibility of losses—whether related to the natural resource, climate, or civilization; (b) relative suddenness of disruptions (which also indicate the phenomena of nonlinear interactions and discontinuities of relationships among environmental features); and (c) severity of the impacts of the environment on global climate change.

Sustainable development, interpreted in various forms (see chapter 3 and also Rao 1999 for a detailed treatment of the concepts and issues), has been an area of concern for hundreds of years. Some of these concerns have been confined to specific components of the ecosystem and have been built into the traditions in some civilizations and into faiths and religions in a few others. One of these has been the worship of nature. Social customs and norms were considered cost-effective methods for implementing socially desirable activities. The notion that other species might be entitled to their own existence on this planet was also recognized in certain beliefs, religious or otherwise. These viewpoints were also supported by individuals like Henry David Thoreau and George Perkins Marsh in the nineteenth century. Marsh's 1864 contribution, *Man and Nature—or Physical Geography as Modified by Human Action*, analyzed the decline of past civilizations and found that most possessed a single common feature: the civilization collapsed when its demands on natural resources exceeded the land's ability to supply the same. There have been experiences of deforestation leading to desertification and collapse of human life in the specific regions.

These relatively recent (on the geological time scale) experiences point to the role of anthropogenic factors in disturbing the ecological and environmental balances of nature. Accompanying these changes have been those of the climate. Some of the climatic variations are attributable to the planet's own random events, like hurricanes and the eruption of volcanoes. But there are a few important systematic phenomena such as the emissions of greenhouse gases and the resultant greenhouse effect that are largely attributable to the influences of anthropogenic factors: human population, consumption and production patterns, and deployment of alternative technologies in the economic activities, including waste disposal. Interpreted in broader terms, the exploitation of the source and sink capacities of the planet bring about major changes in the planet's environment and climate. These changes are, at the least, destabilizing for the climate and for sources of sustained life; at their worst, the changes constitute systematic adverse influences with catastrophic and irreversible consequences. The following section notes the history of scientific understanding of relevant issues during the past century.

1.2 Svante Arrhenius and Later

Earth's temperature is the net result of the planetary radiational balance, and the latter is the outcome of the absorption of incoming solar radiation adjusted by the outgoing terrestrial radiation. The latter is affected by the "albedo factor," subject to anthropogenic influences like the changing concentrations of greenhouse gases. This is rather widely appreciated toward the last decade of the twentieth century, about one hundred years after the findings and predictions of the Swedish scientist Svante Arrhenius. Among the first published contributions were those of Arrhenius (1896). Arrhenius's concern was to explain temperature variations during the glacial and interglacial periods over thousands of years. Several years before Arrhenius's contribution, the French scientist Joseph Fourier (1824) first introduced the notion of the atmosphere as a glass bowl, which lets in sunlight and retains a part of it (the infrared radiation), causing a warming effect—later called the greenhouse effect (GE). Arrhenius used the term "hothouse" to describe this effect, and he assessed that fossil fuel combustion and industrial emissions of carbon dioxide (CO_2) could lead to the GE. It is useful to note at this stage that unless otherwise stated, the GE referred to in this book is the GE contributed by direct and indirect anthropogenic influences. In much of the literature, the nature-induced GE is sometimes called the "natural GE," and the human-induced GE is called the "enhanced GE"; we refer to the latter simply as the GE.

The contributions of Swedish geologist Arvid Hogbom (for details see Berner 1995) to the understanding of the carbon cycle were found useful in the climatic studies of Arrhenius, who pointed to the key features of the Sun-atmosphere-Earth surface systems in the study of long-term climate changes. The asymmetric roles of carbonic acid and water vapor in their ability to allow incoming solar radiation while affecting the outgoing reflections of these light rays were recognized. These constituted the essential foundation for the GE, whether natural or enhanced. Some of these details and recent understanding of the phenomena will be discussed in chapter 2.

Several improvements to the structural model formulation and the scientific underpinnings of the Arrhenius study were made in the recent past. To illustrate a few of these, let us begin with a study by Moller (1963), who considered the effect of the change in the water vapor content of air that results from the CO_2–induced warming of the troposphere: CO_2–induced increase of surface temperature raises not only the temperature of the troposphere but also its humidity, further enhancing the increase in the downward flux of terrestrial radiation at Earth's surface. In Moller's study, the net upward radiation at Earth's surface did not increase significantly with increasing surface temperature because of the assumption of constant relative humidity. The limitation of such studies brought to light the limitation of the surface radiation balance approach, which does not take into account the CO_2–induced changes in other components of the surface heat balance. The surface temperature in radiative-convective equilibrium with a given distribution of relative humidity is almost twice as sensitive to an increase in the concentration of CO_2 in the air than the equilibrium temperature with a given distribution of absolute humidity (details can be seen in Manabe 1997). Ramanathan and Vogelmann (1997) demonstrated that the water vapor feedback amplified the surface warming in Arrhenius's model by about 30 percent. This premise is supported in more recent scientific findings (see chapter 2). As these investigators observed, the successes of Arrhenius's model are many—even when judged by modern-day data and computer simulations.

A number of important studies emerged after the concern of the 1992 Earth Summit in Rio de Janeiro about the environmental problems and the constitution of the United Nations Framework Convention on Climate Change (UNFCCC). The work of the Intergovernmental Panel on Climate Change (IPCC) led to the coordinating forum for the series of the Conference of Parties (COP); the latest one—the fifth in the ongoing series—was held in Bonn in November 1999. The IPCC published its First Assessment Report in 1990, and the Second Assessment in 1995, which concluded that "the balance of evidence suggests that there is a discernible human influence on global climate" (IPCC 1995). The COP is primarily concerned with the problems of global climate change and the role of greenhouse gases (GHGs) in that context. The GHGs and their dynamics are governed by the features of their sources, sinks, and biogeochemical cycles operating in the oceans, on land, and in the atmosphere. The most important sources are combustion of fossil fuels, burning of biomass, nitrification, and industrial emissions. Sources of these gases include ocean absorptions, chemical conversions in the atmosphere, forest sequestration of carbon, and changes in land use. Environmental problems continue to remain the concern of a wide variety of multilateral, governmental, and other institutions. Most problems of global climate change are rooted in the governance of global commons, explained below.

Global commons are defined (see also Rao 1999) as the global environmental resources that cut across national boundaries and that are affected across all regions owing to direct and indirect interventions in any one or more regions. The global commons possess varying features over time because of evolving human interaction with the environment. The main factors of concern in the global commons are the following: atmospheric gases that cause the greenhouse effect and global warming; thinning of the ozone layer leading to increased ultraviolet-B (UV-B) radiation; transboundary pollution in the air and water; and loss of biodiversity.

The roots of anthropogenic contributions in the global commons are largely contained in the open access and free-rider problems of environmental public goods. Thus, the concern in the emerging problems of the global commons tends to focus on the issues of legitimacy of appropriations of sink capacities without any obligations on the part of the users/polluters. These lead to the need to critically examine legitimacy of any exercise of resource appropriations—both of the planet's sinks and sources. Various resources, like fresh water and the biological pool, constitute examples of common property, whereas atmospheric concentrations of greenhouse gases and the ozone layer are examples of global commons with open access. We refer to these commons simply as "global commons." These possess open-access characteristics. Lack of any well-defined and enforceable property rights and of consequent markets makes this vital segment of the planet a potential threat for the survival of humanity.

The phenomenon of the "tragedy of the commons" (Hardin 1968) tends to apply as the sink capacity is tampered with by human appropriators who do not have to pay for such destruction of the sink capacity. This problem is also similar to the "free rider" problem that economists analyze in the economics of public goods, but in those cases the public goods are paid for by some institutions. In the present case, nature provides the goods and services, but she does respond rather belatedly; however, when she does respond she means business: Potential irreversible adverse consequences remain the norm for measuring the impact. The problem of the tragedy of the commons arises not in the context of common property, but in the context of no clearly defined property rights, and that the proper terminology is "free access resources" rather than "common property resources." These features are conventionally applied to the problem of governance of commodities or resources arising from one or more common pools of sources, with no cost to the users.

Hardin sought to explain the processes of extinction of some of the fish stocks in terms of the "philosophy of the commons." However, the reasoning extends to the problems of governance of sinks, which is the main concern. In all such cases, the processes underlying the free-rider and open-access phenomena need to be addressed. Alternatively, from an equivalent economic pricing perspective, the costs of externalities should be internalized. Users or beneficiaries should be made to pay some kind of "tax" based on their value-added "output," loss of sink capacity, and for any losses and damages to the ecosystems or reduction in the ecosystem services. These features will be discussed in chapters 4 and 5.

It is useful to note that any dichotomous treatment of property simply in terms of common (nonprivate) property and private (exclusive) property is an excessive simplification of the issues involved. Is the real alternative to potential problems in the global commons to be seen in terms of globally representative institutions like those under the UNFCCC? The answer is obviously in favor of strengthening such a forum for effective global environmental management. Some of these issues will be discussed in chapter 6.

Global environmental problems have their roots at local, regional, and subregional levels, and at the levels of individual consumers and producers. Accordingly, the features of the tragedy of the commons apply substantially at all these levels. These problems warrant collective coordinated actions where different societies, countries, and individual entities contribute to alleviate common current and potential problems. The problem of global warming and climate change is the single most important problem of sustainability and sustainable development confronting human society at the opening of the twenty-first century.

In the assessment of various characteristics of global commons, we need to focus on the following:

- The roles of human activities in the observed sink problems
- Changes over time; historic and future trends
- Geographic differences in the current state and its likely changes
- Implications of economic activities on global warming
- Impact of changes on the well-being and sustainability of human populations
- The roles of anthropogenic factors in the governance of global commons
- Specific contributions of greenhouse gases in the above factors
- Geophysical and economic explanations of changes
- Institutional aspects of the governance of the global commons
- Provision of incentives and disincentives for both individual and institutional entities' global policies and programs

Anthropogenic Factors

The role of human factors in the problems of the greenhouse effect and global warming may be stated here. The combustion of fossil fuels for consumption and production activities of the human enterprise leads to increases in the concentration of greenhouse gases (GHGs) in the atmosphere: these fundamental factors underlie the global warming process and are attributable to humans (see also Karl et al. 1997). These GHGs are primarily carbon dioxide (CO_2), methane (CH_4), ozone (O_3), and nitrous oxide (N_2O), and halocarbons including chlorofluorocarbons (CFCs). These gases act asymmetrically with respect to sunlight; they let in light rays but tend to insulate the planet against the losses of heat (specifically by trapping infrared radiative energy in the troposphere, the lower atmosphere)—typically the greenhouse effect. Higher concentrations of GHGs imply much greater possibility of global warming, sometimes expressed in terms of the formula for global warming potential (GWP). It was estimated that since about A.D. 1750 (the start of the industrial revolution) humans have altered the natural greenhouse effect by adding 30 percent more CO_2, 145 percent more CH_4, and other gases (IPCC 1995). Most of the GHGs are the toughest to handle because these emissions have a longer life span in the atmosphere, about a century. Also, there are other gases that affect the effectiveness of given levels of the GHGs. These include carbon monoxide (CO), nitrogen oxides (NO_x), and hydrocarbons. The CO_2 emissions are contributed primarily by fossil fuel combustion and deforestation.*

It is also important to note that the interactions or atmospheric chemical compositions and their dynamics are important in assessing the role of CO_2. The concentrations of a set of oxidizing agents such as ozone (O_3), hydroxyl radicals (OH), and nitrogen dioxide (NO_2) affect the rate of conversion of CO into CO_2. The role of the ozone factor remains very significant, and is summarized below; more details can be found in chapter 2.

The Ozone Problem

Let us introduce some of the standard terms used in the discussion. In the atmosphere, the troposphere is closest to the surface of Earth, with an altitude under 15 kilometers (km) from the mean surface level. Similarly, the stratosphere lies in the range 15 to 50 km, the mesosphere in the range 50 to 80 km, and the thermosphere/ionosphere at levels exceeding 80 km in altitude. The stratopause lies between the stratosphere and the mesosphere, and the tropopause is between the troposphere and the stratosphere.

The ozone layer is an important component of the atmosphere; it shields Earth's surface from damaging ultraviolet radiation from the Sun. Ozone (O_3) is continuously generated by the action of solar radiation on atmospheric oxygen and is amenable to destruction by catalytic processes involving trace amounts of free-radical gases like nitrogen oxide. Atmospheric chemists Mario Molina, Sherwood Rowland, and Paul Crutzen won the Nobel Prize for chemistry in 1995 for their diagnosis of the role of chlorofluorocarbons (CFCs) in the ozone layer of the strato-

---

*The former contributes to release of CO_2 via the oxidation process, whereas the latter reduces the carbon sequestration potential (and hence the sink capacity) in addition to contributing to fuelwood or other fuel-burning processes.

sphere. It was found that photo decomposition (due to solar energy) of the CFCs in the stratosphere produces catalysts that destroy ozone. The CFCs, which are very powerful infrared-light absorbers, both destroy ozone and contribute very significantly to the GE. The most important CFCs here are the compounds trichlorofluoromethane (CFC-11) and dichlorodifluoromethane (CFC-12). The atmospheric residence time of the CFCs is about a century, given their slow diffusion into the stratosphere. In general, the ozone depletion features are governed mainly by the interdependent but distinguishable chemical cycles: CFC/O_3, H_2O/O_3, and NO_x/O_3.

Although a number of biogeochemical phenomena are better understood during the 1990s, there are still some unknowns: the response of the terrestrial systems to the changing concentrations of carbonic acid and their interactions with other GHGs like methane, water vapor, and hydrological cycles, climatic feedback mechanisms between oceans and forests acting as sinks for the carbon elements (including some missing sinks), and the spatial distribution of the effects among various regions of the world in different seasons. Also, the interactive effects of other anthropogenic influences like those of aerosols are still not fully understood. The interdependencies of the physical, chemical, and biological processes, and their interactions with land vegetation, ocean and marine resources, atmospheric balances, and flux of nature and related aspects, are only partially understood so far. More detailed explanations of the important linkages and scientific foundations of the phenomena of global climate change will be presented in chapter 2, relevant for the economic analysis to follow later.

1.3 About This Book

Environmental security (or operationally, the avoidance of environmental insecurity) has come to assume great significance in both national and international settings, from both economic and social-survival criteria. It is no longer a luxury to pay attention to environmental issues. It is rather widely recognized that (a) the economy and the environment are largely complementary; (b) any neglect of these issues can result in increasing levels of disasters caused by the consequential climate change and destabilization of ecosystems; and (c) any inertia and lack of preemptive actions could imply irrecoverable losses on many fronts. The long-term damages from climatic change include irreversible biological degradation with implications for human health: the world's fauna and flora will be trapped in a vise. Habitat loss on the land is the major causal factor for the deterioration of tropical biotas, and the climatic warming in addition is particularly harmful for the biotas of the colder areas and polar regions (Wilson 1992). Biodiversity is critical for the sustainability of life on planet Earth. Deploying economic principles that are built on the strongest implicit assumption of a sustainable world is unlikely to be useful for any analysis that addresses potentially cata-strophic phenomena like those of global climate change and loss of biodiversity.

Climate change, whether occurring due to natural causes or human-induced effects, or more likely both, is governed by the changing dy-namics of the stocks and flows of atmospheric chemical elements. The latter evolve according to a number of biogeochemicals. Important among these are the carbon, nitrogen, sulfur, ozone, and aerosol cycles. A de-tailed assessment of these factors enables an improved understanding of the scientific basis of emerging climatic changes and their potential rami-fications. Chapter 2 addresses these issues as well as several salient ad-ditional features. The science and economics of such changes are also important in interpreting the concept and its operational implications of the global warming potential (GWP). It is useful to note that the GWP is very sensitive to the specifications of the time horizon under consider-ation, among other factors. There are several unknowns in the scientific knowledge of the phenomena of global climatic change and its contrib-uting factors, especially the roles of such human activities as land-use change, industrial emissions, and other economic activities. However, pragmatic decision making warrants formulating relevant economic de-cision models and deriving prescriptions for policy based on incomplete information—recognizing the latter for what it is. Otherwise, we will wait several years, during which time irreversible changes and damages could occur to the climatic system, the ecosystem, and other key biogeophysical factors. Any loss of resilience in these systems and their components amounts to the loss of sustainability and potential for con-tinued human development (details can be seen in chapter 3).

Analytical methods of decision making under a system of uncertain-ties, risks, and partial information are some of the tools that assist in arriving at relevant policies. These tools, combined with appropriate eco-nomic analyses, lead to meaningful solutions in the context of the inter-dependencies of the climate-environment-economy systems. Effective integration of the latest scientific findings and advances in economic theory and methods, with a bearing on policy implications, is an important focus of this book. The role of scientific uncertainty is recognized, and socioeconomic decision making is sensitized to such possibilities. Relevant climatic feedback mechanisms and human adaptation as well as economic transition are also recognized in this context. This pragmatism enables societies to incur burdens only to optimal and necessary levels in mitigating the effects of climate change. The economics of GWP remains a debatable issue, and this text advances new insights into the science and economics of the same.

Recent analyses, including the role of nonconstant and endogenous time-discounting and recognition of changing societal preferences (some of these original studies are contributed by the author), tend to influence prescriptions of policy guidelines in the context of global climate change and reduction of greenhouse gas emissions. Win-win solutions and cost-effective approaches to the global problems are examined within a multilevel framework: local, national, and international. These issues remain the focus of chapter 3, in addition to an assessment of the role of transaction costs; transitory and adaptive costs in devising preventive polices to affect the climate; potential valuation methods and the role of benefit-cost analysis; the choice of discount rates in the future valuation of resources; the role of ecotax or "green" tax; and the provision of various incentives and disincentives for optimal policies that balance the needs of the economy and the environment and that lead to the stabilization of the climate.

Most of the existing literature does not seem to address the issues in an integrative framework, except possibly by suggesting the role of integrated modeling exercises with a heavy dose of technical processing. Such efforts may not be sufficient to comprehend some of the facets examined in this book. The focus of the book is to provide analytical bases for pragmatic integrated ecology-environment-economy policies. Only critical factors are empirically examined, and a few essential methods are examined technically. Modeling and data processing are treated as secondary requirements, which should follow, and not precede, the framework provided in the text.

Ecological aspects of the GE are very important. This is because the significance of the ecosystem services must be ensured without any interruptions. The economic factors of GWP are closely interlinked with the choice of discount functions for future valuation of resources or their depletion, and with the direct and indirect effects of various GHGs and influencing factors in determining the magnitudes of the GWP over different plausible time horizons. The role of global warming and worsening temperature variations admits major changes in the biota and hence of the factors affecting human health, with implications on morbidity and mortality. Chapter 4 examines these features and assesses economic damages under plausible scenarios of the climate change and related features. The costs of prevention and of reduction of adverse climatic effects are also examined, both methodologically and empirically. To a large extent, the economics of the GE is inextricably linked to the economics of GHGs, the concern of chapter 5. The economics of climate stabilization, or of the stabilization of the GHGs, has been partly dealt with in analytical economics as an exercise in the modeling of the climate-environment-economy relationship at a very highly aggregate (unisector model) level. Predicting carbon emissions on the basis of the estimates of income elasticities for carbon emissions and energy consumption (see, e.g., Schmalensee et al. 1998) may not offer very useful information unless it is provided with a sufficient level of disaggregation of income groups and can identify the causal factors for changing elasticities. Even the so-called general equilibrium models (GEMs) were not gems of models; they lacked effective integration of relevant climatic feedback effects and of the nonconstant discounting of future valuations of various parameters.

A number of analytical models and their corresponding empirical analyses try to suggest the magnitudes of costs and benefits or other implications of various actions and inactions in stabilizing GHGs, and also the climate, in terms of temperature. These methods are founded on very serious assumptions and tend to magnify uncertainties and unknowns in the scientific, socioeconomic, and terrestrial phenomena governing the global commons. Among the best-known contributions in this context are those of Nordhaus (1991, 1992, 1994). The core model developed by Nordhaus was called the DICE: *d*ynamic *i*ntegrated model of *c*limate and the *e*conomy. The main decision variables were consumption, rate of investment in tangible capital, and the rate of emissions reductions of GHGs. Clearly, these specifications of choice variables are rather narrow and geared primarily to developed economies where an economy is almost fully monetized and driven by private capital investments. In addition, the role of human capital, social capital, and institutions was treated as uniformly constant in the entire global economic system.

The objective in the DICE model was to maximize the discounted value of utility of relevant arguments. The DICE models suggested that the net benefit from pursuing the above model-based optimal policy rather than continuing with a business-as-usual approach (i.e., complete inaction and lack of concern about the sustainability problems) is about $200 billion for the entire foreseeable time horizon. The greatest fallacy of models like the above is that they try to replace the unknowns with estimates of approximated parameters and thus treat the unknowns as knowns. The models addressed the question of what would be the optimal policy to follow if all the parameters were known with certainty. Because all parameters are not known with certainty, the results of these exercises may yield poor policy advice. Conclusions such as stating that the U.S. economy will not be affected by more than about a quarter percent of GDP (gross domestic product) if the emissions of CO_2 accumulate so as to double the 1990 level (Nordhaus 1991) can be very misleading. A program to reduce GHGs would also lead to gains in improvement of the ecological systems and also in sectors like health and agriculture. These aspects as well as a number of noncommercial benefits are lost in the assessments of Nordhaus. Models that do not incorporate relevant feedback mechanisms, including adaptation responses and changing social preferences, may not merit recognition beyond being mechanistic.

Another noteworthy empirically relevant model was developed by the Organization for Economic Cooperation and Development (OECD) (see Burniaux et al. 1991), called GREEN (*general* equilibrium *en*vironmental). This model focuses on the energy sector, and it uses fiscal and carbon tax measures to reduce CO_2 emissions for the time horizon 1985 to 2020, and in later versions to the year 2050. Some of the assumptions of these models include same magnitude of interenergy elasticities of substitution in private and government sectors and identical forms of production functions in all sectors and regions. The problem of mitigating the GE reduces to one of controlling or stabilizing the emissions of the GHGs. New formulations enable remedying such deficiencies, and a framework for these will be suggested in chapter 4.

Robust and comprehensive models to enable devising economic policies for managing the global commons are likely to be more useful. These are a few of the powerful examples of using precision whose ground rules we are not sure of: it is prudent to be approximately right rather than precisely wrong. This position has the implication that the direction of policy is extremely fundamental and the details and mechanics, although very important, should not be allowed to undermine the main focus. The enhanced set of market-based and other policy instruments is useful for effective policy design and operationalization. Cost-effectiveness of alternative measures and their relative significance in both the short term and the long term are assessed to suggest pragmatic options. Cost sharing between different groups of countries using efficiency and equity criteria is one of the issues for analysis in chapter 5.

Institutional mechanisms, especially those involving transboundary ones, are very important in mitigating global climate problems. This requires global actions and international cooperation. Multilateral development institutions and financial institutions possess significant potential to contribute to the effectiveness of some of the policies and operationally meaningful programs. These issues are discussed in chapter 6. Related aspects include an assessment of the role and limitations of a number of initiatives, some of which are market-influenced instruments like the trading of carbon emissions (see chapter 5). Some of the mechanisms involve significant transaction costs, and these must be addressed for the usefulness of the mechanisms. The contributions of the IPCC and of the COP are also examined with the objective of taking stock of some of the experiences and suggesting improvements. Some of these issues are also detailed in the final chapter to provide a perspective. Because the failure of markets in creating an environmentally efficient economic functioning forms a foundation for global environmental problems, it is rather naive to expect that markets or market-based instruments of policy will stabilize the global climate, or that the GHGs are likely to be the main solution to the upcoming problems. Hence the need for a balanced mix of instruments that possess the requisite potential to tackle the problems and accomplish the specified tasks in a cost effective and equitable manner. These are some of the real challenges to be examined in chapters 6 and 7.

The traditional principles of economics, such as the application of marginal cost pricing, prices to reflect environmental costs and possible externalities, regulatory as well as market mechanisms for directing consumption and production activities, and application of marginal cost and marginal benefit equating optimality principles for economic welfare maximization, are not without their foundations. But these are built on a large set of assumptions. The theme of the economics of climatic change requires these implicit assumptions to be brought to light and seeks to modify the foundations. This does not necessarily imply revolutionizing economic theory, but it does mean a modification of the economic approaches and their foundations in order to enrich the same for addressing fundamental issues in the climatological, ecological, and economic sustainability. Some of the proposed improvements of the economic methodology are sought to be incorporated within the context of relatively limited scientific understanding regarding the phenomena, and the application of broad principles of decision making under uncertainty with incomplete information involving long time horizons. In addition, the institutional and policy relevance of most of the suggested solutions is sought to be maintained in much of the analysis to follow.

References

Arrhenius, S. 1896. "On the Influence of Carbonic Acid in the Air upon the Temperature on the Ground." *The Philosophical Magazine* 41:237–276.

Berner, R.A. 1995. "A.G. Hogbom and the Development of the Concept of the Geochemical Cycle." *American Journal of Science* 295:491–495.

Burniaux, J.M. et al. 1991. "GREEN—a Multi-Region Dynamic General Equilibrium Model for Quantifying the Costs of Curbing CO_2 Emissions." OECD working paper no. 104, Paris: OECD.

Fourier, J.B. 1824. "Mémoire sur les températures du globe terrestre et des espaces planétaires." *Mémoires de l'Académie royale des sciences de l'Institut de France* 7:569–604.

Hardin, G. 1968. "The Tragedy of the Commons." *Science* 162:1243–1248.

Intergovernmental Panel on Climate Change (IPCC). 1995. *The Science of Climate Change—IPCC Working Group I Report.* New York: Cambridge University Press.

Karl, T., Nichols, N., and Gregory, J. 1997. "The Coming Climate." *Scientific American* May:78–83.

Manabe, S. 1997. "Early Development in the Study of Greenhouse Warming—The Emergence of Climate Models." *Ambio* 26(1):47–51.

Moller, F. 1963. "On the Influence of Changes in the CO_2 Concentration in Air on the Radiation Balance of the Earth's Surface and on the Climate." *Journal of Geophysical Research* 68:3877–3886.

Nordhaus, W.D. 1994. *Managing the Global Commons.* Cambridge, MA: MIT Press.

———. 1992. "An Optimal Transition Path for Controlling Greenhouse Gases." *Science* 258:1315–1319.

———. 1991. "To Slow or Not to Slow—The Economics of the Greenhouse Effect." *The Economic Journal* 101:920–937.

Ramanathan, V., and Vogelmann, A.M. 1997. "Greenhouse Effect, Atmospheric Solar Absorption and the Earth's Radiation Budget—From the Arrhenius–Langley Era to the 1990s." *Ambio* 26(1):38–46.

Rao, P.K. 1999. *Sustainable Development: Economics and Policy*. Oxford, UK: Blackwell.

Schmalensee, R., Stoker, T.M., and Judson, R.A. 1998. "World Carbon Dioxide Emissions 1950–2050." *Review of Economics and Statistics* 80(1):15–27.

Schneider, S.H. 1997. *Laboratory Earth: The Planetary Gamble We Can't Afford to Lose*. New York: Basic Books.

Wilson, E. 1992. *The Diversity of Life*. Cambridge, MA: Belknap/Harvard University Press.

Chapter 2

Scientific Background

2.1 Introduction

The ten warmest years on record occurred in the past fifteen years. World-wide, the 1990s have been assessed as the warmest decade ever recorded, according to the Goddard Institute of Space Studies (GISS) of the U.S. National Aeronautics and Space Administration (NASA). These phenomena derive partly from the nature of our solar system and terrestrial climate dynamics, but the role played by humans remains nontrivial.

Climate change, to the extent caused by human activities, is fraught with relatively very long time horizons such as a few decades. Accordingly, any effective remediation measures require very substantial time lags. The time lags between the causes and effects of climate changes as well as their interdependence complicate some of the perceptions of the problems and their remedies, even when no serious problems exist of noncooperation of the various constituents of human society. Effective protection of the climate system requires international cooperation, flexibility, and appreciation of perspectives for the future. This raises the issues of efficiency and equity in different categories: local and national, international, and intergenerational. Resolving issues in equity remains important for promoting trust, cooperation, and effectiveness of policy decisions. None of these can be achieved on a realistic basis if the scientific facts of global warming and its contributing factors are not properly evaluated.

This chapter addresses important issues elucidating the phenomena of climate change, issues that both influence and are influenced by the greenhouse effect (GE). The GE primarily stems from accumulations of greenhouse gases (GHGs) with a substantial role of human actions in these phenomena. These aspects, in addition to the ozone and aerosol factors in contributing to global climatic change processes, are explained later in this chapter. Undoubtedly, there are several scientific unknowns and system uncertainties. Pragmatic policy analyses governing global climatic systems require decision making done under uncertainty, and sometimes with only partial information. The risk of waiting for an unknown timetable containing full information is such that it tends to be too expensive or too late because of some of the biogeophysical irreversibilities. Some of these aspects are briefly addressed in a later section of this chapter. The issue of suggesting a framework for optimal policies to achieve climatic stabilization is proposed in later chapters.

2.2 Climatic Renewal and Change

Earth's climate acts interactively among the hydrodynamic and chemical factors affecting the terrestrial atmosphere, the oceans, biota, and stratospheric components, among others. These complex interactions are significantly influenced by solar radiation at different intensities (owing to solar flares or other disturbances). When these influences depict a systematic pattern, the natural question is whether the pattern is determined partly by human-induced changes in the heat-trapping gases that generate the greenhouse effect. Some of the complex interactions are not yet fully understood nor quantified.

In the history of the evolution of scientific thought, Joseph Fourier (1824) and Svante Arrhenius (1896) were among the pioneers studying the effect of increases in atmospheric concentrations of CO_2 on the temperature of Earth's surface. However, Arrhenius is credited with being the first in the quantification of the relationship, which underwent several improvements during the past century. A useful collection of papers was assembled for a special issue of the journal *Ambio* in February 1997, detailing both historical and contemporary scientific perspectives on the theme of the greenhouse effect (GE).

Climate influences all forms of life on Earth, and is influenced by the activities of human beings. The environment and its influence on other components of the climatic system act through a series of interdependent complex relationships, most in the forms of different chemical cycles. These cycles govern renewal and change of the environment, climate, and survival of different life-forms. Hydrological and sedimentary cycles affect dispersion of the six main elements required for life (Schneider

1997): hydrogen, carbon, oxygen, nitrogen, phosphorous, and sulfur. As a result, these elements must be continuously replenished and recycled.

The United Nations Framework Convention on Climate Change (UNFCCC), the key global secretariat for most aspects of study and policy formulations concerning climate change, defines climate system as "the totality of the atmosphere, hydrosphere, biosphere and geosphere and their interactions." The UNFCCC defines climate change as "a change of climate which is attributable directly or indirectly to human activity that alters the composition of the global atmosphere and which is in addition to natural climatic variability observed over comparable time periods." In general, the term "climate variations" refers to fluctuations in the climate as natural events. The UNFCCC definition clarifies the complex interactive roles of ecology, climate, economy, and environmental factors.

Climate includes the rainfall, snowfall, and temperature patterns, among others. These are not simply about averages, and much less about global averages. Winds and storms or weather events are simply by-products of the climatological systems in various regions and seasons. Climate change is influenced not only by natural or planetary and solar system activities but also by human activities. If there is one area of concern for change that is unwelcome, it is climate change, which stands at the top of a list of potential unwelcome changes. This happens to be a consensus view, even if there is not as much agreement on whether or not anthropogenic factors are the main source of global climate change. In a recent study, Rind et al. (1999) examined global temperatures and solar radiative forcing over the past four centuries and concluded that solar radiative forcing by itself was insufficient to lead to the global warming features of the last few decades. The major role is attributable to GHGs during the twentieth century. The most-referred-to source of debate on these issues is the 500-member Intergovernmental Panel on Climate Change (IPCC) constituted by the United Nations and coordinated under its agencies: World Meteorological Organization (WMO) and United Nations Environment Programme (UNEP). The First Assessment Report of the IPCC, published in 1990, provided a scientific basis for UNFCCC, which was launched during the Earth Summit of 1992 in Rio de Janeiro.

The main objective of this Framework Convention was declared in the document's Article 2, namely the "stabilization of greenhouse gas

concentrations in the atmosphere at a level that would prevent dangerous anthropogenic interference with the climate system. Such a level
should be achieved within a time frame sufficient to allow ecosystems
to adapt naturally to climate change, to ensure that food production is
not threatened, and to enable economic development to proceed in a
sustainable manner."

Global climatic change affects both the mean temperature and its variability, thus creating more episodes of extreme weather than ever in the
past. The patterns of rainfall and precipitation, mechanisms of climatological circulation between oceans and land surfaces, levels of sea rise
and flood inundation of coastal and low-lying regions, hurricanes, and
other weather-related disasters are likely to be attenuated as a result of
climate change. Biotic functions and the stability of ecosystems tend to
be significantly affected, and this implies expensive disruption of ecosystem services that are generally freely made available under the pre-
disturbed systems. The El Niño phenomenon is not directly attributed to
human activities, but the effect of GE is such that more frequent El
Niño-like conditions and weather extremities are expected to occur in
several regions of the world (Timmermann et al. 1999).

One of the Synthesis Reports of the IPCC regarding the interpretation of Article 2 of the UNFCCC, based on its Second Assessment Report, stated (para 1.9): "Climate change presents the decision maker
with a set of formidable complications which include the potential for
irreversible damages and unknowns, very long horizons for comprehension and empirical analysis, regional variations in causes and effects,
and various levels as well as types of equity in the incidence of costs and
benefits of any interventions or lack of actions." According to the report
by the IPCC (1995), an observed increase in global average temperature
"is unlikely to be entirely natural in origin" and that "there is a discernible human influence on global climate." This conclusion raises the pertinent question: How much effect, by what sources and what factors,
and what are the likely time-trends in this cause-effect framework? There
are not enough convincing answers with any great precision or certainty.
However, the trends and broad magnitudes of the problem of climate
change and its consequences (with and without human intervention) are
partly answered in some of the IPCC reports and other research studies.

The IPCC reports concluded that in the absence of effective policies and actions to mitigate GHGs, Earth's temperature could increase
between 1 to 3.5 degrees centigrade (about 2 to 6.5 degrees Fahrenheit)

Box 2.1 Important Scientific Concepts

Biogeophysical system The biological and physical system with reference to one or more geological regions.

Biogeophysical feedback This occurs when anthropogenic and natural processes on biota (defined below) and natural resources affect the climate upon which the biota depend.

Biosphere Segments of Earth and its atmospheric surroundings that can support life; in principle, the region on land, in the oceans, and in the atmosphere inhabited by living organisms.

Biota The collection of all living things, including plants and animals.

Carrying Capacity (CC) The maximum size of a specific population of species that a given habitat can support for a specified period of time, without disrupting the long-term equilibrium of the habitat. This is a dynamic concept, and the CC can be expressed in terms of relevant parameters.

Cycles The circulation of biochemical or other elements in the geosphere from the environment to the biological organisms and back to the environment. Biogeochemical cycles include the nitrogen cycle, sulfur cycle, and carbon cycle. These represent the interaction of life, air, oceans, land, and various chemicals. The vigor of atmospheric circulation affects the features governing various phase descriptions of these cycles (for a lucid description of related issues, see Schneider 1997).

Ecosystem The set of all life-forms and their physical environment, including the entire set of interacting entities between them. Ecosystems are products of the interactions of all living and nonliving factors of the environment and the biosphere. The functioning of an ecosystem results in several interactions, and these lead to what is known as "balance of nature" at any given time.

Ecosystem services These include (a) maintaining biodiversity and production of ecosystem goods, such as food, fiber, biomass fuels, pharmaceuticals, industrial products, and their precursors; (b) life-support functions such as environmental cleansing, recycling, and renewal; and (c) provision of intangible aesthetic and cultural benefits (for a detailed description of the ecosystem and its functions, services, and potential approaches to their evaluation, see Daily 1997).

Threshold limits The limits of factors beyond which growth and equilibrium/stability of populations, or other survival features of life-forms and organisms, are likely to be adversely affected. These limits constitute critical levels for sustainability and survival.

by 2100. Some of the major consequences include serious health problems, ecological instability, and a rise of sea level by about 15 to 95 centimeters (6 to 38 inches), with potential to inundate several low-lying coastal regions. Climate change is expected to adversely affect human living conditions and health as a consequence of temperature extremes, expanded tropical diseases, floods, storms, dislocation of human habitats, and disturbances of ecological systems (directly and indirectly affecting food security and ecological system services). In financial terms, any estimate of such damage tends to be of the order of dozens of billions of dollars. It was also predicted that a 1-meter rise in sea level as a result of global warming could lead to loss of coastal land to the extent of 6 percent in the Netherlands, and about 17 percent in Bangladesh (with only about 0.3 percent of global contributions to the GHG emissions), among several other countries and small islands likely to be adversely affected.

The relation among the GE, climate variability in different regions of the planet, and rainfall/precipitation remains a complex one. However, most models predict reduced precipitation in southern Europe and south Asia, for example, as a result of increased GHGs. In tropical and subtropical regions, rainfall has decreased over the past few decades, especially in parts of the Sahel in Africa and eastward to Indonesia (see Karl et al. 1997). These are weather externalities caused by spatially distributed sources of anthropogenic GHG emissions, a powerful example of economic and climatological externalities. The relative roles of current and historical emissions of GHGs by each country in these disastrous phenomena are not fully understood. Lack of requisite accountability tends to allow continued exploitation of the ecological space, with features obeying free-rider or open-access systems. The economics of climate change warrants proper attention to the complex interdependencies in the physical and economic systems (see Rao 1999a for more details). It is important to note that atmospheric water vapor is a greenhouse gas and a primary determinant of Earth's surface temperature. A warming climate will contribute to more atmospheric moisture owing to evapotranspiration, enhance the GE further, and add a positive reinforcement of global warming and climatic change (Rind 1999).

A partial offsetting factor in this process is a potential increase in vegetation in some parts of the world and the radiative effect of the same. However, any significant increase in terrestrial vegetation may be constrained by the role and limitation of N (nitrogen), according to

Rastetter et al. (1997). It was argued that in the short term, carbon is sequestered in vegetation by increasing the vegetation C/N (carbon/nitrogen) ratios; in the longer term (a century or longer), carbon sequestration by ecosystems may be sustained by an increase in total availability of N in the ecosystem in both vegetation and soils. Thus the continued and only partly understood interactions perpetuate a state of climatological disequilibrium.

The long-term study of radiative forcing (expressed in watts per square meter [W/m^2]), the principal influence on global warming, due to the main factors for the period 1600 to 1990, is summarized by Bengtsson et al. (1999): the primary GHGs are 2.11, tropospheric ozone 0.39, direct sulfate aerosols −0.35, and indirect sulfate aerosols −0.91. The roles of feedback mechanisms remain increasingly important in any nonstationary climate system. Some of the GHG-induced and/or global warming-induced feedback systems include water-vapor feedback, snow–ice feedback, and cloud feedback. The last feature remains significantly affected by the role of aerosols as well (see Section 2.6). An estimate of global mean temperature increase due to a single doubling of the atmospheric CO_2 implied (in centigrade scale) 1.3 degrees without incorporating water-vapor feedback and 2.1 degrees when solar water-vapor feedback was included (National Academy of Sciences 1992).

The IPCC Second Assessment of 1996 confirmed most of the previous IPCC conclusions, including (a) climate has changed over the past century, with discernible human influence in this phenomenon; (b) GHG concentrations have continued to increase; (c) anthropogenic aerosols, like airborne particles as in coal-burning dust, tend to produce negative radiating forces that could marginally cool down Earth's temperature. The IPCC Summary for Policymakers did admit the prevalence of uncertainties relating to the parameters of the biogeochemical cycles, climatic feedbacks associated with clouds and vegetation endogenous to the rise in temperatures, and some of the characteristics of global atmospheric circulation models. The single most important message sought to be conveyed is to reduce GHG emissions, with particular reference to CO_2, given the long atmospheric lifetime of this gas. It is hard to disagree with this imperative, even by the standards of most critics of the science of global warming (see also Kerr 1997). Also, in a recent econometric study, Schmalensee et al. (1998) found that most projections of the carbon emissions in the IPCC reports could be underestimates, and thus require an upward adjustment.

The GHGs possess lifetimes that are usually sufficiently long enough to allow their mixing throughout the troposphere and lower stratosphere, so their concentrations vary only a little from their corresponding global mean (Mitchell and Johns 1997). The greenhouse effect tends to be partially counteracted by the role of aerosols, the second most influential set of anthropogenic effects on Earth's radiating budget. Fuel combustion methods generate GHGs as well as aerosols. Whereas the GHGs, especially CO_2, have an atmospheric residency time of over a century, aerosols have atmospheric residence times usually less than a week and thus are concentrated at their sources (Karl et al. 1997), whether these are fuel-burning locations or regions of volcanic eruption. Burning of fossil fuel leads to the release of sulfur, which oxidizes and forms hydrated sulfate aerosols. These particles tend to cool climate as they scatter sunlight. Aerosols produce a global-scale cooling that peaks in the northern midlatitudes of the planet where the aerosol loading or emission is greatest, and also in high altitudes in winter owing to feedbacks between sea-ice and temperature, as observed by Mitchell and Johns, who also concluded that some of the changes in hydrology predicted to occur with increases in greenhouse gases may be less extreme in the short- and medium-term future (several decades). It was also concluded that the situation may not prevail in the longer term because sulfate concentrations will be maintained only as long as sulfur emissions continue, whereas CO_2 has a lifetime of about a century. Accordingly, GHG concentrations will remain high for many decades to come.

The global carbon cycle is important in its role of connecting the carbon pools or reservoirs, functioning as sources and sinks. Land-use changes, especially conversion of forests into other uses, are among the primary causes of disturbing the equilibria of carbon sources and sinks (detailed studies in this regard can be seen in Dale 1997, and Adger and Brown 1994). As a causal factor, land-use changes influence radiative fluxes with their multiplier effects on global warming, with changes in radiative forces caused by positive feedback effects. The capacities of land biosphere as sinks for carbon sequestration are altered, and the sinks instead become sources of carbon release. In Dale's analysis, the following concepts were used: (a) land-use effects on climate change include both implications of land-use change on atmospheric flux of CO_2 and its consequential impact on climate and alteration of climate change effects through land utilization; (b) effects of climate change on land use include both land-use alterations caused directly by climate change and the endogenous land management strategies in response to climate change. It was assessed that the former effect is currently significant relative to the latter. Mitigation strategies focusing on forestry and carbon sequestration are among the issues discussed in detail in chapters 4 and 5.

Anthropogenic disturbances with an ever-increasing trend to exhaust the sources of ecosystem services and the sink-carrying capacity need modifications to sustain an uninterrupted supply of nature's services. Table 2.1 provides a brief summary of the sources and sinks affected by human influences.

The CO_2 concentration in the atmosphere increased by about 80 parts per million by volume (ppmv) over the past two centuries, increasing Earth's radiative forcing by 1.6 watts/m^2. The two major carbon pools are the oceans and the land biosphere. Currently, the buildup of CO_2 in the atmosphere averages about 3 Gt C (1 Gt C = 10^{15} grams, or one billion tons, of carbon), an imbalance between sources and sinks of carbon by this magnitude unparalleled in the known geological past (Ciais 1999). According to some theories, terrestrial ecosystems or land biospheres provide an additional negative feedback (constituting a partial explanation to the missing-sinks phenomena to explain global carbon accumulations). This is because carbon accumulates in vegetation as a result of warming-enhanced mineralization of nitrogen in soil organic matter (and the critical roles of C/N ratios [carbon/nitrogen]). Data regarding variations over time in carbon balances do not fully correlate with temperature changes. It is posited (Houghton et al. 1998) that the existence of multiple mechanisms in the land biosphere working with opposite effects in carbon release and accumulation lead to a resultant net accumulation of carbon. In this argument it is also suggested that a positive feedback between global warming and the release of carbon to the atmosphere by terrestrial respiration seems likely to grow significantly in affecting the global carbon balance. These clarifications by themselves may not lead to actionable programs, but the role of enhanced global warming effects of deforestation and other carbon-release activities appears to contribute to multiplier effects. Anthropogenic influences on the global nitrogen cycle and their consequences on the interactive effects among various greenhouse gases (GHGs) are noteworthy; see Vitousek et al. (1997) for a detailed investigation and analysis.

The mechanisms responsible for the global carbon accumulations are not entirely clear yet. However, many of "these mechanisms are ex-

Table 2.1

Sources and Sinks Affected by Human Influences

	Sources	Sinks
Carbon dioxide	Land-use change, deforestation, fossil fuel combustion, biomass energy	Forests, ocean biota, moist soils
Nitrous oxide	Farm fertilizers, land-use change, biomass combustion	Soil-use change, conversion to N
Methane	Rice cultivation, wetlands, landfills, coal mining, biomass combustion	Oxidation in soil and atmosphere
Sulfur oxides	Fossil-fuel and biomass combustion	Acid deposition

pected to become less effective in the future, leading to a diminished sink" (Houghton et al. 1998). Similarly, Joos et al. (1999) argued that the rising atmospheric CO_2 leads to increased radiative forcing, which leads to higher sea-surface temperatures. These features affect the marine carbon cycle; the end result may be reduction in ocean carbon uptake and hence a potential acceleration of the net carbon accumulation on planet Earth. Various projections of the IPCC concerning future carbon accumulations in the atmosphere ignored the significant feedback relationship between climate change and oceanic uptake of CO_2. "The setting of emission targets as part of a global effort to stabilize the atmospheric CO_2 concentration may depend on accounting for the feedbacks between climate change and the oceanic uptake of CO_2," (Matear and Hirst 1999). Matear and Hirst provided an estimate in the potential reduction in the oceanic uptake at about 0.3 Gt C per year during the interval 1995 to 2010. It was suggested that this nearly corresponds to the target of the Kyoto Protocol (see chapters 5 and 6). Thus, the achievement of these targets could only mean offsetting the multiplier effects of net carbon accumulations rather than making a net impact on the increases in the latter.

The global carbon balance equation assessed by Houghton (1999) is the following:

atmospheric increase $= a + b - c - d$

where $a =$ carbon emissions due to fossil fuel consumption (3.3 ± 0.2 Gt C), b = net emissions from changes in land use (2.0 ± 0.8 Gt C),

c = oceanic uptake (2.0 ± 0.8 GT C), and

d = residual terrestrial sink (2.2 ± 1.3 Gt C).

The figures in parentheses indicate the corresponding estimate and its possible range of variation on either side.

Many of the problems of GHG emissions and the GE are rooted in the problems of lack of property rights in global environmental factors, and the lack of fair or equitable governance of the global commons. "Global commons" are defined here as the global environmental resources that cut across national boundaries and that are affected across all regions due to direct and indirect interventions in any one or more regions. The global commons possess varying features over time owing to changing human interface with the environment. The main ingredients of concern in the global commons are the following: atmospheric gases that cause the greenhouse effect and global warming; thinning of the ozone layer leading to increased ultraviolet-B radiation; transboundary pollution in the air and water; and loss of biodiversity.

The roots of anthropogenic contributions in the global commons are largely founded in the open-access and free-rider problems of public goods. Thus, the concern in the emerging problems of the global commons tends to focus on the issues of legitimacy of appropriations of sink capacities without any obligations on the part of users/polluters. These lead to questions about the legitimacy of any exercise of property rights. Property configurations can be broadly classified in terms of private property, state property, common property, and open access. Various resources like fresh water and the biological pool constitute examples of common property, whereas atmospheric concentrations of greenhouse gases and the ozone layer are examples of global commons with open access. We refer to these commons simply as "global commons." Unless otherwise stated, these possess open-access characteristics.

Lack of any property rights and consequent markets make this vital segment of the planet a potential threat for the survival of humanity, inasmuch as it currently is nature's benevolence that provides these avenues as opportunities for survival of all life-forms on Earth. Ironically, even the believers in the universal role of free markets for resource allocation and efficiency (of one type or other) fell short on the issue of creation of a fair global market for a relatively scarce resource. Emissions trading is a mechanism suggested strongly, but creation of benchmarks for the initial market conditions are far from resolved. It is not the presumption here that markets are the only suitable forms of global governance for the sustainable management of global commons. Both institutional and market factors are required for this purpose. There are hardly any features of property in the open-access case unless some restraints like emissions trading and quotas are institutionally imposed.

The problems relating to the global commons do not possess solutions from any one set of economic activities or individual or institutional categories for general application. The poorer regions contribute to the problems with their continued deforestation and combustion of fossil fuels for survival and economic growth, whereas the more developed regions draw upon the fossil fuels for industrial activities to fulfill higher levels of consumption directly and through industrial products for export revenues. The levels of efficiency of resource use and technology adoption for emission control and waste reduction are usually higher in the latter than in the former regions. However, the problems of limited international cooperation; "free riders;" and the roles of government regulations, market factors as well as voluntary compliance, and environmental consciousness require detailed analysis. Some of the issues of interface between trade and environment, debt and environment, and of environmental components of international trade have been examined in Rao (1999a, 1999b). The design of the institutional ramifications of the emissions and other problems of the global commons will be examined in chapters 5 and 6.

Global commons need to be evaluated not only for what these features depict in biogeophysical terms but also in terms of the accompanying costs of different levels of these features to the socioeconomic system. A single comprehensive measure of the status of the global commons is hard to conceptualize for any operationally meaningful purpose. However, some of the components might be amenable for such quantification. The most significant initiative in this direction concerns the GHGs and their contribution to the global warming problem, discussed in section 2.3.

Tragedy of the Commons

The phenomenon of the "tragedy of the commons" (Hardin 1968) tends to apply as human contributors tamper with the sink capacity without having to pay for such a destruction of the sink capacity. This problem is also similar to the "free rider" problem that economists analyze in the economics of public goods, but in those cases the public goods are paid for by some institutions. Nature provides a number of free goods as long as nature is not tampered with beyond natural threshold limits, and nature does respond rather belatedly with potentially irreversible and/or severe adverse consequences.

The problem of the tragedy of the commons arises not in the context of common property, but in the context of no clearly defined property rights, and because the proper terminology is "free access" resources rather than "common property" resources. These features are conventionally applied to the problem of governance of commodities or resources arising from one or more common pools of sources, with no cost to the users. Hardin sought to explain the processes of extinction of some of the fish stocks in terms of the "philosophy of the commons." However, the reasoning extends to the problems of governance of sinks, which is the main concern. In all such cases, the processes underlying the free-rider and open-access phenomena need to be addressed.

Alternatively, from an equivalent economic pricing perspective, the costs of externalities should be internalized. Users or beneficiaries should be made to pay some kind of "tax" based on their value-added "output," loss of sink capacity, and for any losses and damages to the ecosystems or reduction in ecosystem services.

Any dichotomous treatment of property simply in terms of common (nonprivate) property and private (exclusive) property is an excessive simplification of the issues involved. Another categorization, "anticommons," was suggested in Heller (1998) as an added alternative: Anticommons is a property regime in which multiple owners hold effective rights of exclusion to a scarce resource, and the ownership of anticommons property includes the ability of each owner to prevent other owners from obtaining a core bundle of rights in an entity. In this direction of inquiry, nonprivate property may be analyzed as follows: (a) anticommons property if the predominant feature is one of rights of exclusion in the use of resources, and (b) commons property if the exercise of privileges of inclusion remains the dominant feature.

No doubt global environmental problems have their roots at local levels, regional and subregional levels, and at the levels of individual consumers and producers. Accordingly, the features of the tragedy of the commons apply substantially at all these levels. These problems warrant collective coordinated actions where different societies, countries, and individual entities contribute to alleviate the common current and potential problems. Any such requirement of coordinated or cooperative effort presumes that all potential contributors to the problems tend to participate and that there are common perceptions, objectives, and comparable means of achieving the objectives among participants. To the extent that commonalities could be derived, the approach merits its adoption for devising policies, programs, and actions for implementation. The analytics of strategic cooperative behavior draw upon game-theory formulations, and some of these analyses suggest that in repeat transaction settings with interface between countries (possibly coordinated under agreements like the Montreal Protocol) there is much greater scope for cooperative behavior. This institutional arrangement is particularly relevant when the valuation of the future is not heavily discounted, or the decisions are not too myopic in their evaluation of alternatives.

Because the problem of global warming and climate change is the single most important problem of sustainability and sustainable development confronting human society at the beginning of the twenty-first century, we deal primarily with the first aspect in the remainder of this chapter. Other issues are discussed in various other sections of the text.

In the assessment of different characteristics of the global commons, we need to focus on the following (Rao 1999a):

- The roles of human activities in the observed sink problems
- Changes over time, historical and future trends
- Geographic differences in the current state and its likely changes
- Implications of adverse developments for global warming
- Impact of changes on the well-being and sustainability of human population
- The roles of anthropogenic factors in the governance of the global commons
- Specific contributions of greenhouse gases in the above
- Geophysical and economic explanations of changes
- Institutional aspects of the governance of the global commons
- Scope for devising relevant policies and programs

2.3 The Science of Global Warming

The natural greenhouse effect and the corresponding temperature dynamics on Earth are part of the phenomenon of life on this planet: If there were no natural greenhouse effect, Earth would remain so cold that it could not sustain any form of life. The question that concerns us in the debate on global warming is that of an *enhanced* greenhouse effect (GE). Unless otherwise stated, GE refers to this process. The role of the GE behind global warming remains a matter of serious concern, but not that of the natural greenhouse effect. History of climate change clearly indicates the effects of natural cooling and consequences of the ice ages. Thus, if global warming beyond the levels of recent years is disastrous or unwelcome, global cooling is also an undesirable event. The science behind the latter never attributed to the phenomenon a partial influence by anthropogenic (human) factors. The current debate, however, attributes a nontrivial role of human actions in the global warming processes. This role is played primarily via the GE. Greenhouse gases (GHGs) contribute toward a warm climate by "reducing the efficiency with which longwave radiation escapes to space. In most cases . . . they are well mixed throughout the troposphere and lower stratosphere, so their concentrations vary little from the global mean" (Mitchell and Johns 1997).

The role of human factors in the problems of greenhouse effect and global warming may be stated here. Combustion of fossil fuels for the consumption and production activities of the human enterprise leads to increases in the concentration of greenhouse gases in Earth's atmosphere: These are the fundamental factors underlying the global warming process and that are attributable to humans (see also Karl et al. 1997). These GHGs are primarily CO_2, methane (CH_4), ozone (O_3), and nitrous oxide (N_2O), and halocarbons, including chlorofluorocarbons (CFCs). These gases act asymmetrically with respect to sunlight; they let in the light rays but tend to insulate the planet against the losses of heat (specifically, they trap infrared radiative energy in the troposphere, the lower atmosphere), typically causing the greenhouse effect. Higher concentration of the GHGs implies much greater possibility of global warming. It was estimated that since about 1750 (the start of the industrial revolution) humans have altered the natural greenhouse effect by adding 30 percent more CO_2, 145 percent more CH_4, and various other gases (IPCC 1995). Most of the GHGs are the toughest to handle because many of these emissions have a longer life span in the atmosphere, about a century. In addition, other gases influence the effectiveness of given levels of GHGs. These include CO, nitrogen oxides (NO_x), and hydrocarbons. The CO_2 emissions are contributed primarily by fossil fuel combustion and deforestation (see Table 2.2).

Several scientific uncertainties relate to the specific roles of the contributing factors in the GE and global warming phenomena. Some of

Table 2.2

Time Trend of CO_2 Emissions

Year	CO_2 Emissions (million metric tons)	Cumulative Total (million metric tons)
1755	11	55
1805	33	953
1855	260	5,928
1905	2,433	56,217
1930	3,935	140,111
1955	7,471	277,398
1965	11,457	372,574
1975	16,902	521,395
1985	19,800	709,959
1986	20,504	730,462
1987	20,969	751,431
1988	21,790	773,221
1989	22,178	795,399
1990	22,383	817,783
1991	22,636	840,419
1992	22,292	862,711
1993	22,178	884,889
1994	23,054	907,943
1995	23,838	931,781

Source: Carbon Dioxide Information Analysis Center of the Oak Ridge National Laboratories, Oak Ridge, Tennessee, USA.

these include the magnitudes of aerosol contributions (natural and anthropogenic) that counteract the global warming effects of GHGs; the forecasting or predictive abilities of different global circulation models (GCMs) depicting the long-term behavior of the climatic factors incorporating all important feedback mechanisms; the role of individual GHGs like CH_4 in the short and long term (direct and indirect effects); changes in soil carbon retention potential with changes in climate; role of nitrogen changes in the carbon sequestration mechanisms with forestry programs and related aspects of the dynamics of carbon source and sinks. The issue of the direct roles of the GHGs in global warming and global warming potential is examined in the next section.

2.4 Greenhouse Gases and Global Warming Potential

Curtailing GHGs entails costs in some sections and regions. Policymakers attempting to find cost-effective methods of containing global warming or GHGs need to know the relative contributions of each of the main GHGs to target their reduction or stabilization, with regulation, market mechanism, and institutional cooperation. The relative unit cost of such reductions can possibly be compared among the constituent GHGs, and some trade-offs can be derived.

There is an increasing concern about the definition and role of the conventional measure of global warming potential (GWP) due to several difficulties in its ability to guide policy formulation or evaluation. To begin, let us draw upon the contributions of the IPCC reports to this vital debate. The original aim of the GWP index was to offer a simple characterization of the relative radiative effects of various combinations of gases in the atmosphere. The index was created in order to enable policymakers to evaluate options affecting the emissions of various greenhouse gases by avoiding the need to make complex calculations.

The GWP is a measure of the globally averaged warming effect arising from the emissions of a particular greenhouse gas, and is defined as the time-integrated change in radiative forcing due to the instantaneous release of 1 unit weight of a trace gas expressed relative to that from the release of the same unit weight of CO_2 (IPCC, 1990, 1992). The calculation requires a number of important specifications, including the following:

1. The radiative forcing of the reference gas and of the other species, per unit mass of concentration change at different levels of operation
2. Atmospheric lifetimes of various gases under consideration and of the reference gas
3. The time horizon over which the radiative forcings have to be integrated
4. The levels of future concentrations of other gases that form the background for interactive effectiveness
5. Global meteorological parameters for the current and future time periods.

A review of the initial formulations and their revisions will be useful in the understanding and refinement of the concept of GWP.

The GWP is essentially an assessment of a given GHG's contribution to heat trapping over its lifetime (or, atmospheric residency life interval), and this is normalized for comparison purposes, with respect to a corresponding expression for the reference gas. This reference gas is usually taken as CO_2, given its wider significance in the GE.

The formal definition led to one of the early formulations of GWP index I (Lashof and Ahuja 1990; IPCC 1990):

$$I = F/G, \text{ with } F = \Sigma \ f(t) \ C(t), \text{ and } G = \Sigma \ f(t) \ C(t)$$

where the sum is for T periods (time horizon of concern), $C(t)$ is the concentration of gas i at time $t = 0$, $f(t)$ is the radiating force or heat- trapping ability of the same per unit concentration, $C(t)$ and $f(t)$ are the corresponding quantities for CO_2. This index depends critically on the specification of T, and decreases with the choice of higher magnitudes of T for the gases having a shorter atmospheric residence than the average for CO_2.

The radiative heating effects per unit mass of various GHGs (given in parentheses) relative to CO_2 (taken as 1 unit) are as follows (see Harvey 1993): CH_4 (72), N_2O (206), CFC-11 (3970), CFC-12 (5750), HCFC-22 (5440).

Unless otherwise specified, all GWPs are direct GWPs (i.e., those that ignore any radiative effects due to the products of chemical transformation). Because of lack of information on the latter, indirect GWPs are hard to obtain; even those reported in the IPCC (1990) were ignored (IPCC 1992). A number of limitations of the above definition and operationalization are discussed in IPCC (1992), Harvey (1993), and Kandlikar (1996). We propose to deal with these aspects so that alternatives and improvements can be formulated. As pointed out in IPCC (1990), the modeling of radiative transfer within the atmosphere contains uncertainties and also unknowns, and this has major implications on the assessment and interpretation of the GWP. It was also noted (IPCC 1992) that "great care must be exercised in applying GWPs in the policy arena."

The specific limitations stated in the IPCC (1992) report include the following:

(a) since the direct GWP is a measure of the global effect of a given GHG emission, it is appropriate only for well-mixed gases in the troposphere, namely, CO_2, CH_4, N_2O, and halocarbons; different gas combinations can yield varying spatial patterns of radiative forcings;

(b) since in the assumed scientific model (the Siegenthaler–Oeschger model, underlying the GWP assessments) there is only an ocean

CO_2 sink, it is likely to overestimate the concentration changes and lead to an underestimate of both direct and the indirect GWPs; the magnitude of this bias depends on the atmospheric lifetime of the gas, and the time horizon;

(c) changes in radiative forcing due to CO_2, CH_4 and N_2O changes are nonlinear with respect to these changes; the net effect of these nonlinearities is such that, as CO_2 levels increase from present levels, the GWPs of all non-CO_2 gases would become higher than those evaluated by the present method;

(d) for gases that are not well mixed like the tropospheric ozone precursors, the GWP concept may not be meaningful;

(e) the concept does not also apply to inhomogenously distributed gases like aerosols, which have a significant interaction in the solar spectrum.

Although these problems and hence the limitations of the concept and application of the GWP are significant, a few improvements have been advanced recently. These arise from motivations of practical application. If the economics or the physical project lifetime, like a hydropower plant or coal energy production, is limited to a specified time period, say about 100 years, the incremental role of this production and its linkage to the radiating budget of the GHGs is what is of concern in the context of the project development or assessment of its environmental contribution. The role of varying combustion and fuel-use efficiencies in some of the combustible fossil fuels is somewhat complex in this context. The potential CO_2 release differs from its actual release and is a function of the technology in practical use. The products of incomplete combustion or the by-products (for example, CO and CH_4 in traditional biomass and fuelwood burning) of alternate combustion mechanisms are not simply those of CO_2 but a host of other GHGs as well, and these possess varying implications for the GWP.

An alternative GWP index was suggested by Harvey (1993). This formulation makes assessment of the relative contribution for the life of the project on a cumulative basis of accounting for the accumulated emissions over the time horizon. Empirical calculations showed that this method led to a greater role of CO_2 in the global warming phenomenon. This approach does not distinguish the possible economic impact of emissions occurring at different time points in the specified time horizon—that is, the time-discounting of the cost bases, if any, of alternative emission-control policies is irrelevant (Rao 1999a). Any GHG

indices and GWP measures that do not include economic impact considerations, even approximate ones, are of very little use for any policy
analysis. The estimates of conventional GWPs do not account for the
time variation in the economic opportunity costs of incremental values of
radiative forcing, and they do not recognize the economics of discounting
or time value of financial and other resources, as argued by Eckaus (1992).
Thus, the suggested index falls short of possible use in policy analysis
based directly on this index. It is possible to provide an additional transformation on Harvey's (1993) formulation by superimposing a dynamic
cost or a discounting function. In addition to such attempts, several analytical strengths are added in the contributions of Kandlikar (1995, 1996),
and these provide useful approaches to the entire debate.

The formulations reduce to the conventional formula for GWP when
a number of drastic simplifications are imposed; these include zero time-
discount rate and constancy of the damage function with any changes in
the global mean temperature. The formulation is also shown to be useful
in devising a cost-effectiveness analysis, which is required for most policy
analysis. This is carried out by minimizing the total costs subject to a
constraint on the global mean temperature of the form $T(t)$, where $T(t)$ is
an exogenously specified temperature path. Based on empirical analysis, it was found that the discount rate and the degree of nonlinearity in
the damage function continues to be a more critical determinant of the
index than does the temperature path. Other factors affecting the robustness of the analysis were the uncertainty in methane lifetime, and the
costs of abatement of carbon. Kandlikar's (1996) formulations offer a
very useful insight into the role and implications of future expectations
and discount rates into the impact mechanism of GWPs, converting an
otherwise technical and noneconomic problem into an economic and
strategic decision model; the fact that a discount rate may be the key to
climate change policy decisions is also reflected in the measures of GWP
when properly formulated. This is one of several important reasons for
the in-depth analysis of nonconstant and endogenous discounting methods offered in chapter 3.

One of the notable empirical studies using variable time-discounting
is that of Plambeck and Hope (1996), who argued that economic growth
will be affected by varying abatement policies and climate change impacts. Based on the projections of global economic growth and using a
standard formula for social rate of time preference, the authors found,
based on a pure rate of time preference of 3 percent a year, that the

marginal impact of carbon per ton could range from $10 to $48, with an average hovering around $21. These numbers almost double if the pure rate of time preference is brought down to 2 percent, and they go up very substantially (about twentyfold) if the rate is zero. These figures forcefully demonstrate the magnitudes of sensitivities involved with respect to the time-discounting factors. The formulations of Kandlikar (1996) can be strengthened to include the possibilities of nonconstant time-discounting, possibly using an endogenous discount function (see chapter 3), but this may also be seen with an infinite time-horizon model rather than an arbitrarily finite fixed-time horizon.

Any formulation of GWP needs to incorporate the effects of continued emissions of short-lived aerosols, which tend to provide cooling effects even in smaller intervals of time. The minimum that can be done to improvise these effects in the framework of Kandlikar is to allow for a series of time-dependent constants to be subtracted from the numerator of the relevant expressions. However, the magnitudes of adjustments involved are likely to be small.

Although insights into the relative roles of different GHGs in the GWP (direct and indirect) are useful in dealing with individual and collective GHG emissions, we need more analysis of the economics of the phenomenon of the GE for an overview of the problem at the global and regional levels.

The global climate change phenomena are not confined to global warming and GHGs. A broader set of interrelated aspects is that of changes in the ozone level, the theme of the following section.

2.5 The Ozone Factor

Let us introduce some of the standard terms in the debate. In the atmosphere, the tropospheric region is closest to Earth's surface, with an altitude less than 15 kilometers (km) from Earth's mean surface level. Similarly, the stratosphere lies in the range 15 to 50 km, the mesosphere in the range 50 to 80 km, and the thermosphere/ionosphere at levels exceeding 80 km in altitude. Stratopause lies between stratosphere and mesosphere, and the tropopause between troposphere and stratosphere.

The ozone layer is an important part of the atmosphere and shields the planet's surface from damaging ultraviolet radiation from the Sun. Ozone is continuously generated by the action of solar radiation on atmospheric oxygen and is amenable for destruction by catalytic processes involving trace amounts of free radical gases like nitrogen oxide. Atmospheric chemists Mario Molina, Sherwood Rowland, and Paul Crutzen won the 1995 Nobel Prize in chemistry for their diagnosis of the role of CFCs in the ozone layer of the stratosphere. It was found that photo decomposition of the CFCs in the stratosphere produce catalysts that cause destruction of ozone. The CFCs are very powerful infrared light absorbers; they destroy ozone and tend to contribute very significantly to the GE. The most important CFCs here are, CFC-11 and CFC-12. The atmospheric residence time of the CFCs is about a century, owing to their very slow diffusion into the stratosphere.

Ordinary oxygen is common in the atmosphere in the two-molecule form, O_2; another form of oxygen is ozone (O_3), a photochemically active gas. Whether ozone is useful or harmful to humans and other life-forms on this planet depends on its location in the atmosphere. Good ozone and bad ozone differ only in their location in the atmosphere. Ozone is measured in Dobson units (named after Gordon Dobson). In the lower troposphere it is an ingredient in the formation of photochemical smog, and it causes serious problems in air quality and adverse health effects. The ozone one normally refers to, in the context of the problems of the ozone hole and rupture in the ozone shield, is located in the stratosphere and is critically important to shield life-forms from ultraviolet (UV) radiation and its harmful effects. About 90 percent of the total ozone is located in the stratosphere. Skin cancer and other health problems are associated strongly with the effects of UV radiation. It is also useful to note that ozone concentration varies with the seasons and the latitudes around the planet. Roelofs and Lelieveld (1997) observed that (a) the stratospheric O_3 contributes significantly to surface O_3 in winter and spring when the petrochemical lifetime of O_3 is relatively long, and (b) in summer and in the tropics, little O_3 reaches Earth's surface from the stratosphere, owing to strong petrochemical destruction, so that surface O_3 is determined largely by petrochemical production. Ozone from the stratosphere accounts for about 75 percent of that consumed in the troposphere annually. Production of O_3 in the troposphere is limited because of less UV light relative to that in the stratosphere.

An understanding of the specific nature of the relationship between ozone and its two main anthropogenic precursors, NO_x and volatile organic compounds (VOC), in any region is important for devising mitigating strategies. These precursors themselves exhibit complex nonlinear interrelationships. The dependency of ozone on one or both of the precursors varies in location over time, and area-specific predictions remain uncertain. The ozone-precursor relationships are better understood in terms of a distinction between NO_x-sensitive and VOC-sensitive (or VO_x-saturated) chemical regimes (Sillman 1999). These regimes appear in different forms in urban regions, power plant plumes, and polluted rural areas. Considerable additional studies are required for a better understanding of the complexities of these relationships.

The best current estimate seems to suggest that for each 1 percent depletion in ozone, cataract incidence would increase by 0.6 to 0.8 percent (Madronich et al. 1995). The human immune system is adversely affected by the UV-B effects, and thus public health problems, including infectious diseases, are exacerbated by the depletion of Earth's ozone layer. More details are discussed in chapter 4.

Chlorine (Cl) is one of the catalysts that turns O_3 into O_2 units, causing destruction of the ozone layer. Empirical confirmation of the ozone hole was carried out by Farman et al. (1985). CFC-11, until recently used as a refrigerant and propellant, is one of the main CFCs responsible for nearly half the observed depletion of ozone. The CFCs get mixed gradually into the atmosphere and take decades to reach the stratosphere. After arriving there, they are decomposed by UV sunlight, releasing the chlorine that begins attacking the ozone. The chemical-balancing equations relevant here are in the following: Roelofs and Lelieveld 1997; Somerville 1996, 6–23; and Schlesinger 1991.

The catalytic action of Cl is given by the reaction

$$Cl + O_3 \longrightarrow ClO + O_2$$
$$O_3 + UV \text{ radiation} \longrightarrow O_2 + O$$

A link between ozone depletion and an increase in the greenhouse effect was found by Ramanathan (1975): CFCs trap heat the same way that other gases such as CO_2 do, and thus they are also greenhouse gases (GHGs).

The Ozone Factor and Its Effects

Accumulations of CFC-11 and CFC-12 in the atmosphere nearly doubled between 1975 and 1985. It was assessed (WMO 1986 and UNEP 1987) that such a rapid change would reduce the ozone layer by about 9 percent on a global average by 2050 if no measures were initiated. The possibility was that higher levels of harmful ultraviolet-B (UV-B) radiation could reach heavily populated regions of the Northern Hemisphere. It was also assessed that high atmospheric concentrations of chlorine could result in a potentially significant redistribution of ozone, with depletion in the upper stratosphere partially offset by increases in ozone at lower altitudes. The CFCs themselves were hundreds of times more powerful than carbon dioxide in their capability to enhance the greenhouse effect, and these could significantly aggravate the global warming effect.

The roles of the related CFC-113, CFC-114, and CFC-115 and two bromide compounds, halon-1211 and halon-1301, were also considered significant. All these chemicals possess long atmospheric lifetimes and high efficiency in triggering the catalytic reactions that destroy ozone. The halons had a substantially higher potency than did CFCs for the destruction of the ozone layer.

The Montreal Protocol was strengthened with the 1990 London Amendments, which also expanded the list of ozone-depleting chemicals: for 1997 and the following years, levels could not exceed 15 percent of the base levels of 1986, and a complete phaseout by the year 2000 was mandated. Further enhancement of actions in this direction was sought by the Copenhagen Amendments in November 1992; the initial provision of interim substitutes for CFCs, namely hydrochlorofluorocarbons (HCFCs), were also sought to be eliminated along with carbon tetrachloride and methyl chloroform by 1996. The most significant background for effective international collective action came from the scientific evidence in 1985 about the existence of a significant ozone hole and the analysis of factors behind it. The existence of illicit trade for some CFCs in a few countries remains an area of continued concern.

Analytical and institutional dimensions of the Montreal Protocol as a collective public goods issue were examined in Murdoch and Sandler (1997). The provision of incentives under the implementation mechanisms in the developing countries added to the potential impact of the Protocol.

Ozone Depletion

The ozone layer stretches from ten to twenty-five miles over Earth's surface. It absorbs incoming solar shortwave ultraviolet (UV) radiation.

"Thinning" of this biospheric ozone shield is the most significant source of radiation-induced skin cancers for humans; this radiation can also harm all living systems on the planet, including DNA mutation. Ozone is not only present in the stratosphere but also in the troposphere, which is closer to Earth. Bengtsson and colleagues (1999) found that the reduction of stratospheric ozone cools not only the lower stratosphere but also the upper and middle troposphere, and that the cooling from tropospheric ozone leads to a reduction in the greenhouse warming in the upper tropospheric region.

The problem of potential interactions between ozone loss and exposure of marine phytoplanktons to the effects of UV radiation can adversely influence the CO_2 sink features of the oceans and lead to enhanced GE, possibly with another set of positive feedbacks for global warming and other features (Myers 1993). The synergistic interactions of multiple global phenomena pose severe multiplicative effects, once one or more of the environmental thresholds are exceeded. The real issue is to decipher these threshold combinations, which produce acceptable climatological and environmental configurations.

Ozone is continuously being generated by the action of solar radiation on atmospheric oxygen, and it suffers destruction by catalytic processes involving gases like nitrogen oxide and CFCs (Molina and Molina 1992). Photo decomposition of the CFCs in the stratosphere produces catalysts for the destruction of ozone. Less ozone in the stratosphere tends to counteract the greenhouse effect, but the net result of the opposing forces of ozone-depleting substances and UV radiation is not clear. However, what is clear is that the increase in UV-B radiation that follows ozone depletion worsens air quality and leads to increased numbers of deaths from asthma, chronic respiratory disease, and damages to plant life (see also Nilsson 1996).

The U.S. Environmental Protection Agency (USEPA) estimated that a 50 percent cutback in CFC emissions from 1986 levels could significantly damage the U.S. economy: $6.4 trillion by 2075 in reduced costs associated with skin cancers alone (USEPA 1987). Every 1 percent loss in ozone is estimated to lead to a 2 percent increase in harmful UV radiation exposure (de Gruijl 1995). Some of the recent studies (1999) by the Goddard Institute for Space Studies and Center for Climate Systems Research suggest that the ozone-depletion phenomenon is continuing despite the curtailment of several harmful substances and that the peak magnitude of ozone depletion might occur about 2010.

The role and function of the stratospheric ozone layer as a cosmic protector against ultraviolet-B (UV-B) radiation (which has wavelengths in the range 315 to 280 nanometers) has been crippled due to anthropogenic contributions of concentrations of CFCs and other ozone-depleting substances: methyl chloroform, halons (used in fire extinguishers), and methyl bromide (generally used in chlorinated pesticides). As already stated, the 1995 Nobel Prize in chemistry was awarded to the three scientists who discovered the relevant mechanisms affecting the ozone layer. Paul Crutzen examined the role of nitrogen oxides in the natural creation and destruction of ozone; Mario Molina and Sherwood Rowland identified the role of chlorine from CFCs in these interactions.

In an important recent study, Crutzen et al. (1999) argued that in situ chemical gross production and destruction of ozone in the troposphere are larger than the downward flux from the stratosphere, thus establishing the significance of in situ tropospheric photochemistry in determining the influence on ozone levels in the lower troposphere. It was argued that ozone may be produced or destroyed in amounts largely exceeding the downward flux of ozone from the stratosphere to the troposphere, depending on the availability of NO_x catalysts. The stratospheric influx of ozone then assumes only a secondary role. The relatively small roles of local or regional photochemical smog ozone to the global photochemical ozone budget was also assessed in this process. In some of the other studies, it was suggested that it is more efficient to reduce NO_x emissions in low NO_x areas and to reduce VOC emissions in high NO_x areas.

The CFCs are generally used as refrigerants (propane and butane), foam insulation, aerosol propellants (in air-powered spray devices), electronic goods, and degreasing solvents for cleaning. A number of major initiatives, especially the Montreal Protocol and its follow-up actions, are expected to ameliorate the crisis, but the possible continuity of damages to human and biotic health is not expected to disappear for another five decades or more. Various CFCs are being replaced by the substitutes HCFCs, HFCs, and perfluorocarbons (PFCs). The phaseout of CFCs applies also to HCFCs, but these are allowed as interim substitutes, as agreed to in the 1990 London meeting of the parties of the Montreal Protocol. Like the CFCs themselves, HCFCs and HFCs are both potent gases; during a span of a hundred years after these are injected into the atmosphere, a ton of CFC-11 tends to have about 4000 times the global warming potential relative to one ton of CO_2, and a ton of HCFC-22 will have about 1700 times that of a ton of CO_2 (Worldwatch Institute 1997).

According to the Carbon Dioxide Information Analysis Center (CDIAC) (quoted in *World Resources 1998–99*), trends in the atmospheric concentrations of CO_2 indicated an increase from 325.5 parts per million (ppm) in 1970 to 362.6 ppm in 1996. Levels of emissions and concentrations of other gases that have ozone-depleting properties have also changed for the worse. Based on the data from late 1970s, the trends indicate the following: Concentrations of carbon tetrachloride (CCl_4) in the atmosphere rose from 88 parts per trillion (ppt) in 1978 to 99 ppt in 1996; methyl chloroform (CH_3CCl_3) from 58 ppt to 89 ppt; CFC-11 from 139 ppt to 261 ppt; CFC-12 from 257 ppt to 522 ppt; total gaseous chlorine from 1457 ppt to 2731 ppt; and nitrous oxide (N_2O) from 298 parts per billion (ppb) to 310 ppb. In case of CFC-113, the increase was from 26 ppt to 82 ppt between 1982 and 1996, and in the case of methane (CH_4), the increase went from 1600 ppb in 1986 to 1670 ppb in 1996.

In terms of major international policy initiatives launched during the recent decades, it is relevant to note that the Convention for the Protection of the Ozone Layer, held in March 1985 in Vienna, mandated that the ratifiers of the convention study the harmful effects of CFC emissions on the ozone layer and conduct scientific research to find substitutes. The Montreal Protocol extended the Vienna Convention provisions by setting targets and limits on the emissions of CFC-11 and CFC-12, with the provision that other villains of ozone depletion, such as methyl chloroform and carbon tetrachloride, could be included for similar regulations later. The Montreal Protocol came into force on January 1, 1989, with the following features: Countries agreeing to the Protocol must reduce their annual consumption and production of CFCs to their 1986 levels by July 1993; from July 1993 to June 1994 and during each year until July 1998, the annual production and consumption of CFCs should stay below the limit of 80 percent of their 1986 levels; from July 1998 and after, the corresponding production should be limited to 50 percent of 1986 levels.

The Montreal Protocol did lead to effective reduction of use of some of the ozone-depleting chemicals; the major role of trichoroethane (a previously common cleaning solvent) has already peaked. Montzka et al. (1999) stated that the limiting factor in the further reduction of undesirable atmospheric chemicals is halon H-1211, more than any other restricted chemicals covered under the Montreal Protocol. Given the substantial existing reservoirs of H-1211 and H-1301 in fire-extinguishing equipment, continued emissions could affect the ozone layer for a decade or more.

Among the atmospheric changes attributed to partly counter the effects of global warming are those of the aerosols. These issues are discussed below.

2.6 The Aerosols Factor

Next only to the role of GHGs in explaining the operative features of changes in the climate, the significance of aerosols is receiving much greater attention in the 1990s than ever before. Aerosols are minute particles affecting the solar reflection and Earth's albedo. Unlike GHGs (excluding water vapor), aerosols have short atmospheric residence times (less than a week), and they are concentrated near their origin. Burning fossil fuels and reducing soil moisture because of land-use changes are two factors contributing to the release of sulfur into the atmosphere. Sulfur oxidizes and forms hydrated sulfate aerosols. The role of regional patterns of aerosol emissions suggests potential modifications of regional climate occurring in Europe and Southeast Asia (details are given in the study by Mitchell and Johns 1997).

Natural events such as volcanic eruptions and their contribution to aerosols and cooling of the climate need to be recognized as well. Changes in anthropogenically contributed aerosols can affect net radiative forcing of GHGs, but the effect of the latter is considered predominant. Scenarios with high aerosol and GHG emissions contribute to climatic destabilization, with greater uncertainty in mean temperature and a greater likelihood of changes in other climate parameters (see West et al. 1997). Thus, some arguments suggesting that aerosols may be beneficial to counteract global warming (in terms of global averages) due to GHGs is questionable. Some of the studies at NASA's Goddard Institute of Space Studies (GISS) indicated in the late 1990s that aerosols do not just cool; they also absorb sunlight and contribute to some amount of warming of the atmosphere. The effect caused by aerosols on climate is largely to be viewed in terms of their effects through the clouds' albedo. By enhancing the number of droplets in a cloud, aerosols can amplify the reflectivity of clouds, and this can have a net cooling effect on the atmosphere (Kerr 1997). According to an estimate by Rind et al. (1999), aerosols produced a significant negative forcing of about 1.2 W/m^2, with about an equal contribution from direct and indirect tropospheric aerosol effects. However, the magnitudes of these direct and indirect effects differ from those of Bengtsson et al. (1999), stated in Section 2.2.

Sulfate aerosol has been recognized in science as an important con-

tributor to the scattering of sunlight and a major influence in the con-
densation of nuclei in the atmosphere. It is also believed that human
contributions of emissions of sulfur gases are about two or three times
as large as those attributable to natural sources; this ratio is about ten
times in the regions over heavily industrial areas (Rodhe 1999).

However, differences exist between the Northern Hemisphere and the
Southern Hemisphere in the effectiveness of the aerosols factor. The
feedbacks from clouds in radiative forcing plays opposing roles in the
GHG contribution contrasted with the aerosol contribution. LeTreut et
al. (1998) concluded, based on a detailed modeling effort, that aerosols
may have substantially counteracted the climatic effects of the GHGs in
the Northern Hemisphere during the twentieth century. This poses an
added burden on the ethics and liability of the North relative to the South,
namely that the industrial countries could possibly be evading part of
the damaging effects of global warming while contributing most to the
emissions of GHGs. Emissions of aerosols and GHGs tend to be highly
correlated at their source, but their diffusion into the atmosphere is dis-
similar. The GHGs are largely uniformly distributed and well mixed in
the atmosphere, affecting almost all regions of the world equally, but the
effect of the aerosols is different. These cause a different vertical distribution of the radiative forcing distribution, and the anthropogenic aerosol contributions of the North tend to offset the regional warming effects
of the GHGs.

2.7 Scientific Uncertainty and Decision Making

Scientific uncertainty comprises at least two major aspects: uncertainty
in scientific diagnostics of the processes over time and space or other
subdivisions, and scientific inferences made with explicit recognition of
the probabilistic nature of the operation of the phenomena. Some of the
examples of the former include the effect of deforestation on regional
temperature and rainfall over the next ten years, and those of the latter
include rise in global mean surface temperature by 1 degree centigrade,
with, say, 70 percent certainty during the next fifty years. Assessments
about the likely scientific phenomena should be accompanied by the
applicable parameter ranges for their validity, likelihood of their validity under varying initial and changing conditions governing the evolution of the phenomena over time, and cause-effect relationships under
plausible alternative configurations of the systems under consideration.

The costs of accepting different known and unknown risks constitute different exercises, ultimately facilitating an informed judgment about acceptance of a risk bundle with known costs, or reducing the potential risks with an understanding of resultant costs and benefits.

The climate change phenomena are as complex as any phenomenon known to humans. Accordingly, a meaningful understanding of the relevant phenomena with any reasonable degree of certainty requires a very high level of analytical tools involving mathematical and statistical complexity. It is also important to recognize that scientific analyses in themselves are simply inputs in a chain of analytical processes that lead to final practical decisions within the society. The normal mechanisms in this chain include processing scientific inferences in terms of what they imply to the human systems, the costs/benefits of inaction and different interventions, the methods of intervention, stakeholder participation and resource mobilization, and fair methods of distribution of costs and benefits of interventions.

Some of the applicable statistical methods for climatology are provided in a series of studies; see, for example, von Storch and Zweirs (1998). However, literature on the extension of these methods to integrate climate change and policy inference is relatively scarce. A recent contribution by Levine and Berliner (1999) is a useful presentation, but the focus is on improving the precise statistical nature of climate variations and the quality of detection of climate change due to anthropogenic factors. Some of the IPCC reports dealt with the issues of uncertainty, but none came close to integrating scientific uncertainty, statistical uncertainty, and decision making for public policy intervention under varying degrees of uncertainty.

The above discussion becomes even more complex when the relative contribution of human activities, especially different methods of production, in the global warming processes are isolated from the rest of the influences and estimated for the present and for several years into the future. However, some basic principles of decision making and risk aversion remain relevant in the formulation of both global and country-specific policies to curtail climate change. These include a cost-effective risk aversion (CERA), explained partly by the generally accepted Precautionary Principle (PP). The concept of CERA is based on the evaluation of least-cost choices for a given acceptable level of risk of realization of one or more undesirable states of nature. Varying types (or categories) and their magnitudes of risks generate corresponding menu choices for decision making.

The PP is equivalent to "risk averse" behavior in cases that involve irreversibilities or extremely high costs in socioeconomic or biogeophysical or other terms. When applied in general situations not necessarily involving these features, the PP could lead to a caution that may be attained at the expense of substantial potential gains. However, the risk-averse nature of the Precautionary Principle is very relevant if scientific knowledge is too limited to quantify uncertainty and thus cannot establish probability distributions of potential outcomes.

The PP is based on the idea that any uncertainty should be interpreted toward a measure of safeguard. The PP is equivalent to a "no regrets" policy. The Rio Declaration of the Earth Summit 1992, Agenda 21, Principle 15, stated: "Where there are threats of serious or irreversible damage, lack of full scientific certainty shall not be used as a reason for postponing cost-effective measures to prevent environmental degradation. . . . In order to protect the environment, the precautionary approach shall be widely applied by States according to their capabilities." Earlier, the Ministerial Declaration concluding the Second World Climate Conference in 1990 at Geneva stated this principle exactly. The first international formulation of the Principle was at the First International Conference on the Protection of the North Sea in 1984 when the focus was on emissions into the marine environment. The PP has played an increasingly significant role ever since its endorsement by the Second International Conference of the North Sea in 1987.

Because many environmental problems are fraught with system uncertainties and incomplete information about the system characteristics, the PP tends to be equally applicable, especially in problems like greenhouse effects. The increasing role of PP suggests that it is ripening into a norm of international law; some of the key elements of a legal definition rely upon the following: (a) a threshold of perceived threat against which advance action would be deemed justifiable, and (b) a burden of proof on the activity contributor or entrepreneur to show that a proposed action will not cause actual harm (Cameron and Abouchar, 1991). The PP implies current commitment of resources in order to safeguard against the likelihood of future occurrence of adverse outcomes of certain activities. This approach is implicitly seeking trade-offs in the interests of the present with those of the future, and thus depends on implicitly assumed time-discounting and future resource valuation (Rao, 1999a). These factors are usually not examined in the current practices in the application of the PP. This is because the role of the PP is largely confined thus far to providing guidance to policy judgment and offering benefit of doubt in favor of environmental resources.

In general, it is useful to recognize the distinctions in risk assessment and risk management relative to a given risk potential or fuzzy and unknown risk scenarios where only certain qualitative features are known. The role of value preferences, equity of various dimensions, time-discounting and future resource valuations, and a conscious decision expressing preferences of various risk and reward bundles (however imprecisely evaluated) are among the important considerations behind any decision making in the context of public policymaking for climate governance.

2.8 Concluding Observations

The complex dynamic interrelationships between different components of GHGs and other atmospheric gases require improved understanding. Some of these assessments require a time profile "controlled experiment" set up for isolating the relative roles of different factors and their regional dimensions. Pragmatic intervention policies toward climate stabilization and formulation of cost-effective policies become feasible in an integrated framework when the relative efficacies of alternate measures can be gauged in quantifiable terms. Thus, the scientific inputs for decision making remain critical for devising robust environmental and economic policies, including those of choice of appropriate technologies. Based on the scientific foundations, a meaningful economic strategy can be formulated. These issues are the concern of chapter 3. Suffice it to say that accelerated additional scientific research remains a high priority in order to decipher more of the climatological interactive phenomena and multiple factors associated with global climate change.

References

Adger, W.N., and Brown, K. 1994. *Land Use and the Causes of Global Warming.* Chichester, UK: Wiley.
Arrhenius, S. 1896. "On the Influence of Carbonic Acid in the Air upon the Temperature on the Ground." *The Philosophical Magazine* 41:237–276.

Bengtsson, L., Roeckner, E., and Stendel, M. 1999. "Why Is the Global Warming Proceeding Much Slower Than Expected?" *Journal of Geophysical Research* 104(D4):3865–3876.

Cameron, J., and Abouchar, J. 1991. "The Precautionary Principle—A Fundamental Principle of Law and Policy for the Protection of the Global Environment." *Boston College International and Comparative Law Review* 14:1–27.

Ciais, P. 1999. "Restless Carbon Pools." *Nature* 398 (March 11):111–112.

Crutzen, P.J., Lawrence, M.G., and Poschl, U. 1999. "On the Background Photochemistry of Tropospheric Ozone." *Tellus* 51(A–B):123–146.

Daily, G. (ed.). 1997. *Nature's Services.* Washington, DC: Island Press.

Dale, V.H. 1997. "The Relationship Between Land Use Change and Climate Change." *Ecological Applications* 7(3):753–769.

de Gruijl, F.R. 1995. "Impacts of a Projected Depletion in the Ozone Layer." *Consequences* 1:13–21.

Eckaus, R. 1992. "Comparing the Effects of Greenhouse Gas Emissions on Global Warming." *The Energy Journal* 13:25–35.

Farman, J.C., Gardner, B.G., and Shanklin, J.D. 1985. "Large Losses of Total Ozone in Antarctica Reveal Seasonal ClO_x/NO_x Interaction." *Nature* 315:207–210.

Fourier, J.B. 1824. "Mémoires sur les températures du globe terrestre et des espaces planétaires." *Mémoires de l'Académie royale des sciences et de l'Institut de France.* 7:569–604.

Hardin, G. 1968. "The Tragedy of the Commons." *Science* 162:1243–1248.

Harvey, L.D. 1993. "A Guide to Global Warming Problems." *Energy Policy* 21:24–34.

Heller, M.A. 1998. "The Tragedy of the Anticommons." *Harvard Law Review* 111(3):621–688.

Houghton, R.A. 1999. "The Annual Net Flux of Carbon to the Atmosphere from Changes in Land Use 1850–1990." *Tellus* 51B:298–313.

Houghton, R.A., Davidson, E.A., and Woodwell, G.M. 1998. "Missing Sinks, Feedbacks, and Understanding the Role of Terrestrial Ecosystems in the Global Carbon Balance." *Global Biogeochemical Cycles* 12(1):25–34.

IPCC. Intergovernmental Panel on Climatic Change. 1996. *The Science of Climate Change—IPCC Working Group I Report.* Geneva: IPCC/WMO.

———.1992. *Global Climate 1992–A Supplementary Report*, New York: Cambridge University Press.

———. 1990. *Climate Change—The Scientific Assessment.* New York: Cambridge University Press, published for the IPCC.

Joos, F., et al. 1999. "Global Warming and Marine Carbon Cycle Feedbacks on Future Atmospheric CO_2." *Science* 284:464–467.

Kandlikar, M. 1996. "Indices for Comparing Greenhouse Gas Emissions—Interpreting Science and Economics." *Energy Economics* 18(4):265–281.

———. 1995. "The Relative Roles of Trace Gas Emissions in Greenhouse Abatement Policies." *Energy Policy* 23:879–883.

Karl, T., Nichols, N., and Gregory, J. 1997. "The Coming Climate." *Scientific American*, May:78–83.

Kerr, R.A. 1997. "Greenhouse Forecasting Still Cloudy." *Science* 76 (May):1040–1042.

Lashof, D.A., and Ahuja, D.R. 1990. "Relative Contributions of Greenhouse Gas Emissions to Global Warming." *Nature* 344:529–531.

LeTreut, H., Forichon, M., Boucher, O., and Li, Z-X. 1998. "Sulfate Aerosol Indirect Effect and CO_2 Greenhouse Forcing: Equilibrium Response of the LMD GCM and Associated Cloud Feedbacks." *Journal of Climate* 11(7):1673–1684.

Levine, R., and Berliner, L. 1999. "Statistical Principles for Climate Change Studies." *Journal of Climate* 12:564–576.

Madronich, S., et al. 1995. "Changes in Ultraviolet Radiation Reaching the Earth's Surface." *Ambio* 24(3):143–152.

Matear, R.J., and Hirst, A. 1999. "Climate Change Feedback on the Future Oceanic CO_2 Uptake." *Tellus* 51B:722–733.

Mitchell, J.F.B., and Johns, T.C. 1997. "On Modification of Global Warming by Sulfate Aerosols." *Journal of Climate* 10(2):245–266.

Molina, M.J., and Molina, L.J. 1992. "Stratospheric Ozone." Pp. 24–35 in *The Science of Global Climate Change*, ed. D.A. Dunette and R.J. O'Brien. Washington, DC: American Chemical Society.

Montzka, S.A., Butler, J.H., Elkins, J.W., Thompson, T.M., Clarke, A.D., and Lock, L.T. 1999. "Present and Future Trends in the Atmospheric Burden of Ozone-Depleting Halogens." *Nature* 398 (April):690–694.

Murdoch, J.C., and Sandler, T. 1997. "The Voluntary Provision of Pure Public Good—The Case of Reduced CFC Emissions and the Montreal Protocol." *Journal of Public Economics* 63:331–349.

Myers, N. 1993. *Ultimate Security—The Environmental Basis of Political Stability.* New York: W.W. Norton.

National Academy of Sciences (U.S.). 1992. *Policy Implications of Greenhouse Warming.* Washington, DC: National Academy Press.

Nilsson, A. 1996. *Ultraviolet Reflections: Life Under a Thinning Ozone Layer.* New York: Wiley.

Plambeck, E.L., and Hope, C. 1996. "PAGE 95—An Updated Valuation of the Impacts of Global Warming." *Energy Policy* 24(9):783–793.

Ramanthan, V. 1975. "Greenhouse Effect Due to Chlorofluorocarbons—Climatic Implications." *Science* 190:50–52.

Rao, P.K. 1999a. *Sustainable Development: Economics and Policy.* Oxford: Blackwell.

———. 1999b. *World Trade Organization and the Environment.* London: Macmillan.

Rastetter, E.B., Agren, G.I., and Shaver, G.R. 1997. "Responses of N-Limited Ecosystems to Increased CO_2: A Balanced-Nutrition, Coupled-Element-Cycles Model." *Ecological Applications* 7(2):444–460.

Rind, D. 1999. "Complexity and Climate." *Science* 284 (April):105–107.

———. Lean, J., and Healy, R. 1999. "Simulated Time-Dependent Climate Response to Solar Radiative Forcing Since 1600." *Journal of Geophysical Research* 104 (D2):1973–1990.

Rodhe, H. 1999. "Human Impact on the Atmospheric Sulfur Balance." *Tellus* 51(A–B):110–122.

Roelofs, G.-J., and Lelieveld, J. 1997. "Model Study of the Influence of Cross-Tropopause O_3 Levels." *Tellus* 49B(1):38–55.

Schlesinger, W.H. 1991. *Biogeochemistry-An Analysis of Global Change*. New York: Academic Press.

Schmalensee, R., Stoker, T.M., and Judson, R.A. 1998. "Wprld Carbon Dioxide Emissions 1950–2050." *Review of Economics and Statistics* 80(1):15–27.

Schneider, S.H. 1997. *Laboratory Earth*. New York: Basic Books.

Sillman, S. 1999. "The Relation Between Ozone, NOx and Hydrocarbons in Urban and Polluted Rural Environments." *Atmospheric Environment* 33:1821–1845.

Somerville, R. 1996. *The Forgiving Air—Understanding Environmental Change*. Berkeley: University of California Press.

Timmermann, A., Oberhuber, J., Bacher, A., Esch, M., Latif, M., and Roeckner, E. 1999. "Increased El Niño Frequency in a Climate Model Forced by Future Greenhouse Warming." *Nature* 398 (April):694–698.

UNEP. 1987. *The Ozone Layer*. Nairobi: UNEP Secretariat.

USEPA. 1987. *Assessing the Risks of Trace Gases That Can Modify the Stratosphere*. Washington, DC: USEPA.

Vitousek, P.M., Aber, J.D., Howarth, R.W., Likens, G.E., Matson, P.A., Schindler, D.W., Schlesinger, W.H., and Tilman, D.G. 1997. "Human Alteration of the Global Nitrogen Cycle: Sources and Consequences." *Ecological Applications* 7(3):737–750.

von Storch, H., and Zweirs, F. 1998. *Statistical Analysis in Climate Research*. Cambridge: Cambridge University Press.

West, J.J., Hope, C., and Lane, S.N. 1997. "Climate Change and Energy Policy—The Impacts and Implications of Aerosols." *Energy Policy* 25(11):923–939.

WMO. 1986. *Atmospheric Ozone 1985–Assessment of Our Understanding of the Processes Controlling Its Present Distribution and Change*. Geneva: WMO Secretariat.

World Resources Institute. 1998. *World Resources 1998–99*. New York: Oxford University Press.

Worldwatch Institute. 1997. *State of the World 1997*. Washington, DC: Worldwatch Institute.

Chapter 3

Economic Approaches

3.1 Introduction

Much of the global climatic change is currently influenced by human-induced economic and noneconomic factors. Some of the latter have been discussed in chapter 2. Each one of the scientific factors of global climate change is affected directly or indirectly by human actions (and inactions). In all these cases, one would like to decipher the direct and indirect roles of economic forces so that a conscious choice of cost-effective policies might be feasible. The concept of "cost" must be far more general than what the traditional economic literature would suggest (see Rao 2000 for a detailed treatment). This requires considerable improvement in dealing with the issues of global climate change. Trans-action costs, for example, could include significant costs of adjustments to both expected and unanticipated changes in the climate.

Climatic impacts are usually inequitably distributed across different regions of the world, and across various subsystems of the biogeosphere. The broad question in the global context is: When climatic factors are adversely influenced by a set of known and spatially distributed actions, but the climatological responses are unknown, random, and unrelated in geographic incidence to the global sources of the problems, what accountability can be fixed on the disturbance-causing entities? In other words, when there exist indivisibilities in the "output" function of the climate and its impacts, what are the rational mechanisms for various institutions and their provision of economic incentives to mitigate the impacts, preferably equitably? Most of these issues cannot be answered simply in terms of the traditional economic approaches. The effect on human morbidity due to climate-influenced changes in public health, for example, is one of several costs of adjustment. Moreover, there are additional costs of transition and adaptation. Most of the cost elements are derived not only from market characteristics but also from nonmarket features, varying from time to time.

Economic aspects of global climate change are largely related to the economics of greenhouse gases (GHGs). Some of the important economic dimensions relevant for assessing the phenomena underlying global climate change, and in mitigating its effects, are explained in this chapter. It is important to integrate the debate on climate change with the issues of sustainability and sustainable development so as to provide a human-development perspective. These issues are also required to be integrated with the ecological and biogeophysical aspects of sustainability. These details follow in the next section.

A meaningful policy framework cannot emerge without an appropriate assessment of costs and valuations of resources, including environmental sink features. The discussions in Sections 3.3 and 3.4 address these aspects. The valuation of resources over time into rather long horizons, and appropriate discounting, remain extremely important and complex issues. These critical problems are examined in Section 3.5. A new Green Golden Rule is derived in Section 3.6, which offers insights into the role of human adaptation and changes in preferences in ensuring environmental and economic sustainability. The role of carbon taxes (or green taxes/ecotaxes) is an emerging area of policy intervention to mitigate the effects of environmental externalities at both national and local levels. Various ramifications of this instrument of policy are examined in Section 3.7. A multilevel policy framework incorporating market and nonmarket institutional aspects is proposed in Section 3.8. Appendix 3A provides technical details of the derivation of an analytical result, which suggests that, under uncertainties of cost, a low discounting of future valuations is rational for risk-averse decision-making situations as in the case of global climatic changes. Appendix 3B offers a broad framework for devising optimal incentive and disincentive mechanisms geared toward stabilization of the climate-governing systems and the greenhouse gas regimes.

3.2 Sustainability and Sustainable Development

An ecological basis of survival enables the assessment of relative roles of disturbances to the climate and other systems in their ability to restore or permanently disturb system resilience. Any disturbance to an equilibrium state can lead to new transitory equilibria, and eventually to a new set of equilibria with little possibility of reversal to the old set. The dynamics of ecosystems tend to depict a vastly different set of phenomena relative to economic dynamics. Although the existence of multiple equilibria and adaptation are common in both ecology and economics, the tendency to aggregate valuations and utilization of a monetary metric simplifies the treatment in much of economics. The roles of irreversibility and uniqueness of most biological species and their interdependencies with the ecosystem are among the significant distinguishing features of the ecosystem. These irreversibilities tend to contribute toward a flip from one class of ecological equilibria to another, and the process of the original resilience of the system to withstand small disturbances is lost. This contributes to disruption of ecosystem services and enhances, very significantly, the adaptation costs. Climate change has the potential to adversely affect the ecosystem and its resilience. Neither the conventional economic equilibria nor the presumed availability of ecosystem services hold any longer. In such configurations, human welfare tends to be compromised in rather unforeseen ways.

Let us state some of the concepts and definitions of sustainable development that integrate ecological and economic regimentations. These concepts suggest that sustainable development is (a) to maximize simultaneously the biological system goals (genetic diversity, resilience, biological productivity), economic system goals (meeting basic minimum needs, equity, etc.), and social system goals (social justice, stakeholder participation, effective rule of law and property rights, or other goals) (Barbier 1987); (b) improving the quality of human life while living within the carrying capacity of supporting ecosystems (World Conservation Union, UNEP, and World Wildlife Fund for Nature 1991).

A broadly accepted ecological economics definition states that sustainability is a relationship between dynamic economic systems and larger dynamic, but normally slower-changing, ecological systems, in which (a) human life can continue indefinitely, (b) human individuals can flourish, and (c) human cultures can develop, but in which the effects of human activities remain within bounds, so as not to destroy the diversity, complexity, and function of the ecological life-support system (Costanza et al. 1991). This definition comes close to a reasonable definition of sustainable development, and not simply of sustainability. This could possibly offer useful directions for further improvements of the concept. An application of the biogeophysical definition of sustainability would normally require the creation and preservation of physical and biological resources that possess the potential to maintain undiminished human well-being as well as balance the coexistence of other species for the entire future time horizon.

Various theoretical perspectives on sustainability are seen in the literature. Most of the perspectives are concerned with resource and environmental issues, and hence human sustainability rather than sustainable development. The latter would call for a whole range of balances and exercise of value judgments: potential trade-off among growth, social justice, and intragenerational as well as intergenerational equity of living standards or quality of life. In the Rawlsian theory (Rawls 1972) of social justice, persons in one generation cannot have overriding preferences over members of any other generation. In general, each generation acts as a trustee for future generations and a beneficiary of past generations, although the magnitudes of direct and indirect transfers are not entirely equitable even when they are intended to be so. This is because of several unknowns in the interdependencies of biogeophysical systems and their evolution. The key issue is to devise operationally meaningful principles that reflect the concerns of the future, based on current information at each successive time instant. If an impending climate change is recognized by the current population, it is the moral obligation to address this issue so as to mitigate the effects for the current as well as future generations. Wood (1996) argued: "Because climate is a common resource shared by both present and future generations, it does not belong exclusively to living generations." A common basis for addressing these concerns emerges from the adoption of principles of sustainable development, explained below.

A Broad Definition

The report of the World Commission on Environment and Development (The Brundtland Report of 1987) contributed to much of the ongoing concern for sustainable development. It stated (p. 43):

> Sustainable development is development that meets the needs of the present without compromising the ability of future generations to meet their own needs. It contains within it two key concepts: the concept of "needs," in particular the essential needs of the world's poor, to which overriding

priority should be given; and the idea of limitations imposed by the state of technology and social organization on the environment's ability to meet present and future needs.

Many economists transformed the above concept and suggested that nondeclining per capita consumption measure would be a suitable indicator of sustainability. This was not suggested as an indicator of sustainable development, however. This narrowed-down specification implicitly allows for the status quo ante scenarios governing socioeconomic inequities, resource ownership and income distribution systems, or other structural and institutional impediments to equitable and judicious resource management.

The Brundtland definition needs to be followed up in several more directions to enable greater precision and applicability. This is done with several explorations into different postulates and their implications for one form or another of sustainability. Because the role of capital remains very important in the development processes, it is useful to examine the ingredients of various forms of capital, its stocks and flows. It is possible to carry out a disaggregation of resources in terms of various components of capital relevant to development.

Some economists suggest that a free-market-oriented economic approach to sustainability could potentially incorporate the importance of the environment. This was because of an argument which suggests that if the features of the environment (in terms of the economic significance of the source and sink characteristics) reflect adversely on the health of the economy and other systems, the economy will receive the feedbacks necessary to adjust itself. This presumes the existence of policy and institutional mechanisms (especially the efficient functioning of markets) for such corrections. It was stated in Rao (1999): "Even if this position is accepted, the time frame over which the self-correction feedbacks might affect is not expected to be synonymous with that relevant to preserve the ecosystem resilience. The attainment of such a pseudo-sustainability could be consistent with massive environmental degradation and climate destabilization." The narrow economic approach to sustainability usually yields a precise definition, but one not useful enough to meet the objective from an earthly problem-solving approach incorporating various important interlinkages.

A number of economic definitions are offered in the literature that define economic approaches to the theme of sustainable development.

For example, Mitlin and Satterthwaite (1990) defined sustainable development to imply that development sustainable at the level of countries or at the global level requires that societies, in seeking to achieve development objectives, also seek to maintain a constant stock of environmental assets for use by future generations and to avoid irreversible damage to any single asset. This approach suggests an attempt to balance ecological and economic considerations. However, the specification of avoiding irreversible damage may not be good enough when we recognize the interdependencies of ecological features whenever thresholds are crossed. It is desirable to focus on the latter, in addition to the economic criteria.

The concept of sensible sustainability was originally intended only to allow limited substitutability within allowable limits, between different forms of capital. We require that for any sustainability, each component of the ecological capital vector be equipped with certain critical threshold levels, dictated by the requirements of avoiding stresses and maintaining system resilience. A number of components of natural capital and other forms of capital are allowed substitution, subject to preserving these critical levels. We refer to this process as "sustainability." Much of the above discussion is largely centered around sustainability, and not sustainable development. Hence, the need for a meaningful concept that is built on sustainability approaches but also stipulates development aspects (see also Rao 1999).

Shadow prices are those costs/values related to the specification of objectives, derived from a general socioeconomic philosophy. Shadow prices reflect the opportunity costs and thus the real worth of a resource. This is easier stated than done—usually there exists a range of values assignable as shadow prices. This is because these are sensitive to the explicit and implicit assumptions governing the specifications of the objectives and constraints. Do we value a dollar income for the poor at the same level as for the rich? Is the CO_2 assimilating capacity, for example, of a forest in Kenya a free good for the world and thus worth zero, or do we assign this function a value based on the opportunity cost of controlling CO_2 emissions by alternate means? Whose costs are valued or for whom are the benefits worth? Many similar questions need to be addressed in the context of assessing the shadow prices. Even though this may seem like raising more questions than answering them, the direction of analysis enables greater clarity regarding the evaluation framework and a conscious approach to map directions of progress.

The ecological definition of sustainability can be narrowed down to the implications for the economic arena. This approach suggests that we can draw upon the economic and ecological resources to such an extent that the generalized economic capacity (the productive capacity that includes all forms of ecological capital) to produce material well-being of the human population is retained intact forever. This concept has an important feature, explained below. The "rental" or "return" on this generalized capacity, when partitioned into relevant time periods (typically on a yearly basis) and applied to individual national economic systems, leads to an approximation of an adjusted net national product (NNP), this being the consumption adjusted gross national income. This is based on a specific set of assumptions, and it corresponds to the definition below, based on Rao (1999).

Sustainable development (SD) is the process of socioeconomic development that is built on the sustainability approach (defined above), with an additional requirement that the worth of the capital stocks vector (valued at applicable shadow prices) is maintained constant or undiminished at each time interval forever.

The well-known concept of sustainability advanced by Solow (1994) stands closer to the SD approach when it states that a society that invests aggregate resource rents in reproducible capital is preserving its capacity to sustain a constant level of consumption. Solow argued that a concept of sustainability implies a bias toward investment with a general interpretation: just enough investment to maintain the broad stock of capital intact. It does not mean to maintain intact the stock of every single thing. Substitution of resources is essential for continued economic progress. This statement does imply the need for continued technical progress, and continued improvements in the resource-use efficiencies. This seems a pragmatic economic approach, largely confined to generalized economic capacity so as to enable capital reproducibility and to maintain a constancy of consumption.

Economic Growth and Sustainability

An "all important equation" expressing the relationship between environmental impact and human activity was suggested as the IPAT model by Holdren and Ehrlich (1974). Although several improvements exist in the original framework, it is useful to discuss the early formulation as a starting point. The relationship is expressed as

$$I = P\,A\,T$$

where I is the environmental impact, P is population, A is affluence or economic activity per person (in other variations, this A could be per capita consumption), and T is the environmental impact per unit of economic activity and is a function of the technology used for the production of goods and services and by the institutional, social organization influencing deployment of technology.

If the world's population approximately doubles by the year 2150, as estimated in some studies, the resultant effect on I is not doubling, but is affected by a multiplier factor. This factor is the product of effects of consumption (which is also influenced by any changes in income inequalities) and of technology (which is subject to changes from improved technical efficiency in production and in the treatment of industrial or other pollution). Thus, the above formulation can be generalized to account for at least two more multipliers, each one corresponding to changes in consumption and technology. An attempt in this direction is seen in the study discussed below.

One of the recent and significant studies in this direction of inquiry is that by Dietz and Rosa (1997). The above formulation (I = P A T) is converted to its stochastic version to account for potential discrepancies and uncertainties in the relationship or in data observations (or both) and applied to the specific environmental component: carbon dioxide emissions.

The model is specified as

$$I = a\,P_i\,A_i^b\,e_i^c$$

where the subscript i refers to the observation item; the coefficients a, b, c, e are to be obtained as statistical parameters using the data. The coefficients b and c determine the net effect of population and affluence on impact, and a is a constant that scales the model; technology (and other social, institutional, and cultural factors) is modeled as a residual term e. This version allows for identification of diminishing or increasing impacts due to increases in population or in affluence and thereby improve the original framework. The empirical results, using data for 1989 for 111 countries, suggested that the effects of affluence on CO_2 emissions reach a maximum at about $10,000 in per capita gross domestic product, and that these decline thereafter. It is useful to note that 84 of the

111 countries in the study possess per capita income of less than $5000. This finding has a clear policy message: In the absence of active measures to reduce CO_2 emissions, the problem will continue to be exacerbated during the next several years owing to economic growth in most parts of the world.

In both of the above formulations, one robust formulation that remains generally intact is the postulate of some proportionality between I and P, A, and T or e; the constants or the nonconstants of proportionality and the degree of proportionality vary over regions and time intervals. Technically, a nonlinear statistical estimation methodology is required to identify the parameters involved. Even when some of the above formulations identify relative roles of the contributing factors, this analysis is carried out at a very high level of aggregation and may not suggest substantive policy guidelines. Reducing population, consumption, and improving technology could be a solution, but these constitute a rather trivial prescription (Rao 1999). Planet Earth did have less of the first two for a very long time, but the quality of life (by present-day understanding and standards) was not apparently great. Let us consider the major ingredient of the quality of life, namely the life expectancy or its component, infant mortality rate, which was substantially less during the nineteenth century than in the current period in most regions of the world.

The question that remains important is, even after such advancements in the quality of life, if life itself is unsustainable on this planet, what good are those other life-span achievements? Human capital and its infrastructure (including knowledge, education, morbidity, and mortality) are not fully reflected in the above framework. To illustrate the importance of these factors, let us ask this question: Is it implausible that we could have increasing population, greater affluence (especially in less developed regions) and yet be innovative enough to accomplish goals of sustainability in terms of taking due care of source-and-sink problems of the planet?

Sustainability and National Income

The implication of sustainability on national income or an approximation to this income is a relevant macroeconomic issue. When we deal with largely monetized/marketized economies, we tend to apply the concepts of income, interest, and monetized values of net national product and related economic parameters. Building upon such a background, several attempts to incorporate environmental accounting and valuation can be advanced (see Rao 1999 for details).

Weitzman (1976) demonstrated that under optimal growth with certain assumptions, the NNP (net national product) should be seen as income in the Hicksian sense. This forms a useful beginning in interpreting economic sustainability.

Under these assumptions, the reasoning led to the expression:

$$NNP\ (t) = r\ W(t)$$

where r represents the rate of return on national wealth, W, for each time instant (usually year t). The NNP is thus the return on the magnitude of generalized wealth, without diminishing the wealth and its productive capacity. It is thus an indicator of sustainability: NNP measures the maximum current level of satisfaction of human consumption that can be sustained indefinitely.

The above interpretations are not universally valid, for example, in the presence of continually or occasionally changing preferences reflected in interest rates, unforeseen technological innovations, and other uncertainties. Under such configurations, NNP is not an indicator of sustainability. A significant set of insights into economic approaches is advocated using the well-developed theories of "optimal development," which are founded on neoclassical economic growth theories, development economics, and institutional economics.

An important aspect of sustainable development involves production of knowledge. It is reasonable to assume that the growth of the stock of knowledge is itself a function of deployment of relevant resources in a production sense. It is in the context of creation of knowledge that both enhanced efficiency and improved use of resources with environmental upgradation are facilitated. This is the most powerful counterargument to the "entropy law" advocated in Georgeuse-Rogen (1971). Without the creation of new knowledge, economic growth could lead to negative net returns to the society when all the inputs are properly accounted.

The single most important factor to be reflected in any valuation of the resources is to recognize that these are relatively fixed and scarce, and thus the economic institutions must be sensitive to the natural constraints. This warrants an interdisciplinary approach and integrated ecology-economy models. The ability of the ecosystem to retain resilience is unlikely to be reflected in a linkup of the system with current consumer preference-based economic systems. These preferences are usually endogenous to existing mechanisms of resource allocation, institutions, and legal entitlements governing the same. These features call for an appreciation of broader elements of transaction costs, including externalities.

3.3 Externalities and Transaction Costs

For many years, the focus of issues in the field of environmental economics has been in terms of environmental or other externalities caused by economic activities. Such an approach leads to finding methods to mitigate the effects of externalities. These include appropriate provisions of taxes, penalties, and administrative regulations. These approaches continue to be relevant, but they form only a part of the larger set of ecological and economic management issues and instruments of their management.

The elements involved in assessing costs must reflect the concerns of sustainability and thus cover implications of ecological and economic dimensions in a comprehensive manner. The costs of transition and transaction are significant and should be incorporated in any cost-benefit analysis.

Transient Costs and Equilibrium Costs

Any assessment of costs and benefits is based on a pattern of equilibrium that enables such assessment. However, in a relatively long-term (ten or more years) framework, it is important to recognize that the equilibrium is not expected to remain invariant to the continued disturbances to the systems involved and the significant possibilities of mechanisms of adaptation. In other words, it is not only the common forms of uncertainty that alter the equilibria, but also the systematic feedback mechanisms and adaptation responses of the components of the system that lead to transient equilibria. The effects of such changes on relevant costs and benefits are sometimes viewed in terms of substitution or other effects, but these cover a partial set of adaptations involved.

Comprehensive Cost Assessment

Hardly any economic studies are comprehensive enough to accommodate all relevant costs. In general, the following cost-assessment criteria will be relevant.

General Cost $G_1 = T_1 + T_3 + T_5$
Shadow/True Cost $G_2 = T_2 + T_4 + T_6$

where T_1 represents transaction costs; T_2 their shadow value; T_3 transition/adaptation costs; T_4 their shadow value; T_5 market value or nonmarket value of resource costs; and T_6 their shadow value.

Some of the elements in each of the odd-numbered Ts can be illustrated here. T_1 includes costs of enforcement of regulations, and of institutional mechanisms for internalizing externalities; T_2 includes costs of compliance, hedging, and uncertainty in future regulations and of changing technological implications, adjustment costs in forgoing consumption or other benefits, reduction in profits due to possible higher costs of production, price-income-consumption effects on consumers, and cost-price-profit effects on producers; T_5 includes costs of resource inputs, costs of usage of sources and sink capacities, and other ecological costs of consumption and production. A few select approaches to methods of valuation and of cost-benefit analysis are explained in the following section.

3.4 Valuation of Resources and the Environment

Climatic stabilization is a prerequisite for ecosystem and environmental stability, ensuring the provision of various goods and services. Thus, the functional utility of climate is partly reflected via the utility of these goods and services. It is important to view the significance of global ecological and environmental resources in terms of the service function in converting flows of services into the consumption sector with or without depleting their known or unknown stocks and interrelationships with the value of their services. The least that can be done is to assign a positive value to any services that have some relation to one or more of the stocks of environmental and ecological capital, whether or not these stocks are quantified in monetary terms.

The utilitarianism approach allows valuation; it embraces both direct use values and indirect use values, for consumptive and nonconsumptive uses; it also includes nonuse values (values that do not involve any actual direct or indirect physical involvement with the natural thing in question). The many services provided by ecosystems span all of these category values. Pest-control and flood-control services they offer have direct use value to nearby agricultural producers. Their provisions of habitats for migratory birds implies an indirect use value to people who enjoy bird watching; depending on whether such fowl are watched or hunted, the indirect user value can be consumptive or nonconsumptive.

Some of the relevant concepts of nonmarket valuation are briefly stated below. Willingness-to-pay (WTP) is regarded as the measure of satisfaction. Nonuse values comprise two components—existence value and option value. Existence value is the value that derives from the sheer contemplation of the existence—apart from any direct or indirect uses of goods and services; survey approaches such as contingent valuation assessments may be relevant. Option value can be interpreted in two ways. In the first, option value refers to a premium that people are willing to pay to preserve an environmental amenity, over and above the mean value (or expected value) of the use values anticipated from the amenity. This premium reflects individual risk-aversion. In the absence of the latter, people's WTP would equal the mean use value, and option value would equal zero.

In the second approach, the future value is not necessarily assessed by individual members of the society, but the system realizes the benefits, as in the medicinal value of a plant variety that might be commercially exploited at some future time point.

Reliance on any assessment of WTP can be misleading and sometimes useless for any policy assessment or valuation of a resource. This is because (Rao 1999) individuals are not necessarily fully informed of some of the structural linkages and their worth in a long-term sense; also, depending on the specific society and sample of people involved, their degree of self-interest can be highly significant and subject to large variations. Finally, this approach tries to convert a public-goods issue into a consumer-sovereignty problem and thus misplaces the entire focus. Let us consider an illustration of the last component. If a society prefers to discount the future at an extremely high rate, is that a meaningful method of assessing the parameters for any further use?

We now proceed to define another concept. Total economic value (TEV) has been a useful concept, and it is defined (see also Serageldin 1995) as the sum of use value UV (direct plus indirect), option value OV, existence value EV, and other nonuse value ONUV:

$$T E V = UV + OV + EV + ONUV.$$

The EV is not the same as preservation value; the latter corresponds to the continued existence of an entity for reasons other than any expected benefit for those valuing it. It is thus meaningful to expect the preservation value to be reflected in the ONUV. Nonuse values comprise two components—existence value and option value. Existence value is the value that derives from the sheer contemplation of the existence— apart from any direct or indirect uses of goods and services; survey approaches such as contingent valuation assessments are considered relevant. Option value can be interpreted in two ways. In the first, OV refers to a premium that people are willing to pay to preserve an environmental amenity, over and above the mean value (or expected value) of the use values anticipated from the amenity. This premium reflects individual risk-aversion; in the absence of the latter, people's willingness to pay would equal the mean use value, and option value would equal zero.

Valuation of environmental goods and their related ecosystem services (which will be lost if there is widespread degradation of the environment) requires a full understanding of the ecosystem services that are so benevolently provided by nature. Ecosystem services are the conditions and processes through which natural ecosystems and their living creatures sustain and enrich human life (for a good narration of details, see Daily 1997). In a crude approximation of the value of nature's services, Costanza et al. (1997) observed that for the entire biosphere, the value of nature's services annually was no less than about $16 trillion (at 1994 prices) and could be in the range of $54 trillion, compared to the global GNP of about $18 trillion a year in the mid-1990s. The seventeen ecosystem services included in the study are regulation of greenhouse gases, climate regulation, regulation of environmental disasters, regulation of hydrological cycles, water resource supply, control of soil erosion and sedimentation retention, soil formation, nutrient cycling, waste treatment and assimilation, botanical pollination, biological control and regulation, refugia applicable to various species, food production, raw materials, genetic resources, recreation, and cultural opportunities.

Cost-Benefit Analysis

When considering future costs and benefits of actions/inactions and alternative projects, society can generally be risk-neutral relative to individuals. This is because in the society, a large number of people tend to share the burden of costs and provide some kind of risk pooling; some activities can be very productive and some can be a drag on the system. However, these arguments do not help analyze some of the components of the global climate change or such other problems of global commons where collective doom is a real possibility of either inaction or wrong actions.

Cost-benefit analysis (CBA) has assumed a role in various aspects of public and private decision making. In the context of environmental issues, especially global commons and related policies that arise largely in the public arena, the methods require considerable further strengthening because of the following factors: the time scale involved is usually hundreds of years or longer; there is no unitary decision-making mechanism; most factors to be considered are largely outside market parameters—as they are not necessarily affecting the market signals at the present time; there are unusually predominant unknowns and uncertainties in the cost and benefit configurations; assigning numerical values to bring the multiple factors to a common numeraire and scale is extremely complex and possibly founded on many arbitrary assumptions.

Much of the application of CBA presumes some type of "commensurability." This tends to make sense in a pure corporate private-sector context, but not in general. Strong commensurability assumes the existence of a common numeraire that allows assigning numerical values to each factor and function involved in the decision-making context, models, and policies. Preferences are usually based on the magnitudes of the numerical values assessed. The numbers also assist in arriving at trade-offs, wherever necessary, in compromising otherwise conflicting objectives. None of the approaches can make sense devoid of the institutional implications, constraints, and effectiveness. The market and the state form the background, but their effectiveness makes the difference as to how far they can operate in an ecologically rational manner.

The methods of CBA must take into account sustainability requirements at different stages of valuation, and one of the key elements in this process is to choose an appropriate discount function; the relevant details of this critical issue are given in subsequent sections in this chapter. It is also important to note that valuation of environmental and other resources must first be done within a framework of sustainability and then converted into appropriate equivalents using a common numeraire like consumption. This broader approach is usually ignored when tried by some of the conventional but controversial methods like contingent valuation (CV) and surveys of willingness-to-pay (WTP). Some of the valuations for various resources that generated numerical values seen in part of the literature, which also claims to deal with sustainability issues, are usually carried out in a very narrow context. These ignore any sensitivity of values with respect to the market and nonmarket institutional settings where these numbers or methods of valuation might have relevance and may not therefore be applicable in a wide variety of settings worldwide without major modifications. Besides, the valuations are usually made based on existing unsustainable conditions and then sought to be applied for obtaining some variant of sustainability (Rao 1999). These methods could possibly achieve precision where one can be precise up to the fifth or higher decimal but basically wrong on the premise; this is one of the scenarios where one could be precisely right if only one is right at all! It serves no useful purpose to generate such numbers and use them for project valuation or CBA. The critical ingredients required to be clarified are in terms of the analytical or logical decision model or structure (with or without extensive mathematical methods), which clarify the objectives, constraints, factors and institutions, in addition to the choice of appropriate discount factors. Only such a framework can lead to consistent valuations (and shadow prices) relevant for addressing issues under global climatic change regimes.

The standard financial methods of cost-benefit calculation draw upon the calculation of the discounted stream of cash flows, both the sequences of costs C_t and of benefits B_t, for the period of concern T for a project or component of economic activity. The discounted lump sum is called the "net present value" (NPV) and depends on the choice of the discount rate r. This is given by the expression

$$N P V = \Sigma (1 + r)^{-t} [B_t - C_t]$$

where the summation of the discounted monetized values extends to the horizon of the project or of concern.

If the inflation needs to be taken into account, r is replaced by $r - i$, where i is the rate of annual inflation. The new measure $r - i$ corresponds to the real rate of interest whenever the formulation is carried out only in financial terms.

In general, CBA can play an important role in devising legislative and regulatory policy measures for protecting and improving health and the natural environment; it can provide a framework for consistently organizing information. It was also suggested that if "properly done,"

CBA can be of great help to agencies participating in the development of environmental, health and safety regulations and can be useful in evaluating agency decision making and rule making. It is not uncommon that CBA is a traditional economist's workhorse widely used even under very restrictive (and often without even their full realization) assumptions. An interdisciplinary approach could enrich the considerations involved in the evaluation and ensure robust validity of analyses rather than focus on a false sense of precision; such an emphasis could enhance its standing as relevant tool in multicriteria decision making.

However, one of the major impediments to some of the formal models is to ensure what is known as "time-consistency": to ensure that future decision-making systems will, in fact, respect the continuity and ensure furtherance of the future interests at every point of time, or point of start, of new decision horizons in an intergenerational setting. There may not be many technical answers to this issue that are stronger than the biogeophysical requirement of maintaining climatic stability as a prerequisite for sustainability and sustainable development.

In the project evaluation methods for exhaustible resources, the original classical formulation of Hotelling (1931) had been a good start and was considered useful for a long time. This approach draws on discounted utility maximization subject to appropriate constraints on the boundedness of resources of concern. Clearly, the framework of sink capacity or nature's assimilative constraints have not been part of the concern in these conventional formulations. Minor modifications such as incorporating more arguments in the utility function, like the quality of environment, are rather straightforward. A major effect of improvising the sustainability constraints is to raise the shadow price of exhaustible resources as well as other environmental resources like sink capacity change or climate change. The same effect can be seen in lowering the discount rate.

In the context of climate changes, the above assessments need to take into account the potential dislocation of ecosystem services. Thus, when climatic thresholds are exceeded, system resilience is lost and hence the loss of ecosystem services or steep increases in the scarcity values of these resources. Application of any formulae of benefit-cost analysis needs to incorporate the implications of such potential system discontinuities or nonlinearity of the cost functions. Only in such a framework can the real worth of the withdrawal of resources of the sources and sinks of the planet stand a possible accounting and provide guidance for policy alternatives. Time discounting or valuation of future resources is critical in this context, and the relevant aspects of these features are explained in the next section.

3.5 Discounting Over Time

Valuation of resources requires a comprehension into a single dimension, as is done in the cost-benefit analysis. An economic model concerned with long-term issues like climate change or global warming can hardly justify its existence if it is built on the presumption of constant rate of social time preference or stationarity of preferences over the entire horizon of relevance. Because the benefits of reducing atmospheric emissions today would be realized primarily in a half-century or more, even small differences in the discount rate used can lead to large variations in the results. At 4 percent annual discount rate for the future values, an amount of $7.106 billion in the year 2050 is worth $1 billion in the year 2000, whereas with 7 percent annual discount rate an amount of $29.457 billion is required in 2050 to be worth investing or forgoing a benefit of $1 billion in 2000. In this illustration, a mere 3 percentage points lead to over a fourfold difference in only 50 years.

In another example to explain the critical role of discounting, at 1 percent annual discount rate it may be possible to justify about $130 million today in order to avoid $1 billion in damages in the year 2200, and with no discounting the justifiable present investment could be the full $1 billion rather than $130 million (which also goes down to about $35,000 if the discount rate is 5 percent a year). Thus, longer time horizons amplify very small differences to huge deviations. Let us also note that the application of a constant discount rate implies the discount factor at any time instant is independent of the underlying consumption path, which is not a realistic feature in long-horizon analysis. The need for an adjustable rate of discounting becomes obvious in this discussion (see Box 3.1).

The conventional time-separable additive utility functions imply that the marginal rates of substitution between two time instants depend on the corresponding levels of consumption at those two instants only. Recursive utility functions were sought to recognize the notion of "impatience" with these properties: (a) the functions account for partial complementarity in intertemporal consumption, and (b) they allow flexible rate of time preference endogenously evolved according to the underlying consump-

---

Box 3.1 Economic Concepts and Definitions

Certainty equivalent The comparison of an uncertain quantity X in relation to the probability of its attainment of different values and then comparing the resultant with its certainty c—that is, if the expected value E (X) = c, then X is considered the certainty equivalent of c. In the discrete version case, the expected value is given by the sum p x + p x + ... + p x where p are the probabilities of realization of values x in all the n states that cover the possible alternatives.

Consumer surplus The additional utility that might be available to a consumer as a result of a change in price or nonprice intervention relative to the scenario without such a change.

Exogenous Any variable or influence that is prescribed without any direct influence of the system under its influence.

Expected value The added sum of the products of quantities with their corresponding probabilities of occurrence or realization.

Endogenous The dependent entity that responds to an evolving or changing feature or structural relation in the system affected by the factor or the entity under consideration.

Nonadditive utility Utility levels that do not simply add from one period to another without their interperiod dependency.

Recursive utility The emergence of successive periods of utility in terms of the preceding ones.

Risk-averse behavior The decision-making approach where the certainty equivalence is not enough to offset the involved uncertainties, and the decision situation warrants greater risk premium g to compensate for the uncertainties, i.e., E (X) + g = c.

Risk-taking behavior The converse of the above. Here E (X) – g = c.

Risk-neutral behavior Being indifferent between the certainty equivalent quantity and the corresponding level of quantity with certainty.

Shadow price Opportunity cost or "true worth" of a resource.

Time-consistency Sticking to the multiperiod decision at the end of each successive period as if the original decision still holds for the remaining periods even with new information or other changes.

---

tion stream. As noted by Joshi (1995), recursive utility formulation achieves a separation between risk aversion (behavior toward risk) and the degree of intertemporal substitution (ranking of deterministic consumption programs) if there is nonindifference to temporal resolution of uncertainty.

Time preferences are not simply current versus future consumption preferences. In general, these preferences comprise two components: (1) relative weight placed by the consumer or the decision maker on present versus future consumption depending on the relative consumption levels—called consumption impatience; and (2) for a given consumption path or a constant consumption path, both present and future consumption are distinguished by the element of time impatience. A similar argument was advanced by Becker and Mulligan (1997) without an accompanying dynamic endogenous model to isolate the two effects. The models in Rao (1998a, 1998b; 1999) provide these insights.

Much of the economic debate in the fields of environmental and resource economics was concerned with a preset question: Is it desirable to discount (if at all) the future when evaluating various streams of costs and benefits of project activities, at a "low rate" or "high rate" (both these rates were presumed constant) in relation to private market rate of return? Various investigators were concerned about complexities of handling variable discount rates, especially if they were sought to be endogenized with respect to relevant functions of consumption, capital growth, or variable interest rates at different points of time. Even though a select few contributions offered an analytical framework to deal with the problem, they fell short in providing computable formulae of methods enabling application in realistic economic systems.

Choice of Discount Rates

Ecological and environmental issues brought the theme of discounted valuation of future benefits and costs to the forefront of debate in the 1990s, much more than ever before. It is not only the complexity of uncertainty and incomplete information that bothers the analysts but also the need to deal with infinite or extremely long time horizons for valuation. This horizon issue alone discourages any positive discounting because after a few decades anything gets ignored to null valuation by the "tyranny of discounting." A number of economic efficiency and intergenerational ethical issues are involved in this context. The existing literature tends to fall short of requirements to prescribe a meaningful policy. A few improvements are in progress, and the sections that follow include the approach of endogenized discounting as a possible improvement.

Broome (1992) offers a detailed narration of objections to discounted valuation over time. Broome stated that the real problem in discounting the future is the same as discounting future well-being; consumer interest rate is not necessarily good as it does not take into account the effects of preferences of future generations; the producer rate of interest is not considered useful because the production of goods and services is involved with environmental damages affecting sources and sinks, especially emissions of the GHGs—and thus does not reflect the true opportunity cost of products and services. Broome's solution was to adopt a zero discount rate. Clearly, this number is just as indefensible as any other number.

In a detailed paper, Goodin (1982) suggested that discounting methods are possibly devoid of sound logic. Contrary to the notion of Goodin (1982) that discounting amounts to ignoring the future generations, productive utilization of resources at current and foreseeable future periods gives scope for accommodating the interests of the present and future if only the resources are properly utilized and due attention is paid to future generations. An enlightened and/or egalitarian society can do better than others. Let us also note that a society that does not discount the future at all but is capable of efficiently utilizing its resources is unlikely to protect the interests of the current as well future generations. There is or should be little disagreement on the issue whether or not the discount rate should be the same in each future period: The answer is clearly negative. Discounting may be applied only to "interest bearing" resources, according to some, but this position presumes that the resources are readily monetized in the valuation process. It was also suggested (Goodin 1982) that the rate and structure of discounting applied to nontradable goods should match the corresponding features of investments in those goods. This position presumes the existence of investments in the nontraded goods, an unlikely or unusual scenario in environmental features like GHGs.

Discount rates or interest rates in competitive markets reflect the substitution or rates of transformation of marketed and marketable goods of one time instant in terms of those at another time instant in future. However, these do not possess the relevant information content to facilitate guidance for nontraded goods or those scenarios with missing markets. Problems of global climatic change warrant a much greater comprehensive framework than ever addressed in the economics literature. The most serious impediment in the application of traditional cost-benefit analysis is the lack of commensurability of valuations at different distant time points when the underlying ecosystem (and hence the economic system, the corresponding set of goods and services, consumption baskets and other features) undergoes changes whenever the environmental/ecological thresholds are altered. It is useful to raise a question from a report by the National Academy of Sciences (see Stern et al. 1992, 112): "If current economic activity destroys the life support systems on which human life depends, what investment or at compound interest could ever recoup this cost?"

Changing Preferences and Discounting

In the conventional intertemporal utility maximization approach, the independence arises from the strong separability property of utility: Marginal rates of substitution for consumption at any two time instants are independent of the rest of the consumption profile. A constant time-discounting does imply that the discount factor at any instant is independent of the underlying consumption path.

An ingredient in the definition of sustainability is a possible change relative to the present in preferences of future generations about consumption and environmental assets (see also Solow 1992). These observations suggest the need for specifying discount factors that are endogenized with respect to consumption and resource stock levels at different future time instants. The discount rate must reflect the rate of return on alternative sustainable uses, and not any uses, of capital if we are to have a policy consistent with sustainable development. If an industrial project is estimated to yield a return on capital at 10 percent a year, and an alternative project like forest plantations gives a corresponding return of 5 percent, the basic question remains: Do we accept the 10 percent case as preferable even though a multitude of such projects can contribute to environmental unsustainability and hence to lack of climate stability? This issue cannot be resolved without clarifying the role of the owners of the projects or of the investors. Assuming both the examples above are in the public sector, the issue then becomes one of greater comprehension of costs of the project and accounting for all the elements of costs and benefits over a long period of time—such as infinity. One premise is clear, however: The efficiency allocation rule of maximizing present value can subvert the goal of sustainable development by application of an unsustainable discount rate—that is, a discount rate based on alternate uses of capital that are unsustainable (Daly 1991, 255).

In an interesting contribution in the modeling and analysis of the global commons, Nordhaus (1994, 122) believed that the DICE model used in the investigations could not accommodate gradual change in tastes and also stated that "no issue has raised more concern and confusion than the question of the appropriate discounting of the future." If the discount rate were zero percent, the optimal abatement path would cut atmospheric emissions by 50 percent from baseline by the year 2100, compared with 10 percent reduction at the 3 percent discount rate (Plambeck et al. 1997).

What constitutes a discount rate? This can be defined as the rate of fall in the value of the numeraire against which goods are valued each time instant (this could also be each year, for example); the numeraire and the discount rate need to be considered together. A rigorous analysis of the theoretical issues in this framework can be seen in Dreze and Stern (1987). The shadow discount factor in their analysis is the valuation of the discount factor in accordance with the underlying objective function or net benefit computing formulation. It can be seen as the marginal social value of a unit of numeraire accruing in year t. The shadow (own) rate of return on the numeraire is generally known as the social discount rate (SDR).

The social value of a project or activity is a discounted stream of social benefits expressed in terms of a common numeraire. The shadow discount rate is a scalar number defined as the rate of fall of the discount factor D (. . .), which is an implicit function of time, given by the expression:

$$= -(d/dt) \log D (. . .).$$

This also depicts the rate of fall in the marginal social value of the numeraire. It can be seen that when the shadow discount rate was a constant, the discounting formulation reduces to the conventional inversion of the compounding formula for n periods, as in $(1 + r)^{-n}$.

The application of social discount rates (SDRs) requires that all relevant effects of an activity or project be transformed into their equivalents in a common numeraire, usually consumption. This implies that it may be difficult to avail this ingredient as such in a situation like global climate change where the conversion of everything or entity into consumption equivalent may not be feasible. Social discount rates are to be viewed as percentage rates of change of intertemporal relative shadow prices of the consumption bundle. Relevant proxies for SDRs are but a few: (a) the application of the concept of social rate of time preference (SRTP), explained below; (b) real rates of risk-free interest; and (c) variable endogenous discount functions that reflect changing preferences and consumption levels, and possibly additional factors. These are not usually equated with SDRs because of the assumptions regarding the nature of pure capital appraisal in perfectly competitive markets, and neglect of missing but important long-term factor markets.

In the conventional approach, SRTP can be estimated using the utility-based discount rate. In this framework, the SRTP (observed from the consumption rate of interest) and the opportunity cost of private capital (observed from the marginal rate of return on private investment) are both the same and equal the market rate of interest in a perfectly competitive ideal nondistortionary economy. This follows from Solow's (1970) derivation, explained below.

The optimality criterion is to maximize W, the discounted social value of all future utility streams U of consumption. Let ρ be the pure time preference factor, n the rate of growth of population, and c per capita consumption.

The first-order necessary condition for optimality yields the expression

$$d/dt \ [U^I] \ / \ U^I = - \ \{r * (t) - \rho\}$$

which upon differentiation leads to the following

$$\{U^{II} (c *) \ \cdot \ d/dt \ (c *)\} \ / \ U^I(c *) = - \ \{r * - \rho\}$$

This is summarized as

$$r (t) = \alpha \ g + \rho$$

where α is the absolute value of the elasticity of the social marginal utility of per capita consumption, and g the growth rate of consumption.

The above expression makes it clear that the discount function r is a composite effect of three factors: (1) the pure time preference or time-impatience; (2) the consumption-impatience represented through the elasticity parameter; and (3) the growth effect. Thus, r is not simply a time-discounting factor as sometimes referred to in the literature, but is a measure of discounting of goods. This is the one that should be used in any cost-benefit analysis. If one suggests that the welfare of future generations should not be heavily discounted, the suggestion is simply that ρ, the pure time-preference factor, should be low, and not that r should be low for that reason. Solow (1996) emphasized that along any optimal path, the appropriate discount rate to apply to goods has two components: (1) the pure rate of time preference and (2) the factor which depends on the marginal product of capital (thus allowing transformation of goods into greater quantities of goods over time. The second component usually dominates the first, except in very inefficient economies. These features provide a fundamental explanation to the suggested phenomenon in Becker (1998): preferences and rates of economic growth are correlated partly because factors like a lower rate of preference for present utilities are more conducive to rapid economic growth.

From the above expression for r(t), it is readily observed that even when the utility rate of discount is set equal to zero, the SRTP will be positive as long as consumption is growing over time. The consumption rate of discount need not equal the utility rate of discount. Thus, discounting benefits and costs at a positive rate does not necessarily entail lesser weight to the welfare (as measured by utility) of future generations or the future itself. There is no contradiction between those who claim that the well-being of future generations should not be discounted and those who argue that future incomes should not be discounted at a positive rate. However, this reasoning may not entirely hold sway in economies where future prospects of higher consumption levels are bleak.

Optimization and decision frameworks should be capable of responding to new information and should take into account the option value of alternate courses of action from time to time. This can be carried out with an endogenized discount function and recursive utility framework. In general, time preferences comprise at least two effects: (1) relative value attached to present consumption (in relation to the level of consumption), and its comparative valuation of a future specified level of consumption at a specified time point, and (2) impatience as defined by pure time preference (for a given level of consumption).

Discount Factors and Discount Rates

The use of discount rates is closely tied to the implicit and explicit framework governing the configuration of CBA. It is important to note that a constant rate of time-discounting does imply the independence of the discount factor at any time point of the underlying consumption path (and hence, also, of the corresponding changes in other related factors). Where there exist significant income distributional effects of policies and compensation adjustments not automatically attainable with the deployment of other policy instruments, Bradford (1997) suggested that simple aggregation of gains and losses, in grand-scale programs like control of GHGs, is unlikely to provide a convincing basis for action, as an ethical matter, or predictor of policy in political economy. The implications of very high discount rate are that too little value is placed on future possibilities like global warming; conversely, a very low discount rate could lead to too much investment in the control of potential global warming problems and thus drive out possibly more efficient or better uses of resources. A study by the U.S. National Academy of Sciences (Stern et al. 1992) concluded that (1) if current economic activity tends to destroy the fundamental life support systems on which human survival depends, no amount of investment at compound interest could ever recoup this cost; and (2) market-based discount rates like interest rates do not usually correspond to social valuation of the long run, the horizon relevant in global climate change issues.

The standard economics under uncertainty and risk give the result that the expected value of marginal utility is greater than the marginal utility of expected income. The Intergovernmental Panel on Climate Change (IPCC 1996) recommended that on this basis "there would be grounds for reducing the growth-based component of the SRTP under circumstances of risk. Because the risk in predicting per capita growth on scale horizons of centuries is high, this consideration is particularly relevant for problems of global warming" (p. 137).

A number of alternative formulations of nonconstant discounting functions can be seen in Harvey (1995), including "slow discount functions." These have a main characteristic of changing preferences, and these preferences are also classified into different main categories: relative timing constant, slow timing averse, and decreasing timing averse. Although these are interesting and possess desirable properties, like declining over time and not exponentially declining to zero at fast speed (as in regular exponential discounting functions), the models based on these may not always possess meaningful or rational optimal solutions. However, more analyses into some of these directions and improvements thereof are expected to yield rich dividends in choosing right discounting approaches, both prescriptive and positive (in the sense of accounting for real-life descriptive behavior of societies and individuals).

The discount functions of the type given below are special cases of the above hyperbolic class and were suggested in the class of proportional discounting/"relative timing preference" (Harvey 1986), and depict inverse proportionality with the distance of time element from the present time.

Measuring time by equal proportional increments rather than equal absolute values is sometimes referred to as "logarithmic discounting." This discounting function attaches greater weight to time and valuation of resources at distant time points unlike in the case of conventional exponential discounting.

From the viewpoint of socioeconomic decision making and appraisal of various actions and inactions, the analysis relies very heavily on the explicit and implicit time-valuation of associated benefits and costs over a lengthy time horizon. The intergenerational preferences and trade-offs are directly relevant. The critical parameter that affects choice of policies in this setup is the discount rate over time.

A number of researchers have argued in favor of choice of low (but constant) discount rates so that the distant future may not be ignored; there are others who argue the opposite so as to enhance the current efficiency levels of resource use and possibly reap the benefits for the future. A more useful approach is to make endogenous the discount function. An endogenized nonconstant discount function approach is suggested in Rao (1998a,b) where discount rates are revised with changing consumption level, environment-production linkages, and social time preferences.

Uncertainty and Discount Rates

There has been considerable debate and disagreement regarding the choice of discount rates for environmental projects, especially those affecting the global commons associated with climate change and global warming. There are several unknowns and uncertainties. Moreover, ecological and environmental changes occur relatively exogenously (see, e.g., Myers 1995). All these unknowns, information and event uncertainties, imperfect perceptions and analyses suggest a cautious approach in the design and implementation of policies and programs aimed at the control of the phenomena and their adverse consequences.

The standard economics under uncertainty and risk give the result that the expected value of marginal utility is greater than the marginal utility of expected income. The IPCC (1996) recommended that on this basis, there would be grounds for reducing the growth-based component of the SRTP under circumstances of risk, and that this consideration is particularly relevant for problems of global warming because the risk in predicting per capita growth on a scale of centuries is high.

Under uncertainty, the simplistic view of treating costs as negative benefits does not hold any longer (see also Rao 1999). If there is any risk-averse attitude, the benefit stream should be discounted higher than in the certainty case or the certainty-equivalent case. For a risk-averse decision maker, the expected utility of initial wealth plus the random increment is less than the utility of the expected value of the initial wealth plus the random increment. This follows from the well-known inequalities applicable when the utility function U possesses the properties of a strictly concave function:

$$E\,[U\,(W_t + W_{t+1})] < U\,[E\,(W_t + W_{t+1})] = U\,[W_t + E\,(W_{t+1})].$$

The above inequality shows that the certainty-equivalent of the random wealth W_t is less than the expected value of W_t. Enhancement in the certainty-equivalent is possible with increased discount rate. Similarly, in risk-averse decision making, if the costs are ranked under uncertainty, the converse holds: Lower the discount rate for valuing costs over time. Rigorous technical support for these assertions in the risk-averse cases is given by Prelec (1998).

An application of the Precautionary Principle (PP) or risk-averse decision-making approach leads to a lower discount rate in assessing costs under uncertainty relative to the certainty case or the certainty-equivalent case. A robust derivation of this assertion is given in Rao (1998b) with an endogenized variable discount function; the discount rates are revised with changing consumption level, environment-production linkages, and social time preferences. See Appendix 3A for details.

Environmental resource valuation with long time horizons continues to remain a very complex subject, and the assumptions behind any one valuation make significant differences with another and can lead to different policy inferences. More emphasis is required in devising robust sets of assumptions and methods of assessment, in addition to increased sophistication in the decision model. The latter is needed in the sense of comprehensive consideration of stocks and flows of environmental resources and environmental externalities, technological externalities, and changing preferences as well as nonconstant discount rates in an infinite-horizon decision framework. The choice of discount rates or time-discounting of future is a very critical area of valuation of resources and the future. The least that needs to be done at this juncture seems to be to do away with assumptions of constant discount rate, which is usually constrained by current information or historical considerations. A rigorous proof of the argument that a low discount rate for assessing costs is a rational necessity, in the face of biogeophysical system uncertainties and economic uncertainties associated with intervention strategies, is given in Appendix 3A.

3.6 The New Green Golden Rule

We would like to investigate the analytical properties or requirements for achieving an eternal constancy of marginal utility of consumption when the utility function depends on consumption, environmental quality, and time factor itself (to account for changes in technology, and in the phenomena of externalities). A sustainable development model or an optimal GHG stabilization model permits optimal control-theoretical formulation (see, e.g., Clark 1993) of the decision model for optimal consumption, environmental improvement, and other relevant features. To gain some insights, let this be initially modeled as an undiscounted optimizing formulation. Assuming an optimum exists, the relevant policy and response functions are expressible only as functions of time, after appropriate substitution of optimal stationary values, assuming stationary preferences. Let the resultant time-function depicting the objective function be given by $f(t)$. Let λ denote a constant rate of time-discount or interest. The sustainability criterion generally requires constancy of annual rental on wealth-like magnitude, that is,

$$\underset{t \to \infty}{\text{Lt}} \lambda \int_0^\infty \exp\left[-\lambda \tau\right] f(t) \, dt = c, \text{ a constant.}$$

This also represents the annuity-equivalent value of f and sustainability. Abel's Theorem in Laplace transform gives the following (see, e.g., Doetsch 1971):

If $\underset{t \to \infty}{Lt} f(t) = d$, then there exists 1 such that

$$\underset{t \to \infty}{Lt} \lambda \int_0^\infty \exp\left[-l\,t\right] f(t) = d$$

In other words, if the long run is to possess a finite positive worth or value rather than be nullified as a victim of time-discounting tyranny, then there exists a corresponding low discount rate that provides an annual rental on the wealth L [f(t)] and this rental is constant; here L denotes the Laplace transform operator. An alternative interpretation of the above is to state that as long as there exists net technical progress, the return at every time instant to this factor will be a constant when the rest of the system is treated as stationary in an aggregative sense (usually referred to as weak sustainability). Also, the above theorem allows fixing any two of the parameters and obtaining the third as a resultant: discount rate (λ), exogenous technical progress function f(t), and the required finite felicity in the long run (δ). The entire discussion so far presumes the existence of a constant discount rate based on stationary preferences. When this does not hold, we need to formulate endogenized discount functions (Rao 1998), and the Laplace transform method ceases to apply.

The Green Golden Rule given by Chichilinsky et al. (1995) reduces the long-run undiscounted utility maximization problem to a static optimization problem and is given by the rule of equating the ratio of marginal utilities of environment and consumption to the negative of the marginal change in the environmental improvement. This amounts to equality between the marginal rate of transformation and marginal rate of substitution between consumption and environment across steady states (Chichilinsky et al. 1995). This result is based on stationary preferences over the entire infinite horizon.

We transform this problem into a corresponding decision model with endogenous preferences.

Let $D = D(C, E, t)$ be the discount factor.

The discount function at time t is given by

$$D^t = \exp\left[-\int_0^t D(C, E, t)\, dt\right]$$

with

$$D_t > 0, D_E > 0, D_C > 0, \text{ and } \underset{t \to \infty}{\text{Lt}} D^t = 0.$$

In the long run the stock of capital is not considered here a major limiting factor, as in Chichilinsky et al. (1995). Technically, however, this aspect can be incorporated within the current framework.

The relevant formulation of the model in our setup is

$$\text{Max} \int_0^\infty D(C, E, t) \, U(C, E) \, dt$$

subject to

$$E = \alpha C + R(E), C < 0 \text{ constant}, E(0) = E \, 0 \text{ given.}$$

In the above, the utility function U depends on usual consumption factor as well as on the environmental quality and is assumed to possess regular properties; C, E are continuous functions of t. The dynamics of E above represent the resultant emissions and renewals of the pollutant.

The relevant Hamiltonian is given by the following:

$$H = D(C, E, t) \, U(C, E) + \lambda_1 [C + R(E)] + \lambda_2 [-D(C, E, t)]$$

where λ_1 and λ_2 are costate variables representing the shadow values of environment and discount factor, respectively (see Rao 1998b for details).

An application of Pontryagin's Maximum Principle gives a set of first-order conditions (see Rao 2000), leading to the following interpretations. The shadow value of environment is the negative of the discounted marginal utility of consumption per unit (adverse) impact of consumption on environment, or per unit emission arising out of consumption activities.

This is a useful relation linking the growth rate of marginal utility of consumption with the discount factor, the productivity of environmental improvement function, the coefficient of consumption effect on environment, and the relative marginal utilities of environment and of consumption. If the above growth rate is zero, as is the case with stationarity, we derive the New Green Golden Rule (NGGR):

The ratio of the marginal utility of the environmental features to the marginal utility of consumption is proportional to the difference between marginal renewal of the environment function (or environmental improvement coefficient) and the growth of the discount factor. The proportionality factor is the coefficient of emissions in the consumption function. In other words, NGGR is that marginal utility of consumption that is (a) directly proportional to the marginal utility of environment and the negative of the emission coefficient of consumption, and (b) inversely proportional to the difference between the growth of the discount factor and the marginal renewal of the environment. The marginal utility of consumption is constant if either all the factors in (a) and (b) are constant, or the factor in (a) is constant and the difference stated in (b) is constant. The above NGGR clearly suggests that for a given discount factor, enhancement in the renewal of the environment, or, equivalently, enhancement in the climatic stability factor, contributes to the enrichment of marginal utility of consumption.

The following section elucidates the role of ecotaxes, sometimes referred to as "green taxes" (or, more narrowly applied, "carbon taxes"), in the preservation and stability of the environment and climate, respectively.

3.7 Economics of Ecotaxes

Various economic instruments and incentives merit their application for regulating and stabilizing GHGs. Some of these, like trading emissions permits, are proposed for discussion in chapter 4 in connection with the issues of GHG abatement and stabilization. This section deals with ecotaxes for general environmental problems. The terms "ecotaxes," "green taxes," "environmental taxes," and "pollution taxes" are interchangeably used here for the present, although they do not precisely mean the same. These categories include "carbon taxes," but the converse does not hold. Historically, Pigou (1932) was among the first economists who advocated pollution taxes. A Pigouvian tax is a tax levied on each unit of pollution or emissions output, and the tax equals the marginal damage the pollution causes to the economic system, at an efficient level of production system or output level. This tax tradition may have some feasibility if the source of pollution and its relative contribution and damage are known.

Baumol and Oates (1985) classified two alternative bases within the above tradition of taxes: (1) assessment of tax on the basis of optimal production (implying an "optimal tax rate"—which may not provide an incentive to the polluting firm to alter the emission pattern of pollution; and (2) levy of tax rate iteratively adjusted to relate it to the current magnitudes of marginal damages—which may provide incentives to the polluter to alter the magnitudes of pollutant emissions. Both these approaches to taxation are built on serious limitations arising out of information limitations and practical implementation problems or enforcement difficulties. These considerations did not bother some economists who carried out some arithmetic to venture an approximation of global average carbon tax estimates on the basis of some notion of global damages due to global warming and to divide the cost with current CO_2-equivalent emissions.

Much of the literature on Pigouvian taxes did not address the issue of revenue mobilization or the consequent decisions of levying pollution taxes. Pollution taxes promise the potential to offer a better tax structure for any given economy and also enhance environmental quality, if the tax instruments are properly formulated and implemented: a case of double dividend!

The Principle of Polluter Pays (PPP) has its application and this was institutionally advocated by the Organization for Economic Cooperation and Development (OECD) (1975) for adoption in its member countries, which are typically industrial and advanced economies. The OECD document stated: (1) the principle for allocating costs of pollution prevention and control measures to encourage rational use of scarce environmental resources and to avoid distortions in trade and investment is the "Principle of Polluter Pays"; the costs of these measures "should be reflected in the costs of goods and services which cause pollution in production and/or consumption"; and (2) when the environmental costs are taken into account, the market fails to reflect these costs in the price system. Despite these broad principles, the issue of internalizing environmental costs in dealing with international trade in goods and services remains a contentious issue. If the Principle of Polluter Pays were applied as broadly as it should be, to include the transboundary pollution problems and consequent damages, we could possibly have avoided the current environmental mess regarding the GHGs and climatic instabilities.

In recent years public policy in the industrial countries favored some form of ecotax or green tax or pollution tax, partly to offset the personal tax burden and simultaneously to achieve some degree of dampening of pollution emissions. An element of revenue-neutrality is also contemplated in this tax-shift pattern. In a revenue-neutral tax reform, it is possible to increase progressivity elsewhere in the economy or in the tax system to at least offset the regressivity inherent in the green taxes or carbon taxes; reductions in the lowest tax rates under the income tax system can, for example, address this objective (Oates 1995).

The phenomena of "dividends" of various types were also touted in support of various kinds of environmental tax measures.

> *(Single) Dividend*: Environmental taxation increases total welfare of the society by reducing or eliminating negative environmental externalities.
>
> *Double Dividend*: Shifting the tax burden from personal taxation to environmental resources reduces the relative cost of labor and augments employment.
>
> *Triple Dividend*: The process leads to reduction of tax distortions and increases economic output toward more efficient paths—economically and environmentally.

However, in the presence of existing tax distortions, new green taxes can sometimes outweigh the efficiency gains from revenue recycling—no double dividend in such cases! When new taxes are introduced—especially the provision of green taxes—existing twisted tax systems can take advantage of some of the tax regimes and countries to correct the previous distortions and come on track for a more sensible, efficient, and equitable system; whether such an approach will in fact be adopted is to be answered in terms of political and socioeconomic factors.

In a useful survey, Goulder (1995) examined the theory and empiricism of environmental taxation and various forms of dividend propositions; the rise and fall of the double dividend claim is included. Some of the major conclusions are summarized below. First we define the concept of "gross costs" here: These are the welfare sacrifices associated with environmental tax policies—under this criterion the overall efficiency change from a policy initiative is the welfare benefit arising from the change in environmental quality (the gross benefits) minus the gross costs. Three forms of double dividend are distinguished:

1. *Weak form*: Environmental taxes are used to finance reductions in marginal rates of an existing distortionary tax; cost savings are achieved relative to the case of transfer of tax revenues to the taxpayers in lump-sum fashion;
2. *Intermediate form*: Revenue-neutral substitution of the environmental tax for a distortionary tax is used in such a way that this results in zero or negative gross cost;

3. *Strong form*: The revenue-neutral substitution for the environmental tax for typical or representative distortionary taxes involves a zero or negative gross cost.

The overall effect of the tax consists of (a) the Pigouvian (or the partial equilibrium) effect; (b) the tax interaction effect; and (c) revenue recycling or, more generally, the fiscal effect. The basic partial equilibrium analysis of optimal environmental tax invokes the Pigouvian method, where the optimal tax rate equals the marginal external costs or marginal environmental damages (MED); this implies the gross marginal cost or marginal abatement cost associated with an environmental tax equals the tax rate.

In a more comprehensive and a general equilibrium analysis, Bovenberg and de Mooji (1994) established that the presence of prior taxes imposes higher gross costs from the environmental tax, even when revenues are recycled through cuts in the distortionary tax. The results presented by Parry (1995, 1997) support the above conclusions; the tax interaction effect is of greater magnitude than the revenue recycling effect under plausible values of parameters; the optimal environmental tax works out to about 70 percent of the Pigouvian tax, or of the MED. The Nordhaus (1993) model and its results do not capture the interactive effects of existing taxes.

In contrast, the results of Bovenberg and Goulder (1996) suggest that the optimal carbon taxes decline with the level of preexisting taxes. The interactive effects of taxes, innovations, and incentives for research and development (R&D) contribute to the final outcome regarding the efficiency of pollution containment.

Reverting to the relevance of environmental taxes, even the studies that cast doubts on the existence of significant double dividends did not have much difficulty in arriving at the conclusion that as long as the tax yields an environmental benefit, it offers an overall welfare improvement. Goulder (1995) concluded that any evaluation of green taxes cannot be carried out independent of environmental benefits assessment. According to Goulder, "The difficulty of establishing the strong double dividend does not contradict the common numerical finding that an environmental tax can promote higher national income when revenues are earmarked for capital formation" (p. 176). This conclusion was derived by dropping the stronger requirement of welfare improvement and replacing it with the weaker income criteria.

In terms of relevant methodologies for optimal environmental taxation with due recognition of existing taxes and their roles, a very useful general equilibrium analysis methodology and also a few empirical results are contributed by Bovenberg and Goulder (1996), who extend previous analyses with the inclusion of pollution taxes like carbon taxes on intermediate inputs of the economy (such as fossil fuel inputs for energy and transportation fuels). A more recent analytical work by Denicolo (1999) compares the effects of effluent taxes and pollution permits in a deterministic economic setting. One of the results of this analysis suggests that taxes may be superior as policy instruments relative to pollution permits when the socioeconomic damage associated with pollution emissions is not too high or environmental externality is small. In the latter case, permits may be preferable.

To summarize, the main findings of recent significant contributions to the study of environmental taxation are (see Rao 1999): (a) there are merits in levying these taxes; (b) because of the tax interaction effect with the prevailing taxes in the economy, the magnitudes of optimal environmental taxes tend to be about 10 to 30 percent less than those dictated by traditional partial equilibrium analyses; (c) depending on the revenue recycling or other patterns of utilization of these tax revenues, the net effect of the tax levies can be progressive or neutral or regressive for various economic classes; (d) the relevance of the tax instruments (relative to pollution permits) can be assessed in relation to the changing levels of the marginal environmental damages of one or more pollutants, in addition to the role of transaction costs associated with alternate policy regimes.

Taxes are but a set of instruments, usually considered in the category of disincentives for environmental degradation or spread of externalities. The broad framework for economic incentives and disincentives is given in Appendix 3B. In the application of any of these instruments, one must be conscious of the role of transaction costs in effectuating the policies to meet the desired objectives. It is not difficult to list a set of potential candidates for each of the categories of incentives and disincentives, but it is usually very difficult to enforce the same without significant costs. The need for a multilevel framework becomes evident in any policy context.

3.8 Economic Policies: Multilevel Approaches

Traditional methods of taxation, regulation, and nonmarket reliance for environmental compliance are of relatively less significance if we consider the comprehensive list of potential economic instruments. These instruments are necessarily aimed at ensuring better compliance in a cost-effective manner, but they are also proactive in going beyond compliance. In other words, ecological and economic integration, combined with a comprehensive institutional framework, tends to provide a cost- effective approach, where costs include the total costs (explained in Section 3.3). In terms of institutions, we need to recognize markets, governments, and societies/individuals/nongovernmental organizations. Both public education and environmental consciousness are likely to be some of the most cost-effective methods of proactive environmental activity toward global climate stabilization. It is desirable to address relevant problems in a multilevel framework with built-in feedback mechanisms so that continuous improvements are possible. Government institutions are usually more effective in the enforcement of incentives for environmentally friendly activities, although their role in regulating and enforcing legal provisions is equally important. At the national level, scrupulous deployment of environmental accounting, in addition to the traditional national income accounting practices, will pave the way for an environment-climate-economy enhancing complementary methods of economic activities. Similar steps at the corporate level, possibly based on the new standards ISO 14000 devised by the International Standards Organization, will be very relevant.

A number of formal and informal levels come to interact in the concordance or otherwise of environmental management. Combined with this institutional aspect, the features of the environment itself might require attention at the local (such as point-source and non-point-source water pollution), regional (such as transboundary pollution emissions between Mexico and the United States), and global (e.g., GHGs) levels. It is useful to adopt a multilevel approach to various environmental and economic development issues, even if the levels are not necessarily coterminus with powers of decision making or geographic or such similar well-defined boundaries. The purpose is to deal with each package of internally consistent policies and programs so as to be integrated with similar frameworks from the rest of the components or subsystems of the global system.

Every country would do well to undertake a comprehensive assessment of its status and perspectives on environmental sustainability and sustainable development. It is useful to note that climate stability is a necessary but not sufficient requirement in this context. The result can form, at its worst, a good beginning in the right direction. Some of the highlights of the U.S. Federal and Intersectoral Approach Recommendations are illustrated in the policy recommendations (adding up to a few dozen) of the President's Council on Sustainable Development (1996). These include the following: The federal government should cooperate in key international agreements—from ratifying the UN Convention on Biological Diversity to taking the lead in achieving full implementation of specific commitments made in international agreements to which the United States is a party.

Broader aspects of climate stabilization via sustainable development hinge heavily on the knowledge sector, with its engine R&D. The trends in the share of government expenditures on environmental R&D in the total expenditure (measured in "purchasing power parity" dollars for various OECD countries) for the period 1981 to 1992 seem to suggest (see OECD 1996) that there are a few countries, such as the United States, Greece, Belgium, and Norway, that have reduced expenditures in this area. This could be a source for concern, although the private sector is expected to invest substantial resources in this sector during the next few years. Government support is justified on the grounds that there is underinvestment in environmental R&D by corporations because of the following factors (OECD 1996):

1. externalities associated with environmental research, where individual firms are unable to capture sufficient benefits from R&D to justify their expenditure, but social returns on investment are high;
2. possibly larger than normal business uncertainties about the existing markets and future markets for new products;
3. uncertainties in local and international regulations and environmental laws affecting products and processes in demand from time to time.

In addition to the need for enhanced and accelerated investments in relevant R&D support from the governmental sector, a number of other technical and managerial innovations need to be supported and implemented. These include various types of eco-efficiency measures, design of environment approaches in structures, and systems of technologies and industrial ecology.

The tools of "greening" include design for eco-efficiency (DFE), environmental accounting, life-cycle analysis (LCA), full cost pricing to include environmental costs, recognition of the industrial and human ecology of the environment, and scientific information gathering and analysis of environmental parameters (local and global). The interaction of science and policy in atmospheric science is advancing at an unprecedented rate as we enter the twenty-first century, and there are sufficient reasons to believe that this process will continue for the next several years in search of more definitive answers to some of the questions of global warming and the relative role of anthropogenic pollution. The essential basic meteorological infrastructure of individual countries needs to be strengthened and maintained.

Economywide integration of environmental issues, with a bearing on the local climate (as in urban concentrations or deforestation) and on transboundary pollution (as in the emissions of GHGs or reductions in the forest sinks of CO_2), is an important prerequisite to identify and realize the potential cost savings while achieving desired goals. Intersectoral, interregional, and multilevel identification of potential areas of intervention for climate stabilization will be a comprehensive and practicable approach. Details of some of these aspects will be explored in chapter 5.

3.9 Concluding Observations

Some of the significant conclusions arising from the discussions in this chapter include the following:

1. The economics of global climate change need to be viewed within the framework of sustainable development if policy measures are to be derived for climate stabilization or any modulation of climatic variations; this enables a meaningful interpretation of the valuation of the climatic and consequential resources like those of the ecosystem services and other environmental goods and services;
2. global warming is but a part of the problem of climate change, and control of greenhouse gases as well as other influencing factors in the ecology-economy interlinks must be fully explored to ensure resilience of the biogeophysical system;
3. traditional methods of assessing costs of climate change or of its control are rather narrow; this is because these have generally neglected various important ingredients like transaction and adaptation costs, effects of feedback mechanisms, and transition costs; a comprehensive concept of costs and also of benefits is necessary to derive an operationally meaningful policy framework;
4. resource valuation needs to recognize the finiteness of sink capacities

of planet Earth; this will enable proper valuation of traditionally "free" resources; global commons are governed by open-access features leading to potential catastrophe; economic instruments can play a major role at the global and national levels in controlling such processes;

5. the critical issue of time-discounting or valuation over time for long horizons requires, unlike in most studies, recognition of variable discounting with requisite endogenization of the discount function;

6. risk-averse behavior warrants low discount rates for costs and high discount rates for benefits in the evaluation of an environmental or climate change program;

7. ecotaxes continue to merit their expanded role; if designed and implemented properly, these taxes could be effective instruments of environmental policy; and

8. considering the marginal value of information in reducing climatic unknowns and their uncertainties, it remains a cost-effective priority to invest in the understanding of the phenomena for prevention and control of anthropogenic influences adversely affecting the climate, environment, and the economy.

References

Barbier, E. 1987. "The Concept of Sustainable Economic Development." *Environmental Conservation* 14(2):101–110.

Baumol, W.J., and Oates, W.E. 1985. *The Theory of Environmental Policy.* Englewood Cliffs, NJ: Prentice-Hall.

Becker, G. 1998. *Accounting for Tastes.* Cambridge, MA: Harvard University Press.

Becker, G., and Mulligan, C. 1997. "The Endogenous Determination of Time Preferences." *Quarterly Journal of Economics* 112(3):729–758.

Bovenberg, A.L., and Goulder, L.H. 1996. "Optimal Environmental Taxation in the Presence of Other Taxes—General Equilibrium Analyses." *American Economic Review* 86:985–1000.

Bovenberg, L., and deMooji, R.A. 1994. "Environmental Levies and Distortionary Taxes." *American Economic Review* 84(4):1085–1089.

Bradford, D. 1997. "On the Uses of Benefit-Cost Reasoning in Choosing Policy Toward Global Climate Change." Working Paper no. 127, Center for Economic Studies, University of Munich.

Brockett, P.L., and Golden, L.L. 1987. "A Class of Utility Functions Containing All the Common Utility Functions." *Management Science* 33:955–964.

Broome, J. 1992. *Counting the Cost of Global Warming.* London: White Horse Press.

Chichilinsky, G. et al. 1995. "The Green Golden Rule." *Economics Letters* 49:175–179.

Clark, C. 1993. *Mathematical Bioeconomics.* New York: Wiley Interscience.

Costanza, R. et al. 1997. "The Value of the World's Ecosystem Services and Natural Capital." *Nature* 387 (May 15):253–260.

————. 1991. "Goals, Agenda, and Policy Recommendations for Ecological Economics." In *Ecological Economics: The Science and Management of Sustainability*, ed. R. Costanza, 1–20. New York: Columbia University Press.

Daily, G., ed. 1997. *Nature's Services: Societal Dependence on Natural Ecosystems*. Washington, DC: Island Press.

Daly, H.E. 1991. *Steady-State Economics*. Washington, DC: Island Press.

Dasgupta, P., and Heal, G. 1976. *Economic Theory and Exhaustible Resources*, 244–246. Cambridge: Cambridge University Press.

Denicolo, V. 1999. "Pollution-Reducing Innovations Under Taxes or Permits." *Oxford Economic Papers* 51:184–199.

Dietz, T., and Rosa, E. 1997. "Effects of Population and Affluence on CO Emissions." *Proceedings of the National Academy of Sciences* 94:175–179.

Doetsch, G. 1971. *Guide to the Application of the Laplace and Z-Transforms*. New York: Van Nostrand.

Dreze, J., and Stern, N. 1987. "The Theory of Cost-Benefit Analysis." Chapter 14 in *Handbook of Public Economics*, Vol. 2, ed. J. Auerbach and M. Feldstein, 909–989. New York: North-Holland.

Eeckhoudt, L. et al. 1996. "Changes in Background Risk and Risk Taking Behavior." *Econometrica* 64(3):683–689.

Georgeuse-Rogen, N. 1971. *The Entropy Law and the Economic Process*. Cambridge, MA: Harvard University Press.

Goodin, R. 1982. "Discounting Discounting." *Journal of Public Policy* 2(1):53–72.

Goulder, L.H. 1995. "Environmental Taxation and the Double Dividend—A Reader's Guide." *International Tax and Public Finance* 2:157–183.

Harvey, C. 1995. "Proportional Discounting of Future Costs and Benefits." *Mathematics of Operations Research* 20(2):381–399.

Harvey, C.M. 1986. "Value Functions for Infinite-Period Planning." *Management Science* 32:1123–1139.

Higle, J.L. et al. 1990. "Deterministic Equivalence in Stochastic Infinite Horizon Problems." *Mathematics of Operations Research* 15:396–407.

Holdren, J., and Ehrlich, P. 1974. "Human Population and the Global Environment." *American Scientist* 62:282–292.

Hotelling, H. 1931. "The Economics of Exhaustible Resources." *Journal of Political Economy* 39:137–175.

Independent Commission on Population and Quality of Life (ICPQL). 1996. *Caring for the Future*. New York: Oxford University Press.

IPCC. 1996. *Climate Change 1995: Economic and Social Dimensions of Climate Change*. Geneva: IPCC, published by Cambridge University Press.

Joshi, S. 1995. "Recursive Utility and Optimal Growth Under Uncertainty." *Journal of Mathematical Economics* 24:601–617.

Mitlin, D., and Satterthwaite. D. 1990. *Human Settlements and Sustainable Development*. Nairobi: UN Center for Human Settlements Habitat.

Myers, N. 1995. "Environmental Unknowns." *Science* 269:358–360.

Nordhaus, W.D. 1994. *Managing the Global Commons: The Economics of Climate Change*. Cambridge, MA: MIT Press.

————. 1993. "Rolling the DICE—The Optimal Transition Path for Controlling Greenhouse Gases." *Resources and Energy Economics* 15:27–50.

Oates, W.E. 1995. "Green Taxes, the Environment, and the Tax System." *Southern Economic Journal* 61(4):915–922.

Organization for Economic Cooperation and Development (OECD). 1996. *The Global Environmental Goods and Services Industry*. Geneva: OECD Secretariat.

———. 1975. *The Principle of Polluter Pays: Definition, Analysis, and Implementation*. Paris: OECD Secretariat.

Parry, I.W. 1997. "Environmental Taxes and Quotas in the Presence of Distorting Taxes in Factor Markets." *Resource and Energy Economics* 19:203–220.

———. 1995. "Pollution Taxes and Revenue Recycling." *Journal of Environmental Economics and Management* 29:S64–S77.

Pigou, A.C. 1932. *The Economics of Welfare*. London: Macmillan.

Plambeck, E.L. et al. 1997. "The 'Page 95' Model: Integrating the Science and Economics of Global Warming." *Energy Economics* 19(1):77–101.

Pratt, J.W., and Zeckhauser, R.J. 1987. "Proper Risk Aversion." *Econometrica* 55:143–154.

Prelec, D. 1998. "The Probability Weighting Function." *Econometrica* 66(3):497–527.

President's Council on Sustainable Development (PCSD). 1996. *Sustainable America: A New Consensus for Prosperity, Opportunity, and a Healthy Environment for the Future*. Washington, DC: U.S.Government Printing Office.

Randall, A. 1987. *Resource Economics: An Economic Approach to Natural Resource and Environmental Policy*. New York: Wiley.

Rao, P.K. 2000. *The Economics of Transaction Costs: Theory, Methods and Applications*. London: Macmillan (in press).

———. 1999. *Sustainable Development: Economics and Policy*. Oxford and Boston: Blackwell.

———. 1998a. *Is Net National Product an Indicator of Sustainability?* (under review.)

———. 1998b. *Sustainable Development with Endogenous Preferences*. (in press).

Rawls, J. 1972. *A Theory of Social Justice*. Cambridge, MA: Harvard University Press.

Serageldin, I. 1996. *Sustainability and the Wealth of Nations: First Steps in an Ongoing Journey*. Washington, DC: World Bank.

———. 1995. "Sustainability as Opportunity and the Problem of Social Capital." *Brown Journal of World Affairs* 3(2):187–203.

Solow, R.M. 1996. "Comments on Net National Product." Personal communication to the author.

———. 1994. "An Almost Practical Step Toward Sustainability." In *Assigning Economic Value to Natural Resources*. Washington, DC: National Academy Press.

———. 1992. "Sustainability: An Economist's Perspective." The 18th Steward Johnson Lecture, Woods Hole Oceanographic Institution, Woods Hole, MA.

———. 1970. *Growth Theory—An Exposition*. New York: Oxford University Press.

Stern, P.C. et al., eds. 1992. *Global Environmental Change: Understanding the Human Dimensions*. Washington, DC: National Academy Press.

Weitzman, M.L. 1998. "Why the Far-Distant Future Should Be Discounted at Its Lowest Possible Rate" *Journal of Environmental Economics and Management* 36:201–208.

————. 1976. "On the Welfare Significance of National Product in a Dynamic Economy." *Quarterly Journal of Economics* 90:156–162.

Wood, J.C. 1996. "Intergenerational Equity and Climate Change." *Georgetown International Environmental Law Review* 8(2):293–332.

World Bank. 1995. *Mainstreaming the Environment: Fiscal 1995.* Washington, DC: World Bank.

World Commission on Environment and Development: The Brundtland Report. 1987. *Our Common Future.* Oxford: Oxford University Press.

World Conservation Union, UNEP, and World Wildlife Fund for Nature. 1991. *Caring for the Earth—A Strategy for Sustainable Living.* Gland, Switzerland: IUCN (World Conservation Union).

Appendix 3A
Analytics of Low Discount Rates
for Stochastic Costs

The following derivation helps establish a rigorous proof of the need for low discount rates when valuing environmental costs under uncertainty over a lengthy time horizon.

Let r be the market-influenced discount rate, such as the competitively determined perfect capital market-based rate of interest. Assume r exhibits random behavior that admits the following characterization of the (certainty) equivalent interest rate r* (EIR) (see Higle et al. 1990):

$$E\left[\exp\{-rT(z)\}\right] = \exp\{-r^* E[T(z)]\}$$

for each state z of the stochastic process $\{T(z), z > 0\}$. \hfill (1)

Using the well-known Jensen's inequality, it can be shown (Higle et al. 1990) that $r^* < r$—that is, the stochastic nature of the dynamic process $\{T(z), > 0\}$ has the same effect on the decision-making process as does reducing the discount rate in the deterministic problem, as long as $\{T(z), z > 0\}$ is a process with stationary independent increments (as, for example, Brownian motion commonly used in a number of stochastic economic models).

Let us introduce the A class of utility functions given by Brockett and Golden (1987). These utility functions possess important useful properties, namely decreasing absolute risk aversion (DARA) and proper risk aversion (Pratt and Zeckhauser 1987).

When we deal with the A class, the Laplacian ordering of utilities generates stochastic dominance ordering of the von Neumann–Morgenstern utility functions. Moreover, this process allows an ordering of corresponding EIRs, and hence the results that suggest lowering of EIRs in relation to ascending uncertainties of the system as its evolves over time, as in the case of global environment and global warming.

Let us note that the left-hand side of equation (1) is simply $L[T(z)]$, the Laplace transform of $T(z)$.

Let $K = \{T_m : T_m(z), z > 0, m > 1\}$ be a stationary stochastic process with independent increments.

Let $T_1(z)$ and $T_2(z)$ be two stochastic processes that are consistent with the EIRs r^*_1 and r^*_2, respectively. Theorem 3 of Brockett and Golden (1987) states that if

$$L[T_1(z)] > L[T_2(z)], \text{ then}$$
$$E\,U[T_1(z)] < E\,U[T_2(z)]$$

whenever U is the utility function of the class A.

Using the above ordering, $T_2(z)$ is preferred to $T_1(z)$, and $r^*_2 < r^*_1$.

Thus, if there is a choice among r^*s associated with the stochastic process, the lowest r^* is preferred in the above sense.

The arguments above are relevant to a wide variety of decision problems that are not necessarily confined to the models described here. However, application of these findings to the economics of global warming seems to brighten the prospects of resolving the controversies and complexities of choosing appropriate discount rates. It is also of interest to note that Weitzman (1998) arrived at a similar conclusion as in this appendix, using a vastly different analytical approach. Weitzman concluded that uncertainty about future discount rates provides a strong rationale for using "certainty-equivalent social discount rates that decline over time."

Appendix 3B
Optimal Incentives and Disincentives

The provision of proper incentives and disincentives that are compatible with climate stabilization requires an appreciation of the roles of at least two major factors: (1) biogeophysical and behavioral uncertainties, lagged responses to interventions or exogenous influences, and long time horizons; and (2) systemwide assessments of costs and benefits, even from an anthropocentric view. Some of the relevant analytical features to deal with scientific uncertainties were discussed in chapter 2. However, broader assessments require recognition of economic behavioral uncertainties and decision making in such a context. A considerable literature exists to analyze individual economic decision making and enterprise decision making, under various stochastic settings. The analytical requirements differ in dealing with the analysis of a large (perhaps as large it can get on planet Earth) system. It is rather naive to reduce the entire problem of global climatic policy to an aggregative simple optimization problem. The least we can do at this stage of development of relevant knowledge is to seek the best directions for further inquiry and recognize the roles and limitations of any analytical tools we deploy.

Using the approach of the general systems theory, it is easy to observe that the dynamics of nonautonomous (those with the independent role of purely time-related factors) systems models are relevant for any study of the climate and climatic changes. This is because of the role of external factors—not controlled or influenced by humans—in affecting various parameters of the climatic system. The broad scientific consensus is that over time, the main characteristics of the climate are depicting changes with increasing magnitudes of variations (weather extremes, spatial and seasonal variations, geohydrologic variations, and related aspects). Let us call these "background risks." The study of nonautonomous systems and their optimization suggests that the role of the above changes, sometimes clustered under the role of "time," is fundamentally human-welfare reducing as long as there are no offsetting efforts. These human-induced offsets may or may not be in terms of controlling the climate itself. Instead, they could be in terms of innovative efforts for enhancing production and consumption externalities, or minimizing environmental damages.

Focusing on the economic systems, in a dynamic multiagent decision-making system, provisions for incentive-compatible inputs or, equivalently, the design of incentives for economic welfare maximization, are not independent of the underlying institutional configurations. The roles of markets and other economic institutions, of regulatory framework, and of social institutions are such that any assessment of benefits and costs of provision of alternate sets of incentives remains highly sensitive to the incidence of transaction costs, in addition to the usual elements of the cost vector. Transaction benefits are also to be noted in a few cases, but these are essentially the ingredients corresponding to some of the transaction-cost-minimizing activities. Much of the empirical economic literature is impervious to the size and effect of transaction costs in assessing the benefit-cost ratios or other related indicators. This is one of the most significant limitations of such analyses in their usefulness to suggest real-world policies.

Rational economic behavior consistent with a generalized concept of wealth maximization (to include all forms of natural capital) warrants anthropogenic decision making that belongs in the "risk averse" category as long as there exist background risks. Various analytical models relevant in this context can be found in an important contribution by Eeckhoudt et al. (1996). The applicability of operational guidelines like those of the Precautionary Principle (see, e.g., Rao 1999) becomes obvious in such system configurations. In the context of provision of incentives and disincentives for climate stabilization, risk-averse behavioral requirements suggest the need to dovetail such measures to prevent climatic damages—in a cost-effective manner (costs to include transaction costs). Whether disincentives are more relevant than incentives depends on the features governing the institutional alignments for proper implementation of the same: the effectiveness and the corresponding transaction costs. Let us recognize that the transaction costs of an ineffective policy instrument are the sum of the costs of enforcement and of the unrealized potential of the instrument. Ecotaxes, for example, are more likely to work in regimes having efficient income tax mechanisms. Emission quotas and targets under regulatory regimes tend to work if there exists an efficient enforcement system. The complementarity of the quality of institutions and the cost-effectiveness in the implementation of desired incentives and disincentives must be noted.

Chapter 4

Economics of the Greenhouse Effect

4.1 Introduction

The global warming effect of the greenhouse phenomenon, contributed by accumulations of different greenhouse gases, does not lend itself to any simple rules for an assessment of associated costs and benefits. These costs are mainly those of preventing further accumulations, and the costs of inaction leading to enhanced greenhouse effects. The benefits derive from reductions in greenhouse emissions, reductions in net accumulations, and the consequences of these curtailments. Often, one of the guiding economic principles of optimal reductions in these gases and in the net accumulations is expressed in terms of the "marginality principle," a state of environmental management where the marginal cost of reduction equals the marginal benefit of the same.

However, this prescription is much easier stated than applied in practice. The main reasons, apart from the motivations of the involved parties, for limiting its applicability are that assessment of the marginal costs and marginal benefits is founded on dozens of assumptions governing the behavior of the elements contributing to the cost functions in different ranges of their operation, over time, and in varying sectors/regions. Many of the traditional assumptions regarding private-sector economics of ascertaining costs and benefits do not hold in this mega-production system, given the ecological and economic interactions and environmental unknowns. The simultaneous operations of a multitude of economic agents, the dynamics of bioeconomic systems, and the interdependencies of various "noneconomic" systems along with the recognized economic systems are some of the factors that must be considered in any realistic appraisal of the economic parameters.

This chapter addresses the broad foundations and framework for the economics of the greenhouse effect (GE). The focus is on the underlying factors and their comprehension, rather than on oversimplified arbitrary empirical estimates of the costs and benefits. The following section clarifies the economy-ecology interdependencies, which are important in understanding the impact of the GE. The degree of thermal temperature change due to the GE is measured using the methods of assessing the global warming potential (GWP) under plausible assumption regarding the accumulations of different greenhouse gases (GHGs). The GWP in different time horizons and time preferences for various costs and benefits has diverse economic consequences, explored in Section 4.3. The impact of the GE on biogeophysical systems, especially on the health of humans, is of great concern, even if a precise-dollar cost estimate of the impact is not yet within the grasp of most studies. These aspects are discussed in Section 4.4. The damage assessment methods are examined, and the economics of mitigating damages are deliberated in Sections 4.5 and 4.6, respectively.

4.2 Ecological Economic Aspects

The role of the GE is such that it tends to affect both the economic and the ecological systems, even after assuming the role of adaptive mechanisms that adjust to GE-related impacts and changes. None of the adjustments are cost free, although the costs may not entail monetary values in the market sense. Moreover, when the ecosystem loses its resilience, a new set of system dynamics governs the evolution of physical and economic systems and leads to a new set of equilibria (not usually known in advance). The linkages of economy and ecology are thus greatly influenced by changes in the GE, and to a large extent the specific characteristics of these linkages may not be understood until it is either too expensive to remedy undesirable changes or too late because of biogeosystem irreversibilities.

The feature that a market may not exist for some of the products and services provided by nature and by ecosystems does not mean there is no scarcity value nor that they are infinitely available and forever, even with sustained human tampering with the natural systems. It is an issue of defining property rights and liability systems for some of the important environmental goods. Such a mechanism will lend support to conservation and provide incentives for innovation, leading to efficient utilization of resources of all categories. The following two propositions provide useful fundamental insights into the dynamics of the links between ecology and economy.

Proposition 1

Given the conservation of mass, any system generating nonzero residuals will be time varying in its coefficients of production. (Perrings 1997)

"Spaceship Earth" constitutes a closed system, and thus there is no "free" disposal of environmental "goods" or "bads" or any other waste. It may be cost-free for some but expensive for all to indulge in uncompensated or free-for-all disposal of wastes or various environmental emissions. These constrain the sinks and the speed of biogeochemical renewal to such an extent that the sink capacity declines over time and leads to a new set of ecological and biogeophysical equilibria. Underlying input-output relations in various systems, of which the economic production system is one example, depict time-varying changes. These changes are endogenous to various human interventions as well. An active and pragmatic technical innovation and adoption, in addition to various potential adaptation mechanisms, constitute some of the measures to address the adverse effects of changes in the coefficients of production.

Proposition 2

A subsystem within the global economy-environment system may be technologically stationary at equilibrium in the presence of nonzero residuals, if and only if disposal of those residuals is cost-free. (Perrings 1997)

This implies that in the presence of various feedback mechanisms of systems and their subsystems, and with positive costs of residuals and their disposal affecting the sinks of planet Earth, stationary equilibrium does not exist.

Among the related issues is that of the phenomena of climate change where change in averages usually is accompanied by changes in the variability of the parameters or factors of influence in the entire system. As a result of such changes, it is not sufficient to focus on average changes. The socioeconomic welfare implications of climate change models that do not incorporate the effects of changes in climatic variability tend to underestimate the effects of climate change. This feature was demonstrated in a detailed investigation by Dalton (1997), whose observations are particularly relevant in the study of the economics of global warming. Section 4.3 addresses the issues of global warming potential and its economics.

4.3 Economics of the Global Warming Potential

The anthropogenic emissions of CO_2 account for about two-thirds of the global warming potential (GWP) of current anthropogenic GHG emissions. The relative role of methane (CH_4) is estimated at about 20 percent and that of nitrous oxide (N_2O) at about 8 percent. The possibility of changes in the sink-renewal rates in response to changes in GHG concentrations is not yet fully understood. Similarly, the indirect and interactive effects of GHGs in various combinations sustained over different time intervals are not fully known either. These are some of the elements of analysis relevant for assessing the GWP, the details of which are presented below.

The original motivation for devising the GWP index was to offer a simple characterization of the relative radiative effects of various combinations of gases. It was created so as to enable policymakers to evaluate options affecting the emissions of various greenhouse gases by avoiding the need to make complex calculations.

The GWP is a measure of the relative, globally averaged warming effect arising from the emissions of a particular greenhouse gas, and is defined as the time-integrated change in radiative forcing due to the instantaneous release of 1 unit weight of a trace gas expressed relative to that from the release of the same unit weight of CO_2 (IPCC 1990, 1992). The calculation requires a number of important specifications, including the following:

1. the radiative forcing of the reference gas and of the other gases, per unit mass of concentration change at different levels of operation;
2. atmospheric lifetimes of various gases under consideration and of the reference gas;
3. the time horizon over which the radiative forcings have to be integrated;
4. the levels of future concentrations of other gases that form the background for interactive effectiveness; and,
5. global meteorological parameters for the current and future time periods.

A review of the initial formulations and their revisions will be useful in understanding and refinement of the concept of GWP.

The GWP is essentially an assessment of a given GHG's contribution to heat trapping over its lifetime (or, atmospheric residency life interval), and this is normalized for comparison purposes, with respect to a corresponding expression for the reference gas. This reference gas is usually taken as CO_2, given its wider significance in the GE.

The formal definition led to one of the early formulations of the GWP index I (Lashof and Ahuja [1990], IPCC [1990]): I= F/G, with F representing the contribution of the GHG under reference for assessment of its contribution, and G representing the corresponding contribution of CO_2 over the same time period T, the time horizon of concern; F is the weighted sum f(t) x C(t) of reference GHG, for each time period (in the discrete time scale, or its integral equivalent in the continuous time scale) starting from initial time t = 0, with f(t) as the radiating force or heat-trapping ability of the same per unit concentration, and C(t) the corresponding quantity of the GHG. The expression for G regarding CO_2 is analogously defined. This index depends critically on the specification of T, and it decreases with the choice of higher magnitudes of T for the gases having a shorter atmospheric residence than the average for CO_2.

The radiative heating effects per unit mass of various GHGs (given in parentheses) relative to CO_2 (taken as 1 unit) are as follows (see Harvey 1993): CH_4 (72), N_2O (206), CFC-11 (3970), CFC-12 (5750), HCFC-22 (5440).

Some approximations of the GWPs, using the formula given above, are in Houghton et al. (1990). Based on the lifetime (sometimes known as "mean residence time in the atmosphere") of 120 years, CO2 contributes 51 percent of GWP if we take a 20-year time horizon, and its contribution becomes 68 percent if we take a 100-year time horizon. In contrast, a relatively short-lived gas CH_4 with a 10-year lifetime, contributes 37 percent of the GWP in a 20-year time horizon evaluation, and this changes to 17 percent for the 100-year time horizon evaluation.

The modeling of radiative transfer within the atmosphere contains uncertainties and also unknowns, and this has major implications on the assessment and interpretation of the GWP (IPCC 1990). It was also noted (IPCC 1992) that "great care must be exercised in applying GWPs in the policy arena." The specific limitations stated in the IPCC (1992) report include the following (see also Rao 1999):

(a) because the direct GWP is a measure of the global effect of a given GHG emission, it is appropriate only for well-mixed gases in the troposphere, namely CO_2, CH_4, N_2O, and halocarbons; different gas combinations can yield varying spatial patterns of radiative forcings;

(b) because in the assumed scientific model (called the Siegenthaler-Oeschger model underlying the GWP assessments) there is only an ocean CO_2 sink, it is likely to overestimate the concentration changes and lead to an underestimate of both direct and indirect GWPs; the magnitude of this bias depends on the atmospheric lifetime of the gas, and the time horizon;

(c) changes in radiative forcing due to CO_2, CH_4, and N_2O changes are nonlinear with respect to these changes; the net effect of these nonlinearities is such that, as CO_2 levels increase from present levels, the GWPs of all non-CO_2 gases would become higher than those evaluated by the present method;

(d) for gases that are not well-mixed, such as the tropospheric ozone precursors, the GWP concept may not be meaningful; and

(e) the concept does not also apply to inhomogenously distributed gases like aerosols, which have a significant interaction in the solar spectrum.

Although these problems and hence the limitations of the concept and application of the GWP are significant, a few improvements have been recently advanced. These arise from motivations of practical application. If the economic or the physical project lifetime, like a hydropower plant or coal energy production, is limited to a specified number of years, say, about 150, the incremental role of this production and its linkage to the radiating budget of the GHGs is what is of concern in the context of the project development or assessment of its environmental contribution.

Global Warming Potential: Formulae

An alternative GWP index was suggested by Harvey (1993). This formulation makes assessment of the relative contribution for the life of the project on a cumulative basis of accounting for the accumulated emissions over the time horizon. Empirical calculations showed that this method led to a greater role of CO_2 in the global warming phenomenon. This approach does not distinguish the possible economic impact of emissions occurring at different time points in the specified time horizon—that is, the time-discounting of the cost bases, if any, of alternative emission-control policies is irrelevant.

Any GHG indices and GWP measures that do not include economic-impact considerations, even approximate ones, are of very little use for any policy analysis. The estimates of conventional GWPs do not account for the time variation in the economic opportunity costs of incremental values of radiative forcing, and they do not recognize the economics of discounting or time value of financial and other resources, as argued by Eckaus (1992). Thus, the suggested index falls short of possible use in policy analysis based directly on this index. It is possible to provide an additional transformation on Harvey's (1993) formulation by superimposing a dynamic cost or a discounting function. In addition to such attempts, several analytical strengths are added by the contributions of Kandlikar (1995, 1996), and these provide useful approaches to the entire debate.

One of the critical issues in determining the GWP of a GHG is the role of the time horizon with reference to which the assessment is made. We encounter the complex and crucial role of time-discounting, discussed in chapter 2. Damages arising over 100 years per unit GHG compared to damages occurring in 20 years per unit of another GHG need to compared on the same scale via GWP or its transformed valuation of economic valuation. This is required because simple technical calculation of the GWP of various GHGs may not offer policy advice for practical purposes. Science itself is of little help in determining relevant time horizons. A shorter time horizon (usually relative to CO_2) implies higher weight to GHGs that affect the global warming over shorter horizons, and consequentially discount the GHGs that continue to accumulate and contribute to global warming over longer time horizons. The following discussion is aimed at more precise and specific quantification of relevant parameters.

The impact of an incremental emission of the GHG at the initial time $t = 0$ can be described by finding the net present value (NPV) of the damages that arise from the emission of that gas unit. Let NPV (i) denote the corresponding measure and E (i) the incremental rise in the emissions of gas i, with the resulting increase in the global mean temperature T (i, t) leading to climate damage function D [T (t)]. Here D need not be dependent on the specific gas i. Let L denote the time horizon of concern; assume for the moment that this L is easily identified; extensions to the infinite time horizon can be made without major hurdles, and these are discussed later. Let a time-dependent discount rate be given by r(t) (a simple generalization of Kandlikar's [1995] constant discounting formulation). Now the NPV (i) can be calculated; for details see Kandlikar (1995). The formula was extended to include GHG cycles, radiative forcing, and climate system response (Kandlikar 1995), but the details are not proposed for discussion here.

Kandlikar (1996) obtained the expression for the GWP using relevant dynamic optimization models, and seeking the optimum level defined as equal to the ratio of damages caused per unit emissions of each gas, equated to the ratio of the marginal costs of abatement of a non-CO_2 with that of CO_2, and evaluated at a reference initial time. Any formulation of GWP needs to incorporate the effects of continued emissions of short-lived aerosols, which tend to provide the cooling effects even in smaller intervals of time. The next step to improvise these effects in the framework of Kandlikar is to allow for a series of time-dependent constants to be subtracted from the numerator of the relevant expressions. However, the magnitudes of adjustments involved are likely to be relatively small.

The studies by Kandlikar (1995, 1996) demonstrated the equivalence of choosing a time horizon to evaluate the GWP with that of choosing a discount rate for any time horizon. This may seem like a simple shift of the problem, but the latter is likely to be better guided by socioeconomic criteria and supplement the scientific criteria to their mutual reinforcement toward devising relevant policies. In the choice of GHG indices or of GWP indices, impact-based approaches may be more relevant for policy formulation than a purely scientific index with partially known scientific phenomena. Considering the complexities of the issues involved, some already stated above, it appears too simplistic when many of the economic studies try to examine the economics of global warming based on an equation that the increment in global average temperature equals the product of the amount of warming of Earth with unit radiative forcing of one or more GHGs, the magnitude of this forcing, and any multiplier effect (as a parameter).

Although the insights into relative roles of different GHGs in the GWP (direct and indirect) are useful in dealing with individual and collective GHG emissions, we need more analysis of the economics of the phenomenon of the GE for an overview of the problem at the global and regional levels.

4.4 Biogeophysical and Public Health Economics

One of the direct results of the greenhouse effect is the heating of surface temperatures and consequent severity of heat waves in most regions of the world. Heat stress is a known drag on the productivity and morbidity of almost all populations, rich and poor. Richer populations could possibly find some safeguard through the help of energy-intensive technologies, only to provide another multiplier effect or enhanced GE. To that extent, the protection against climate change can contribute to enhanced economic as well as environmental externalities. Poorer regions of the world can ill afford any worsening of their climate as their adaptation costs are unaffordably high, and these tend to lose out for want of any meaningful protection against the severity of the climate and its adverse health effects. These effects could be direct or indirect, operating via disease burden, or other indirect consequences such as depleted quantity and quality of water resources and access to productive employment.

Whenever an aggregate estimate of temperature rise due to global warming is estimated, magnitudes such as a third of a centigrade per decade convey only part of the emerging scenario. The implications of such magnitudes in terms of the significant increase in the number of days with higher nighttime temperatures and the implications of a drastic increase in disease vectors transmitting infectious diseases are serious. Mosquitoes, flies, rodents, and other vermin tend to flourish under enhanced warming. Loevinsohn (1994) observed the marked increase in the incidence of malaria in Rwanda during the 1980s in close relation to observed increases in regional temperatures. The mechanism of enhanced transmission of malarial diseases due to climate change was also documented by Lindsay and Birley (1996). Rapid increase in the incidence of serious illness stemming from dengue fever epidemics is predicted from many of the global models (see Patz et al. 1998 for details). Besides malaria and dengue fever, other diseases expected to expand their incidence include potentially fatal ones such as schistosomiasis and onchocerciasis. Global climate models suggest that, in regard to malaria alone, a 3-degree (centigrade) increase in global mean temperature by 2100 could lead to substantial widening of the malarial zones and an addition of 50 million to 80 million cases per annum, globally (Stone 1995).

The emergence of new diseases is tied to changes in the climate, which affect the survival of parasites and which alter the ratios of the prey-predator combinations (see Patz et al. 1996, and Epstein 1995 for several additional details). The emergence of greater variety and incidence of diseases due to global warming is indicated by Bradley (1997). These constitute ever increasing problems when the ongoing phenomena of biodiversity loss reduce the potential for obtaining medical solutions to emerging health problems. The health impact of climate change depends on various interactive phenomena: multiple and continued disturbances to the ecosystem leading to public health effects, variations in the adaptation (autonomous or planned intervention-based) of different societies to health issues and global climatic changes with differential impacts on local areas and systems, and other feedback effects of continued changes. McMichael and Martens (1995) listed the main types of potential health impacts of global climatic change, enumerated below.

> *Direct impacts*: Morbidity and mortality due to increased and severe heat waves; respiratory illnesses as a result of increased air pollution and pollen content of the air; skin and eye problems as a result of increased ultraviolet radiation from stratospheric ozone depletion; aggravated weather extremities leading to destruction of life and property.
>
> *Indirect impacts*: Altered range and diffusion of vector-borne infectious diseases like malaria, and contagious diseases like cholera; adverse effects on the food production systems leading to malnutrition and loss of health; demographic disruption and compromises in the quality of life in most regions.

The integrated approach to any assessment of health impacts of climatic change involves appreciation of the effects of climate change directly, and its effects via environmental alterations. The interactive feedback mechanisms of both climate and environmental changes must be recognized in this context. Direct climatic influences include disturbances to the ecological systems, habitat loss for humans and other biota, agronomic effects on food production and human survival, heat stress and consequent morbidity and mortality. The effects of climatic change that operate via consequential environmental changes include alterations in air pollution chemistry leading to severity of known and unknown diseases; aggravated effects of ozone depletion; enhanced deployment of pesticides of all varieties, which, in turn, tend to contribute to more health problems; and loss of biodiversity and its effects on potential health remedies. In addition, the interaction of climate and environmental changes multiply the above effects in unknown proportions. A set of detailed and potentially significant interactions between climate change and human health features are discussed in McMichael et al. (1996). Some of the relevant integrated analytical models in this context are summarized by McMichael (1997). The state of this knowledge requires both continued and even greater attention from institutions such as the World Health Organization. Box 4.1 summarizes some of the effects of environmental factors on human health; this information is partly based on data from the USEPA (U.S. Environmental Protection Agency).

The problem of extended and accelerated spread of many of the diseases is the expected economic burden in both developed and developing regions worldwide. The magnitude of illness, its effects on productivity, costs of prevention and of treating affected populations, problems of morbidity and mortality, and adverse implications on sustainable development are only a partial list of considerations. Some estimates of monetary costs are proposed in a few studies (some are cited in the special focus issue *World Resources 1998–99*), but none are comprehensive. At this stage, even a qualitative understanding of the likely effects provides greater insight into the economic and human costs of climate change.

Surveillance of public health and ecological changes remains a high priority in most countries as a result of climate and environmental shifts. A comprehensive documentation of emerging public health problems would be very useful for further interpretation.

4.5 Economic Damage Assessment

It is relevant to examine the magnitudes, their likelihood of incidence, sectoral and geographic details, and related components within the context of assessment of damages from GHGs and global warming. It is not entirely valid that there are no gainers in these phenomena, such as warmer temperatures in severely cold regions and the corresponding benefits of moderation of the climate. However, these pockets of potential benefits are minimal, and these areas do not get to reap the potential benefits because of weather extremities induced by climatic destabilization.

Some of the robust observations of Grubb (1997) are relevant: (1) from any "credible economic perspective some abatement action is justified now"; (2) the only condition that seems necessary to support this claim is the assumption that "higher rates and degrees of atmospheric change increase the risk of adverse impacts." These assumptions were seen to be well founded in chapter 2 of this text. The nonlinearity of the nature of relationships between the magnitudes of average temperature increase

Box 4.1 Environment and Health

The roles of various environmental features in their effect on human health can be summarized (mainly based on information from the USEPA and other sources).

Ozone

Source: Chemical reaction of pollutants; VOCs and NO_x
Health effects: Breathing problems, reduced lung function, asthma, reduced resistance to infections, stress on lung tissues

Volatile organic compounds (VOCs)

Source: Emissions from burning fuel; from solvents, paints, glues, and other products
Health effects: In addition to affecting the ozone, many VOCs can cause serious health problems such as cancer.

Nitrogen oxide

Source: Burning of gasoline, natural gas, coal, oil, etc.
Health effects: Lung damage, illnesses of breathing passages and lungs

Carbon monoxide

Source: Burning of gasoline, natural gas, coal, oil
Health effects: Reduces ability of blood to carry oxygen to body cells and tissues, which require oxygen to work; hazardous to people with heart or circulatory problems

Sulfur dioxide

Source: Burning of coal and oil, especially high-sulfur coal from the eastern United States; industrial processes (paper, metals, and other products)
Health effects: Breathing problems; damage to lungs

Lead

Source: Leaded gasoline; paint; smelters; manufacture of lead storage batteries
Health effects: Brain and other nervous system damage; children are at special risk, with irreversible consequences; some lead-containing chemicals cause cancer in animals; lead causes digestive and other health problems.

and the variations in thermal and other climatological processes lends support to these possibilities. Thus, it appears it is less expensive to address the GHG and global warming problems sooner rather than later.

The question of the magnitudes of intervention is to be resolved based on clarifications regarding the validity of the assumptions: (a) greater resource allocation at any stage diverts productive resources to a less productive arena; and (b) the intervention mechanisms could be such as to induce innovation for reducing the adverse effects of the consumption and production systems on the GHGs and GWP at a negative cost, assessed over a relatively long time horizon (see also chapter 3).

Lower-level estimates (during the early 1990s) of the impacts of marginal CO_2 emissions stood at about $4 per ton of carbon (C) in the global averages; the upper-level estimates, depending on the assumptions involved, varied in the range of $45 to $270 per ton C (for details see Hope and Maul 1996). Plambeck and Hope (1996) assessed that the "best estimate" of the marginal impact was $21 per ton C, and that in the uncertainty with 90 percent confidence level, the estimate stood in the range of $10 to $48 per ton C. It was clarified that the role of uncertainty led to nonlinear damage functions (in terms of temperature increases) and hence the magnitudes of higher impact. The critical factors relevant in the assessment of the marginal impact of increased CO_2 emissions include, among others, sectoral, social, geographic, and temporal specifications. A global aggregate carries little information value. Ther is no meangingful socioeconomic or institutional entity that incurs such an impact. The disparate impact of continued increases in the GHGs warrants a fairly disaggregative analysis, a far cry from current state of knowledge. Besides, the choice of an "optimal" time horizon and a meaningful discount function remain crucial issues. Also, the estimates vary widely with the provision of alternate mechanisms of adaptation and adjustment of appropriate costs.

The core model developed by Nordhaus was termed the *d*ynamic *in*tegrated model of *c*limate and the *e*conomy (DICE). The main decision variables were consumption, rate of investment in tangible capital, and the rate of emission reductions of GHGs. Clearly, these specifications of choice variables are rather narrow and are geared primarily to developed economies where the economy is almost fully monetized and driven by private capital investments. Moreover, the role of human capital, social capital, and institutions is treated as a constant uniform in the entire global economic system. The objective in the DICE model was to maximize the discounted value of utility of relevant arguments. The formal representations are given below. As Nordhaus (1991) rightly argued, in weighing global climate change policies, the potential for global warming and the linkage with anthropogenic emissions of GHGs form a key building block. The basic approach of the DICE model is to estimate the "optimal paths" for both capital accumulation and reductions in GHG emissions in the framework of the Ramsey (1928) model of intertemporal choice—the framework that is largely responsible for the foundations of current neoclassical economic growth models (Solow 1956, Shell 1962). In the model, climate change is represented by changes in the global mean surface temperature T(t) at time t.

The structural equations in the DICE model include the following:

$$T(t) = a [g \{M(t)\} - T(t)]$$

and

$$M(t) = \beta E (t) - \delta M (t),$$

where the left-hand side time derivatives are those of, respectively, T(t) the increase in global mean surface temperature due to greenhouse warming since the mid-ninteenth century, and M(t) the anthropogenic atmospheric concentration of CO_2 equivalent GHGs (billions of tons CO_2 equivalent). The notation on the right-hand side is as follows: E(t) is the anthropogenic emissions of CO_2 equivalent GHGs (billions of tons of CO_2 equivalent per year), g [ ] is the equilibrium increase in global mean temperature in response to increasing CO_2 equivalent concentration, α is the delay parameter of temperature in response to radiative increase per year, β is the fraction of CO_2 equivalent emissions that enter the atmosphere, and δ is the annual rate of removal of CO_2 equivalent emissions from the atmosphere.

The first equation above was linearized in Nordhaus (1991) around the mean, for computational convenience. A critical assumption was also made that the economy was in a "resource steady-state," that is, all physical flows in the global economy are constant although the real value of economic activity may be increasing. Thus, all emissions and concentrations of GHGs are constant each year and "the climatic impacts of industrial activity have been stabilized" in this sense. The DICE model allows for "balanced resource-augmenting technological change," that is, the useful goods and services produced by the economy are assumed to grow uniformly in each sector, although the physical throughputs are constant. These are extremely strong assumptions and tend to undermine the real problems of the human enterprise and the planet by simply assuming there do not exist several severe impediments to sustainable development. In addition to the above formulation and assumptions, we need to narrate the specifications of the objective function of the model. This is given as the discounted value of streams of consumption. The optimal programs for allocating resources over time are required to maximize the discounted utility over an infinite time horizon.

The empirical analyses of Nordhaus's (1992, 1994) studies, based on the above formulations and related constraints in the optimization model, indicated the role of a carbon tax. This tax represents the shadow price of carbon, estimated at $5 per ton of carbon or its equivalent in other GHGs at the end of the twentieth century, to increase to $10 by 2025 and to $21 by 2095 (at 1990 prices). The above values double if uncertainties are incorporated in the DICE model. Risk-aversion and concave damage functions enhance these values to higher levels (Tol 1995). The corresponding tax worked out to be $100 in the early twenty-first century in the DICE model, if the objective were to stabilize GHG emissions at 1990 levels. Fankhouser (1994) derived trajectories for the carbon shadow prices, rising from about $20 per ton by 1991–2000 to $28 by 2021–30; his sensitivity analysis with discount rate suggested that moving from 3 percent to 0 percent discounting could increase marginal costs by a factor of 9.

Mabey et al. (1997) observed that the failure of several studies of optimal climate change policy "to account for the irreversibility and unique nature of climate damage has undervalued the cost of climate change for future generations, and resulted in the recommendation of environmentally unsustainable abatement policies." Whereas the irreversibility poses major cost elements in damage assessments, the role of endogenous technical progress or endogenous substitutions in sectors such as energy tend to partly offset the cost of damages. Chakravorty et al. (1997) examined these issues and concluded that some of the projections regarding global warming are overestimates insofar as the factors in continued technical progress and adaption are ignored. However, these factors are themselves to be viewed in terms of by-products of climate change mitigation strategies such as green tax, emissions trading, or other instruments. In other words, there is a significant role for technical progress to offset damages, but there is nothing automatic about such progress; there must be a reasonable impetus or incentives in that direction, and these arise largely as a part of the package of measures catered to mitigate climate change and its impacts.

4.6 Mitigating the Greenhouse Effect and Climatic Changes

The design of optimal policies for mitigating the GE and adverse climatic changes requires a basic methodological or analytical basis. An intertemporal model generally serves as a relevant candidate, but the results of such models depend very much on the specifications and multitudes of explicit and implicit assumptions. The dynamic integrated climate-economy (DICE) model of Nordhaus (1992) was a beginning in a series of alternate models developed during the past decade to suggest a few prescriptions, but a fully developed meaningful model is still to be perfected. The shortcomings of the DICE and several later models are their usage of constant discounting of time at a given rate for the entire time horizon; assumptions of constant-elasticity-of-substitution in the utility maximization objective over the time horizon; and usage of an aggregate damage function to estimate the damage potential due to an aggregate temperature increase and an aggregate estimate of damage (such as percentage of the gross domestic product) due to such thermal changes. These exercises do not carry the full potential of the problem or its mitigating interventions at such aggregate deterministic levels, with little recognition of the active interactions of the human and economic entities to the evolving mechanisms of the biogeophysical, technological, and socioeconomic factors. Global climate change is not simply to be assessed in terms of thermal changes, with little recognition of the variations in the same.

Mean temperature increases are also seen to correlate with increases in the variances or magnitudes of weather extremities, the most important phenomenon associated with global climatic change. Economic calculations such as those of Nordhaus (1992) tend to indicate that the costs of climate stabilization are very high relative to potential gains. This is because of the nature of aggregativeness and exclusion of several important costs associated with climate change. The benefits of climate-control policies such as enhanced technical efficiency and long-term gains of adaptation seem to have played a lesser role in evaluating the costs of policy regimes like carbon taxation. Endogenous treatment of technological development remains an important realistic provision in assessing the impacts of climate change and measures affecting the same.

Decomposing the CO_2 Components

For the reason that CO_2 is the single most important source of the green-house effect, it is relevant to look into the economics of the GE partly in terms of the economics of CO_2: its emissions and also its sequestration via forestry activities. Both the role and the contribution of CO_2 in various consumption and production activities require a disaggregate analysis. One of the simplest methods to conduct this decomposition is to use the chain-rule of calculus. This can be carried out in several alternative expressions, and the formulation is usually guided by the possibility of empirically assessing the ingredients using available data—illustrative examples are given below (see, e.g., Gupta and Hall 1996 for an application of a formulation similar to the first decomposition below using data for India).

Part of the literature (see IPCC 1996) refers to what is now called Kaya identity (Kaya 1989), which does apply the chain-rule to perform the decomposition:

$$CO_2 = (CO_2 /E) * (E/Q) * (Q/POP) * (POP),$$

where CO_2 is its total emissions, E the total energy use, Q total output, and POP the total population in a region or country.

This same decomposition gets expressed in terms of rates of change (as there are no likely discontinuities in the functions or zero levels of their operation—to ensure the existence of relevant derivatives):

$$d(\log CO_2)/dt = d (\log CO_2/E)/dt + d(\log E/Q/dt$$

$$+ d (\log Q/POP)/dt + d (\log POP)/dt,$$

which simply states that the percentage rate of change in CO_2 emissions equals the sum of the rate of change in CO_2 emissions per unit energy, rate of change requirements per unit output, rate of change in per capita output, and the rate of change in population.

Alternative sets of decomposition can also be contemplated (Rao 1999):

$$CO_2 = (CO_2 / CE) * (CE / TE) * (TE / GDP) * (GDP / POP) * (POP)$$

$$CO_2 = (CO_2 / TCE) * (TCE / FF) * (FF / DEF) * (DEF / DEBT) *$$

$$DEBT / GDP) * (GDP / POP) * (POP),$$

where CO_2 represents the total CO_2 emissions in the economy (millions of tons of carbon), CE = coal energy (millions of tons of oil equivalent), TE = total energy usage (millions of tons of oil equivalent), GDP = gross domestic product at constant prices, POP = population (millions), TCE = total commercial energy (millions of tons of oil equivalent), FF = fossil fuel usage (millions of tons of oil equivalent), DEF = deforestation (millions of tons of oil equivalent), and DEBT = total external debt borrowings outstanding (same units as GDP).

The expressions above, or other variants of these, can be deployed to examine the growth of CO_2 in terms of relevant ingredients contributing to such growth, and the latter can be subject to further analyses of costs and benefits of potential alternative changes in their production, consumption, or growth policies.

An empirical study contributed by Han and Chatterjee (1997) used a structural decomposition with a focus on structural changes, as these capture the impacts of development processes on CO_2 emissions. Changes in these emissions are decomposed in terms of changes due to effects of GDP growth, changes in industrial structure, changes in energy sector composition, interactions in these three elements, changes in levels of final consumption, effects of changes in final consumption, effects of changes in the energy intensities of final consumption activities, and effects of interaction of the preceding three elements. The decomposition formulae were used for a set of countries. The summary of results indicated the significant role of growth of GDP in the CO_2 emissions; the structural shifts from a rural economic base to a manufacturing one resulted in increased energy demand.

4.7 Concluding Observations

The economy-ecology linkages remain important in the context of major global changes such as climate change. The usual economic equilibria do not exist under such changes, and ecological equilibria are vastly different from the notions of economic equilibria. The role of adaptation remains significant in either categorization, but the loss of ecological resilience can lead to multiple unknown equilibria. Hence, the need exists for environmental stress management, within tolerable threshold limits, to avoid irreversible damages. The role of climate change in health factors affecting humans is a serious issue. Methods toward economic damage assessment should be capable of integrating multiplier effects and costs of both monetized and nonmonetary damages. It is unlikely that all these damages could be lumped into a single numeraire or parameter and utilized to prescribe climate and environment policies on that basis. However, a multicriteria approach is expected to express the societal concerns for various survival and development objectives of the present and the future.

References

Bradley, D.J. 1997. "From Chilly Summer Afternoon to Global Warming: Climate as a Determinant of Human Disease" (editorial). *Tropical Medicine and International Health* 9:823.

Chakravorty, U., et al. 1997. "Endogenous Substitution Among Energy Resources and Global Warming." *Journal of Political Economy* 105(6):1201–1234.

Dalton, M.G. 1997. "The Welfare Bias from Omitting Climatic Variability in Economic Studies of Global Warming." *Journal of Environmental Economics and Management* 33:221–239.

Eckaus, R. 1992. "Comparing the Effects of Greenhouse Gas Emissions on Global Warming." *The Energy Journal* 13:25–35.

Epstein, P.R. 1995. "Emerging Diseases and Ecosystem Instability: New Threats to Public Health." *American Journal of Public Health* 85(2):168–172.

Fankhouser, S. 1994. "The Economic Costs of Global Warming Damage: A Survey." *Global Environmental Change* 4(4):301–309.

Grubb, M. 1997. "Technologies, Energy Systems and CO_2 Emissions Abatement." *Energy Policy* 25(2):159–172.

Gupta, S., and Hall, S.G. 1996. "Carbon Abatement Costs—An Integrated Approach for India." *Environment and Development Economics* 1(1):41–63.

Han, X., and Chatterjee, L. 1997. "Impacts of Growth and Structural Change on CO_2 Emissions of Developing Countries." *World Development* 25(3):395–407.

Harvey, L.D. 1993. "A Guide to Global Warming Potentials (GWPs)." *Energy Policy* 21(1):24–34.

Hope, C., and Maul, P. 1996. "Valuing the Impact of CO_2 Emissions." *Energy Policy* 24(3):211–219.

Houghton, T.J. et al. 1990. *Climate Change—The IPCC Scientific Assessment.* New York: Cambridge University Press.

IPCC. 1996. *Climate Change 1995—Economic and Social Dimensions of Climate Change.* New York: Cambridge University Press.

———. 1992. *Global Climate 1992—A Supplementary Report.* Geneva: IPCC/WMO.

————. 1990. *Climate Change—The Scientific Assessment.* New York: Cambridge University Press, published for the IPCC.

Kandlikar, M. 1996. "Indices for Comparing Greenhouse Gas Emissions: Integrating Science and Economics." *Energy Economics* 18(4):265–281.

————. 1995. "The Relative Roles of Trace Gas Emissions and Greenhouse Abatement Policy." *Energy Policy* 23(10):879–883.

Kaya, Y. 1989. "Impact of Carbon Dioxide Emission Control on GNP Growth—Interpretation of Proposed Scenarios." IPCC Working Group on Response Strategies, quoted in IPCC 1996.

Lashof, D.A., and Ahuja, D.R. 1990. "Relative Contributions of Greenhouse Gas Emissions to Global Warming." *Nature* 344:529–531.

Lindsay, S., and Birley, M. 1996. "Climate Change and Malaria Transmission." *Annals of Tropical Medicine and Parasitology* 90(6):580–588.

Loevinsohn, M.E. 1994. "Climatic Warming and Increased Malaria Incidence in Rwanda." *The Lancet* 343:714–717.

Mabey, N., Hall, S., Smith, C., and Gupta, S. 1997. *Argument in the Greenhouse.* New York: Routledge.

McMichael, A.J. 1997. "Integrated Assessment of Potential Health Impact of Global Environmental Change: Prospects and Limitations." *Environmental Modeling and Assessment* 2:129–137.

McMichael, A.J., Haines, A., Slooff, R., and Kovats, S. 1996. *Climate Change and Human Health.* Geneva: World Health Organization.

McMichael, A.J., and Martens, W.J.M. 1995. "The Health Impacts of Global Climate Change: Grappling with Scenarios, Predictive Models, and Multiple Uncertainties." *Ecosystem Health* 1(1):23–33.

Nordhaus, W. 1994. *Managing the Global Commons.* Cambridge, MA: MIT Press.

————. 1992. "An Optimal Transition Path for Controlling Greenhouse Gases." *Science* 258:1315–1319.

————. 1991. "To Slow or Not to Slow—The Economics of the Greenhouse Effect." *The Economic Journal* 101:920–937.

Patz, J.A., Epstein, P.R., Burke, T.A., and Balbers, J.M. 1996. "Global Climatic Change and Emerging Infectious Diseases." *Journal of the American Medical Association* 275:217–223.

Patz, J.A., Martens, W.J.M., Focks, D.A., and Jetten, T.H. 1998. "Dengue Fever Epidemic Potential as Projected by General Circulation Models of Global Climate Change." *Environmental Health Perspectives* 106(3):147–153.

Perrings, C. 1997. *Economics of Ecological Resources.* Cheltenham, UK: Edward Elgar.

Plambeck, E.L. and Hope, C. 1996. "An Updated Valuation of the Impacts of Global Warming." *Energy Policy* 24(9):783–793.

Ramsey, F.P. 1928. "A Mathematical Theory of Savings." *Economic Journal* 38:543–559.

Rao, P.K. 1999. *Sustainable Development: Economics and Policy.* Oxford and Boston: Blackwell.

Shell, K. (ed.). 1967. *Essays on the Theory of Optimal Economic Growth.* Cambridge, MA: MIT Press.

Solow, R.M. 1956. "A Contribution to the Theory of Economic Growth." *Quarterly Journal of Economics* 70:65–94.

Stone, R. 1995. "If Mercury Soars, So May Health Hazards." *Science* 267:957–958.

Tol, R.J. 1995. "The Damage Costs of Climate Change—Towards More Comprehensive Calculations." *Environmental and Resource Economics* 5:353–374.

World Resources Institute. 1998. *World Resources 1998–99*. New York: Oxford University Press.

Chapter 5

Greenhouse Gas Regimes and Climate Change

5.1 Introduction

The phenomena governing global climatic changes are varied, as seen in the previous chapters. Various human interventions can mitigate the effects of change, and much more urgently, prevent unwelcome changes. The prevention is largely equivalent to stabilization of the climate, so as to ensure the potential for sustained life and prosperity for humans on planet Earth. This requirement of stabilization is not necessarily well defined and needs clear specifications for evolving operationally meaningful and pragmatic strategies. Alternative measures to define and institute climate stabilization are discussed in the next section. These broader objectives lead to the main imperative: stabilization of concentrations of greenhouse gases (GHGs) that cause the greenhouse effect (GE). The stabilization of GHGs is largely equivalent to reduction of the emissions of GHGs in the current time periods, and possibly bringing the net annual emissions to zero levels. The policy measures in this direction, the economics of some of the alternatives, and the international institutional arrangements governing these features are detailed in Section 5.3.

Reduction of net GHG emissions operates via market as well as nonmarket institutions, and the corresponding policy regimes. These activities can be effective in their applications through sources as well as sinks of the GHGs. Cost-effectiveness and practicability in implementation are the major determinants of the choice of most appropriate instruments. These aspects are discussed in the following sections of the chapter. Because many of the measures to bring about a reduction in net

GHG emissions involve international cooperation and coordination, the issue of cost-sharing among nations, especially between developed and developing countries, require an efficient and equitable strategy. These features are addressed in Section 5.8. Additional analyses of global policies and instruments of climate stabilization policies are proposed for chapter 6.

5.2 Climate Stabilization

The formal definition of climate stabilization can be stated as follows: maintaining climate and its parameters within a reasonable small neighborhood of deviations from their "normal," "desired," or "average" levels established with reference to a base year.

This definition requires additional specifications regarding the reference period for assessing "normal" or "desired" levels, the degree of meaningfully (in a risk-taking sense) allowable deviations (more likely the allowable or tolerable expected temperature rise), and an evaluation of sensitivity of the cost-benefit implications under varying (yet within reasonable ranges) specifications of these and structural dynamics of the entire climate system. The main purpose of this approach of formalization is to simulate alternate possibilities and derive a set of pragmatic choices. In the entire (rather mechanistic) approach, the role of natural variations and related uncertainties cannot be ignored. The anthropological influences, the direction of such influences on the phenomena of global warming and climate change, and a cost-effective, risk-averse approach to mitigate the effects of such changes are the issues that require a qualitative and quantitative assessment. Even the criterion of risk-aversion is founded on parameters governing the type and degree of risk aversion, and this requires further formal specifications and detailed analysis.

One aspect is clear, however. Climate stabilization is a necessary prerequisite for economic prosperity and sustainable development. Conversely, economic stability in the short term may not automatically lead to economic stability in the long term, if emphasis on sustainable development principles is not accorded. In other words, climate stability, economic stability, and sustainable development complement each other. It should be our constant endeavor to exploit these interdependencies. Continued accumulations of GHGs remain an area of greatest concern in any attempt to harmonize the three phenomena. Accordingly, more urgent attention is warranted.

5.3 Greenhouse Gas Reduction and Target Fixation

Kyoto Protocol

The Conference of Parties (COP-3) under the UNFCCC was held in Kyoto, Japan, in December 1997 and this led to the Kyoto Protocol (KP). Some of the important details of this protocol are given in Appendix 5B of this chapter. The KP includes a set of accepted GHG reductions by 39 countries (referred to as Annex I countries in the UNFCCC and as Annex B countries in the KP). The accepted targets for GHG reductions are also given in Appendix 5B of this chapter. These binding commitments come into force as soon as 55 countries of the COP-3 accounting for at least 60 percent emissions have signed and ratified the KP. These commitments are also referred to as "Quantified Emissions Limitation and Reduction Objectives" or QELROs. Developing countries (typically non-Annex I countries) were spared the need to come up with reduction targets at this juncture, but their inclusion at a later date was contemplated. Considering the fact that there exist synergies between energy efficiency improvement and GHG reduction at national and international levels, it remains an issue of initial capital and technological resource availability for the developing countries to accept certain binding commitments in select sectors where the implementation strategies lead to win-win solutions to improvements in technical efficiency, environment, and economy. The role of concessional multilateral lending and technical support remains significant in this context.

The KP suggests usage of QELROs at the individual country levels to allow for the optimal mix of the instruments and their policy regimes concerning joint implementation (JI), clean development mechanism (CDM), and emissions trading. Article 6 of the KP allows Annex B countries to transfer or acquire emission reduction credits resulting from eligible GHG reduction projects. The role of CDM is outlined in Article 12 of the KP. The UNFCCC executive board supervises the implementation. Article 17 provides for emissions trading to fulfill commitments in supplementation (rather than substitution) of domestic GHG reduction activities.

The commitments of the Annex I countries refer to the following GHGs or their carbon equivalent (CE): CO_2, CH_4, N_2O, HFCs, perfluorocarbons (PFCs), and sulfur hexafluoride (SF_6). The sectors considered were energy, industrial processes, solvent and other product use, land use, and waste management. Article 4 of the Kyoto Protocol refers to JI whereby a country in Annex I can jointly implement the GHG reduction as an "additionality" in a country eligible for such participation.

Let us note Article 4 of the KP, which allows a group of countries (from the Annex I list of countries) to fulfill their GHG reductions jointly under the process "joint implementation" (JI). This process is permissible when the effective emission reductions are assessed to be "additional" to already adopted policies for GHG reduction in these countries. The practical interpretations of these provisions, compliance with them, and implications of noncompliance are among the issues of current policy significance.

Kyoto Protocol Article 25

1. This Protocol shall enter into force on the ninetieth day after the date on which not less than 55 Parties to the Convention, incorporating Parties included in Annex I which accounted in total for at least 55 per cent of the total carbon dioxide emissions for 1990 of the Parties included in Annex I, have deposited their instruments of ratification, acceptance, approval or accession.

Article 27

1. At any time after three years from the date on which this Protocol has entered into force for a Party, that Party may withdraw from this Protocol by giving written notification to the Depositary.
2. Any such withdrawal shall take effect upon expiration of one year from the date of receipt by the Depositary of the notification of withdrawal, or on such later date as may be specified in the notification of withdrawal.
3. Any Party that withdraws from the Convention shall be considered as also having withdrawn from this Protocol.

Buenos Aires Plan of Action

A two-year plan of action to reduce GHGs using the basis of the Kyoto Protocol was indicated with few details. About 170 governments participated in the COP-4. It was felt that the aggregate 5 percent reduction (relative to the base year 1990, and reduction to be achieved during the period 2008 to 2012) in the GHGs envisaged at COP-3 was appropriate.

The roles of emissions trading, joint implementation (JI), and clean development mechanism (CDM) were emphasized at the November 1999 meetings of COP-5 in Bonn and details proposed for future deliberations of the COP during the early years of the twenty-first century.

5.4 Market and Nonmarket Policy Instruments

In principle, a wide variety of policy instruments can address the issue of reduction of GHGs with a market-based or regulation-based (or a mix) governance of policy design and implementation. However, the detailed arrangements make greater or lesser sense in relation to the institutional arrangements and corresponding transaction costs to achieve specified objectives and goals. In the international settings, it is not entirely feasible to devise country-specific recommendations in the process of devising global policies for stabilizing GHGs. Thus, the suitability of one or more specific policy instruments and their policy regimes remains an issue to be addressed at the corresponding national levels. The specification of ends rather than means remains the main focus of attention at the global level.

The broad categories of instruments for environmental policy tend to fit it into groups: marketable permits, and regulatory limits on emissions (possibly with specified fees). Baumol and Oates (1988) argued that the marketable permits system has a few merits over other command-and-control-type regulatory policies and regimes. These include the fact that marketable permits lead to more predictable levels of achievement of targets. It was also suggested that in some cases it may be easier to attain least-cost allocation of emissions under a set of fees than under a system of marketable permits. The latter requires two major tasks to be fulfilled in order that the system is useful in the short run and in the multiperiod setting over time: (1) a fair and efficient initial allocation of permits, and (2) provisions that offer incentives, in a multiperiod framework, to achieve pollution management efficiency and technical innovation. An analytical investigation of the relative roles of taxes and regulatory permits in achieving pollution reduction is given in Denicolo 1999.

5.5 Tradable Permits and Carbon Trade

The broad approach of market-based instruments is generally useful in causing reductions in GHG emissions and in the cost-effective governance of the environment. However, this possibility is predicated on the assumption of the existence of low-cost transactions to carry out the policy instruments in practice. This usually is feasible either in traditional organizations of informal management in some of the less developed countries or in the most advanced developed economies. In either case, the role of monitoring and evaluation remains critical in the governance.

Dales (1968) first proposed the concept of marketable permits to allocate pollution-reduction among private entities as a mechanism of cost-effective implementation. The legal origins of the air pollution market in the United States arose from the Clean Air Act of 1970. The U.S. Environmental Protection Agency (USEPA) proposed in 1976 to offset pollution reduction targets aimed at companies but with some conditions. For example, these included: offsets had to be for the same specific pollutant; only new emission sources could enter the market as buyers. The "bubble policy" was also devised. This policy allowed pollution-producing units to develop alternate emission control strategies; sources can belong to a bubble and utilize cost-effective alternatives in meeting pollution reduction targets.

Tradable permits for emissions trading remains a high priority in both national and institutional settings. This is because of the promise of market-based implementation. It is not entirely clear, however, whether these mechanisms can be cost-effective when we consider all the relevant transaction costs and uncertainties in attaining environmental goals via market mechanisms. Using market institutions to correct market failures or externalities is not inconsistent with effective institutional management of the environment. The problem is one of ensuring efficient implementation in a quasi-market framework of trading public goods. The complementarity of government institutions and market institutions in this activity is an essential prerequisite to achieve cost-effective implementation. There exists a positive correlation between the quality of the governmental institutions and that of the private market institutions; the governance of the latter is not independent of the quality of governance of the former. This combined operation is not a common feature in most countries where the general quality of these institutions is still lagging far behind those of some of the developed economies.

The *Economic Report of the U.S. President* (*Economic Report* 1998) argued in the context of domestic (rather than international) emissions trading and the role of tradable emission permits (TEPs): "Any firm that can reduce its emissions for less than the going price of permit has the incentive to do so and then sell its unused permits to other firms for which emissions reduction is more costly . . . ; firms can meet environmental standards at lower cost than under traditional regulation." The problems of market concentration in permits, lack of competitive features, manipulated market price variations, and transaction costs are some of the practical considerations in the evolution of an efficient functioning market for TEP. These features are relevant in both domestic and international market settings. The applicability of Coase's (1960) theorem (see the Coase proposition below), which suggests that the assignment of private property rights could lead to an efficient outcome, is founded on the assumption of zero transaction costs.

Proposition 1

"If there are no transaction costs, there is no need for government intervention to correct for the environmental problems; the most efficient solution is to define clearly the property rights" (Coase 1960).

The Coase proposition is founded on the assumption, among others, of common knowledge among participants in the environmental damage resolution or compensation negotiation. No doubt the absence of well-defined enforceable property rights poses a set of externalities, but application of these property rights does not automatically ensure efficient environmental solutions. Thus, we arrive at the following.

Proposition 2

The existence of property rights is a necessary but not sufficient condition to resolve environmental or economic externalities. The prevalence of significant transaction costs warrants the complementary role of the government to enhance market-efficiency features.

The potentially high transaction costs pose a major hurdle in the emissions trading markets. The existence of high transaction costs and the degree of uncertainty (for details see Montero 1997) in regulatory approval of some of the trading permits even in developed systems like those in the United States suggests that the principle of market-based emission trading may have a long way to proceed before being effective in any sense.

Based on limited incentives for innovative and net efficiency improvement for GHG reduction with undue reliance on emissions trading mechanisms, Driesen (1998a, 1998b) argued that emission taxes may be more effective than emissions trading in meeting environmental objectives. It was stated (Driesen 1998b) that emissions trading functions as a "cheap fix, reducing short-term costs while tending to lessen innovation and thwart democratic accountability." Specific limits to international emissions trading were recommended in order to "avoid undermining the long-term efficacy of the climate change regime."

5.6 Carbon Sequestration and Forestry

Forests serve many purposes, including watershed functions, as fisheries, climate stability, in situ genetic pool preservation, maintaining biodiversity; as a sink for carbon sequestration; recreational and environmental values; source of fuelwood and other forms of timber; forest products to augment food supplies (such as fruits, legumes, and other edible products); as a source of medicinal supplies for both alternative systems of medicine and those of modern medicinal systems; and stability of ecosystems as well as regular functioning of biogeochemical cycles. Forests constitute a major reservoir of resources beyond their national borders. This supply of transboundary resources are generally nonmarketable in their (first order) raw provisions, but these facilitate production of marketable value-added products for societies within and outside the borders of the countries that host large forests. Thus, forests constitute a segment of common property resources (see also Myers 1996). Moreover, these offer subsidies on a global scale in the provision of ecosystem services. The uncompensated supply of these subsidies from forest-rich countries to others must be recognized in any assessment of a fair and equitable cost-sharing method for global climate stabilization.

Houghton et al. (1996) estimated that net emissions from changes in tropical land use and deforestation amounted to an annual average flux of 1.6 GtC, (1GtC = 10^{15} grams, or one billion tons of carbon) and this is higher than the corresponding contributions of all anthropogenic activities (estimated at 1.3 GtC) excluding emissions from fossil fuels and cement production. Thus, the effects of land use change, mainly deforestation, in the emissions of GHGs are significant. The effect is likely to be accompanied by a positive feedback effect when we take into account the consequential soil carbon retention and other changes in the global biogeochemical cycles of both carbon and nitrogen. This is because carbon is stored both in the plant-related biomass above ground level and also in the leafy ground soil, which is affected by the soil composition (including moisture content).

Carbon sequestration costs vary under the assumed values of land and other resource costs, including their opportunity costs. A broad range of $12 to $30 was estimated in some sources (for additional details, see IPCC 1996a, 1996b). However, physical limitations exist on the magnitudes of land resources available to offset the continued emissions of GHGs. Carbon emissions from a 500-megwatt coal-fired power station emits about 0.8 million tons of carbon (Mt C) per year. To offset this, we need to grow a very large new forest area of about 1700 square kilometers, assuming a biomass productivity of 2 to 4 tons per hectare per year over 50 years and a storage of carbon of 100 to 200 tons per hectare in a mature forest (IPCC 1996a). Besides, the credit for forestry is limited in the context of global emissions trading (explained below).

Kyoto Protocol Article 17

The Conference of the Parties shall define the relevant principles, modalities, rules and guidelines, in particular for verification, reporting and accountability for emissions trading. . . . Any such trading shall be supplemental to domestic actions for the purpose of meeting quantified emission limitation and reduction commitments under that Article.

Despite relative prominence of carbon sequestration via forestry as a cost-effective method of stabilizing GHGs, it is also useful to note that there are finite and rather limited possibilities in this direction as well. In other words, this approach forms a measure that could possibly offset GHG emissions in the medium run, but not necessarily in the long run—should the emissions continue to grow as in the past few decades. It was estimated (Watson et al. 1996) that the potential land area available for forest-based carbon conservation and sequestration was about 700 million hectares, and that the corresponding total carbon that could be sequestered and conserved globally by 2050 was but 60 to 87 GtC. It was also stated: "To the extent that forestation schemes yield wood products, which can substitute for fossil fuel–based materials and energy, their carbon benefit can be up to four times higher than the carbon sequestered." Measures to arrest deforestation are a first step in this process. Afforestation, social forestry, reforestation are some of the elements of forestry development. No doubt the programs must be comprehensive enough to address local needs and integrate with the relevant regional and sectoral economies.

5.7 Cost-Effectiveness of Alternatives

An assessment of costs of specific actions must comprise the total transaction cost, and not the direct first-round cost alone. This cost needs to be compared to the total cost of damages due to inaction. The latter must also be weighed in terms of reasonable probability of occurrence of undesirable events or accrual of damages over a period of time. All these involve time-discounted valuation of future costs. The concept of transaction costs (TC) needs generalization here, so as to include adaptation costs (AC) as well. Transaction costs (Rao 2000; Dudek and Wiener 1996) include, but are not limited to, adaptation costs, search costs, information costs, negotiation costs, approval costs, monitoring costs, enforcement costs, costs of externalities arising out of specific transactions, insurance or related costs, opportunity costs of time, or other resources. When adaptation costs involve or eventually lead to higher efficiency (with or without technical innovation), these costs tend to become negative in some of the scenarios, thus becoming net benefits. In other words, what are considered costs in the short term may essentially be viewed as investments for a return in the long run. In this interlinked system, the time horizon makes the difference between costs and benefits if we follow the same set of investments. This assessment is predicated on the continuity of the entities and stability of the biogeophysical systems. The underlying dynamic structures of costs, benefits, production, and climate stability generate such possibilities.

As Grubb et al. (1995) observed, the important question in analyzing technology development is "why it develops in some directions more than others." Both the demand and supply factors affect these developments. The roles of inertia in inflicting a higher cost stream, and of adaptation in smoothing costs of adjustment, are also related to the design of policy regimes for climate stabilization. It is relevant to recall some of the observations of Grubb et al. (1995): "It may be the act of abatement itself which starts to generate the possibility of long-term solutions to the energy/climate problem." It was argued that a delay in present-day responses could lead to marginal increases in GHG emissions, and thus enhance the costs of climatic impacts both in the short run and in the long run. Realistic possibilities of negative mitigation costs in GHG stabilization strategies were indicated in Halsnaes et al. (1998), where some of the energy sector and transport sector units depict considerable "efficiency gaps" in the existing operations.

It is rather well known that it requires an underdeveloped country to afford the luxury of fuel inefficiencies in automobiles, large-scale transmission losses in electricity transmissions, power load shedding and frequent replacement of equipments destroyed in the process, and allow greater air pollution in urban regions where the population can ill afford quality medical facilities. These are double jeopardies of underdevelopment; the underdevelopment trap masks causes with effects and vice versa. This phenomenon is a lagged adjustment response: lack of requisite resources brings down potential for prosperity, and the latter contributes to paucity of resources.

However, there are alternative ways to circumvent this vicious circle, with the influence of exogenous or endogenous economic and technological forces. The point of concern in the present cost-effectiveness and cost-assessment exercise is a realistic understanding of the baseline case and its futuristic profile in the absence of changes required or contemplated under the GHG stabilization strategies. Contrary to the apprehensions of some of the developing countries, their participation in select sectors for GHG reduction will pave the way for an accelerated development and attainment of GHG reduction targets. This is critically dependent on soft finance or other concessional facilities from the industrial countries. The global mechanisms for GHG reduction should avail the agreed-upon CDM or other packages to achieve these potential win-win scenarios, with explicit credit and incentives for the industrial countries to participate actively in these programs.

It is relevant to elucidate the concepts of incremental costs, in their applied contexts. The UNFCCC Article 4.3 distinguishes "full agreed incremental cost" from "agreed incremental cost." The first is meant to cover all costs of an activity and relates to the costs of new activities undertaken by countries, and the second covers only the difference between operating a climate-mitigation strategy and a baseline scenario, as, for example, the cost difference in the case of a power project with a low and a high emission scenario. "Incremental cost" is defined here by the UNFCCC as the additional cost of implementing a climate mitigation project, relative to the cost of the activity that the project replaces (from the baseline or business-as-usual case).

5.8 Cost Sharing and North–South Issues

Some of the differences in the economic standards of the North and the South, or rather equivalently, of developed and developing countries, arise partly from a number of historical factors. Many of the developing nations have been colonized for long periods and their current development levels have this historical background as a partial determinant. Moreover, some of the instruments (market-based or other) of global economic policies and globalization have not been sufficiently sensitive to the genuine aspirations of the South. According to Ekins (1993), among a few others, international trade, debt, and aid worked systematically to the benefit of the North at the expense of the South. The potential positive role of aid was limited by the limited aid-effectiveness. Some of the recent attempts of the richest industrial countries (G-7) to provide debt relief to the poorest indebted countries could form a major break in indebtedness of the recipient countries.

The "development aid" (including project-specific concessional loans) to the South was also limited in its effectiveness. The result of some of these features has been continued poverty in the South, and the effects of the widespread poverty are such as to lead to environmental degradation. Speth (1990) suggested the role of "unwitting complicity" of the North in environmental degradation of the South, especially through the imposition of "development projects" with inadequate environmental safeguards.

The majority of the population in the nations of the South depends directly on the local environmental assets for their survival. Exploitation of land, forests, and natural resources constitutes a necessity for sustenance of life. This exploitation has both local and global externalities. In the absence of alternatives, these phenomena tend to continue. The damage incidence from global climate change is also likely to be greater for the South than for the North. This is partly because of limited infrastructure of many of the developing countries to withstand the effects of climate change, and partly because of greater vulnerability of their life-sustaining natural assets to such changes. Moreover, the inequitous damage incidence is also of concern. Bangladesh, for example, contributes about 0.3 percent of emissions of the greenhouse gases, but could loose 17 percent of its coastal land because of the effects of global warming and rise in the sea level (UNDP 1996).

The UNFCCC recognizes the principle of "common but differentiated responsibilities" among countries, and the provisions of the Convention (especially Article 4) require the developed countries of the North to play a key role in mitigating the climatic change through use of technology and finances (see Box 5.1).

Box 5.1 UNFCCC Article 4 Commitments*

1. All Parties, taking into account their common but differentiated responsibilities and their specific national and regional development priorities, objectives and circumstances, shall:

(a) Develop, periodically update, publish and make available to the Conference of the Parties, in accordance with Article 12, national inventories of anthropogenic emissions by sources and removals by sinks of all greenhouse gases not controlled by the Montreal Protocol, using comparable methodologies to be agreed upon by the Conference of the Parties;

(b) Formulate, implement, publish and regularly update national and, where appropriate, regional programmes containing measures to mitigate climate change by addressing anthropogenic emissions by sources and removals by sinks of all greenhouse gases not controlled by the Montreal Protocol, and measures to facilitate adequate adaptation to climate change;

(c) Promote and cooperate in the development, application and diffusion, including transfer, of technologies, practices and processes that control, reduce or prevent anthropogenic emissions of greenhouse gases not controlled by the Montreal Protocol in all relevant sectors, including the energy, transport, industry, agriculture, forestry and waste-management sectors;

(d) Promote sustainable management, and promote and cooperate in the conservation and enhancement, as appropriate, of sinks and reservoirs of all greenhouse gases not controlled by the Montreal Protocol, including biomass, forests and oceans as well as other terrestrial, coastal and marine ecosystems;

(e) Cooperate in preparing for adaptation to the impacts of climate change; develop and elaborate appropriate and integrated plans for coastal zone management, water resources and agriculture, and for the protection and rehabilitation of areas, particularly in Africa, affected by drought and desertification, as well as floods;

(f) Take climate change considerations into account, to the extent feasible, in their relevant social, economic and environmental policies and actions, and employ appropriate methods, for example, impact assessments, formulated and determined nationally, with a view to minimizing adverse effects on the economy, on public health and on the quality of the environment, of projects or measures undertaken by them to mitigate or adapt to climate change;

(g) Promote and cooperate in scientific, technological, technical, socioeconomic and other research, systematic observation and development

*The excerpts in this section are reprinted by permission of the Secretariat for Climate Change, Bonn, Germany.

of data archives related to the climate system and intended to further the understanding and to reduce or eliminate the remaining uncertainties regarding the causes, effects, magnitude and timing of climate change and the economic and social consequences of various response strategies;

(h) Promote and cooperate in the full, open and prompt exchange of relevant scientific, technological, technical, socioeconomic and legal information related to the climate system and climate change, and to the economic and social consequences of various response strategies;

(i) Promote and cooperate in education, training and public awareness related to climate change and encourage the widest participation in this process, including that of nongovernmental organizations; and

(j) Communicate to the Conference of the Parties information related to implementation, in accordance with Article 12.

2. The developed country Parties and other Parties included in Annex I commit themselves specifically as provided for in the following:

(a) Each of these Parties shall adopt national policies and take corresponding measures on the mitigation of climate change, by limiting its anthropogenic emissions of greenhouse gases and protecting and enhancing its greenhouse gas sinks and reservoirs. These policies and measures will demonstrate that developed countries are taking the lead in modifying longer-term trends in anthropogenic emissions consistent with the objective of the Convention, recognizing that the return by the end of the present decade to earlier levels of anthropogenic emissions of carbon dioxide and other greenhouse gases not controlled by the Montreal Protocol would contribute to such modification, and taking into account the differences in these Parties' starting points and approaches, economic structures and resource bases, the need to maintain strong and sustainable economic growth, available technologies and other individual circumstances, as well as the need for equitable and appropriate contributions by each of these Parties to the global effort regarding that objective. These Parties may implement such policies and measures jointly with other Parties and may assist other Parties in contributing to the achievement of the objective of the Convention and, in particular, that of this subparagraph;

(b) In order to promote progress to this end, each of these Parties shall communicate, within six months of the entry into force of the Convention for it and periodically thereafter, and in accordance with Article 12, detailed information on its policies and measures referred to in subparagraph (a) above, as well as on its resulting projected anthropogenic emissions by sources and removals by sinks of greenhouse gases not controlled by the Montreal Protocol for the period referred to in subparagraph (a), with the aim of returning individually or jointly to their 1990 levels these anthropogenic emissions of carbon dioxide and other greenhouse gases not controlled by the Montreal Protocol. This information will be reviewed by the Conference of the Parties, at its first session and periodically thereafter, in accordance with Article 7.

3. The developed country Parties and other developed Parties included in Annex II shall provide new and additional financial resources to meet the agreed full costs incurred by developing country Parties in complying with their obligations under Article 12, paragraph 1. They shall also provide such financial resources, including for the transfer of technology, needed by the developing country Parties to meet the agreed full incremental costs of implementing measures that are covered by paragraph 1 of this Article and that are agreed between a developing country Party and the international entity or entities referred to in Article 11, in accordance with that Article. The implementation of these commitments shall take into account the need for adequacy and predictability in the flow of funds and the importance of appropriate burden sharing among the developed country Parties.

4. The developed country Parties and other developed Parties included in Annex II shall also assist the developing country Parties that are particularly vulnerable to the adverse effects of climate change in meeting costs of adaptation to those adverse effects.

5. The developed country Parties and other developed Parties included in Annex II shall take all practicable steps to promote, facilitate and finance, as appropriate, the transfer of, or access to, environmentally sound technologies and know-how to other Parties, particularly developing country Parties, to enable them to implement the provisions of the Convention. In this process, the developed country Parties shall support the development and enhancement of endogenous capacities and technologies of developing country Parties. Other Parties and organizations in a position to do so may also assist in facilitating the transfer of such technologies.

6. In the implementation of their commitments under paragraph 2 above, a certain degree of flexibility shall be allowed by the Conference of the Parties to the Parties included in Annex I undergoing the process of transition to a market economy, in order to enhance the ability of these Parties to address climate change, including with regard to the historical level of anthropogenic emissions of greenhouse gases not controlled by the Montreal Protocol chosen as a reference.

7. The extent to which developing country Parties will effectively implement their commitments under the Convention will depend on the effective implementation by developed country Parties of their commitments

under the Convention related to financial resources and transfer of technology and will take fully into account that economic and social development and poverty eradication are the first and overriding priorities of the developing country Parties.

8. In the implementation of the commitments in this Article, the Parties shall give full consideration to what actions are necessary under the Convention, including actions related to funding, insurance, and the transfer of technology, to meet the specific needs and concerns of developing country Parties arising from the adverse effects of climate change and/or the impact of the implementation of response measures, especially on:

(a) Small island countries;

(b) Countries with low-lying coastal areas;

(c) Countries with arid and semi-arid areas, forested areas and areas liable to forest decay;

(d) Countries with areas prone to natural disasters;

(e) Countries with areas liable to drought and desertification;

(f) Countries with areas of high urban atmospheric pollution;

(g) Countries with areas with fragile ecosystems, including mountainous ecosystems;

(h) Countries whose economies are highly dependent on income generated from the production, processing and export, and/or on consumption of fossil fuels and associated energy-intensive products; and

(i) Land-locked and transit countries.

Further, the Conference of the Parties may take actions, as appropriate, with respect to this paragraph.

9. The Parties shall take full account of the specific needs and special situations of the least developed countries in their actions with regard to funding and transfer of technology.

10. The Parties shall, in accordance with Article 10, take into consideration in the implementation of the commitments of the Convention the situation of Parties, particularly developing country Parties, with economies that are vulnerable to the adverse effects of the implementation of measures to respond to climate change. This applies notably to Parties with economies that are highly dependent on income generated from the production, processing and export, and/or consumption of fossil fuels and associated energy-intensive products and/or the use of fossil fuels for which such Parties have serious difficulties in switching to alternatives.

The relative roles of contributions of GHGs arising from "necessary emissions" of the South and "luxury emissions" of the North can also be identified further. As far as the climate is concerned, the atmospheric chemistry cannot differentiate these distinctions (valid or otherwise): the net effect of the emissions obey scientific laws. It is an issue in cost-sharing between the North and the South to prevent accelerated/continued emissions of the GHGs, and also in mitigating damages. Quantitative emission reduction targets remain relevant, but these will be practicable only if the economic incentives are properly formulated for the countries that indulge in "necessary emissions." Some of the mechanisms such as joint implementation (JI), clean development mechanism (CDM), and emissions trading (with appropriate initial entitlement allocations of tradable emission permits) are expected to address the global climate change as well as the dichotomy of the countries of the North and the South. These issues are discussed in chapter 6.

5.9 Concluding Observations

Greenhouse gas reduction and equitable cost-sharing in this process remain high priorities for the management of global climate change phenomena. Optimism about evolving a globally coordinated effort is well founded, considering that within a decade of somewhat sure signs of anthropogenic influences adversely destabilizing the climate, several notable initiatives have been launched. However, the scope for strengthening the initiatives, without necessarily adding additional bureaucratic institutions, remains an area for further attention. Policies and programs that reflect total transaction costs, rather than direct costs alone, are likely to lead to more effective solutions.

References

Baumol, W.J., and Oates, W. 1988. *The Theory of Environmental Policy*. New York: Cambridge University Press.

Coase, R. 1960. "The Problem of Social Cost." *Journal of Law and Economics* 3:1–44.

Dales, J. 1968. *Pollution, Property, Prices*. Toronto: University Press of Toronto.

Denicolo, V. 1999. "Pollution-Reducing Innovations Under Taxes or Permits." *Oxford Economic Papers* 51:184–199.

Driesen, D.M. 1998a. "Is Emissions Trading an Economic Incentive Program? Replacing the Command and Control/Economic Incentive Dichotomy." *Washington and Lee Law Review* 55(2):289–350.

———. 1998b. "Free Lunch or Cheap Fix? The Emissions Trading Idea and the Climate Change Convention." *Boston College Environmental Affairs Review* 26(1):1–87.

Dudek, D.J., and Wiener, J.B. 1996. "Joint Implementation, Transaction Costs, and Climate Change." OECD Document OECD/GD(96)173. Paris: OECD Secretariat.

Economic Report of the U.S. President. 1998. Washington, D.C.: U.S. Government Printing Office.

Ekins, P. 1993. "Making Development Sustainable." In *Global Ecology: A New Era of Political Conflict*, ed. W. Sachs. London: Zed Books.

Grubb, M., Chapuis, T., and Duong, M.H. 1995. "The Economics of Changing Course." *Energy Policy* 23(4/5):417–32.

Halsnaes, K., Callaway, J.M., and Meyer, H.J. 1998. *Economics of Greenhouse Gas Limitations*. Geneva: UNEP Secretariat/Riso National Laboratory, Denmark.

Houghton, J.T., Filho, L.G., Callander, B.A., Harris, N., Kattenberg, A., and Maskell, K., eds. 1996. *Climate Change 1995: The Science of Climate Change*. IPCC report. New York: Cambridge University Press.

IPCC. 1996a. *Climate Change 1995—Impacts, Adaptations, and Mitigation Options*. IPCC report. New York: Cambridge University Press.

———. 1996b. *Second Assessment Report 1995*. New York: Cambridge University Press.

Montero, J.P. 1997. "Marketable Pollution Permits with Uncertainty and Transaction Costs." *Resource and Energy Economics* 20(1):27–50.

Myers, N. 1996. "The World's Forests: Problems and Potentials." *Environmental Conservation* 23:156–168.

Rao, P.K. 2000. *The Economics of Transaction Costs*. London: Macmillan.

Speth, G. 1990. "Toward a North-South Compact for the Environment." *Environment* 32(5):16–20, 40–43.

UNDP. 1996. *Human Development Report 1996*. New York: Oxford University Press.

Watson, R.T., et al., eds. 1996. *Technology, Policies and Measures for Mitigating Climate Change*. Technical report WG2, IPCC; Web site www.gcrio.org/ipcc/techrepI/techsumm.html, October 13, 1998.

Appendix 5A
UN Framework Convention on Climate Change
(Source: UNFCCC Web site http://www.unfccc.de)

The United Nations Framework Convention on Climate Change (UNFCCC) of 1992 states in its preamble that the parties to the Convention were "Concerned that human activities have been substantially increasing the atmospheric concentrations of greenhouse gases, that these increases enhance the natural greenhouse effect, and that this will result on average increase in an additional warming of the Earth's surface and atmosphere and may adversely affect natural ecosystems and humankind," and it was also stated that "States have . . . the responsibility to ensure that activities within their jurisdiction or control do not cause damage to the environment of other States or areas beyond the limits of national jurisdiction." Presented below are some of the important provisions of the UN Convention.

Article 3 Principles

In their actions to achieve the objective of the Convention and to implement its provisions, the Parties shall be guided, inter alia, by the following:

1. The Parties should protect the climate system for the benefit of present and future generations of humankind, on the basis of equity and in accordance with their common but differentiated responsibilities and respective capabilities. Accordingly, the developed country Parties should take the lead in combating climate change and the adverse effects thereof.

2. The specific needs and special circumstances of developing country Parties, especially those that are particularly vulnerable to the adverse effects of climate change, and of those Parties, especially developing country Parties, that would have to bear a disproportionate or abnormal burden under the Convention, should be given full consideration.

3. The Parties should take precautionary measures to anticipate, prevent or minimize the causes of climate change and mitigate its adverse effects. Where

---

The excerpts in this section are reprinted by permission of the Secretariat for Climate Change, Bonn, Germany.

there are threats of serious or irreversible damage, lack of full scientific certainty should not be used as a reason for postponing such measures, taking into account that policies and measures to deal with climate change should be cost-effective so as to ensure global benefits at the lowest possible cost. To achieve this, such policies and measures should take into account different socioeconomic contexts, be comprehensive, cover all relevant sources, sinks and reservoirs of greenhouse gases and adaptation, and comprise all economic sectors. Efforts to address climate change may be carried out cooperatively by interested Parties.

4. The Parties have a right to, and should, promote sustainable development. Policies and measures to protect the climate system against human-induced change should be appropriate for the specific conditions of each Party and should be integrated with national development programmes, taking into account that economic development is essential for adopting measures to address climate change.

5. The Parties should cooperate to promote a supportive and open international economic system that would lead to sustainable economic growth and development in all Parties, particularly developing country Parties, thus enabling them better to address the problems of climate change. Measures taken to combat climate change, including unilateral ones, should not constitute a means of arbitrary or unjustifiable discrimination or a disguised restriction on international trade.

Annex I Countries

Australia
Austria
Belarus*
Belgium
Bulgaria*
Canada
Croatia†
Czech Republic*†
Denmark
Estonia*
European Economic Community
Finland
France
Germany
Greece
Hungary*
Iceland
Ireland
Italy

Japan
Latvia*
Liechtenstein†
Lithuania*
Luxembourg
Monaco†
Netherlands
New Zealand
Norway
Poland*
Portugal
Romania *a/*
Russian Federation*
Slovakia *a/**
Slovenia*/†
Spain
Sweden
Switzerland
Turkey
Ukraine*
United Kingdom of Great Britain and Northern Ireland
United States of America

---

*Countries that are undergoing the process of transition to a market economy.
†Countries added to Annex I by an amendment that entered into force on 13 August 1998, pursuant to decision 4/CP.3 adopted at COP 3.

Appendix 5B
Kyoto Protocol to the UNFCCC
(Source: UNFCCC Web site
http://www.unfccc.de)

Article 2

1. Each Party included in Annex I, in achieving its quantified emission
   limitation and reduction commitments under Article 3, in order to promote sustainable development, shall:
   (a) Implement and/or further elaborate policies and measures in accor-
       dance with its national circumstances, such as:
       (i)   Enhancement of energy efficiency in relevant sectors of the
             national economy;
       (ii) Protection and enhancement of sinks and reservoirs of green-
             house gases not controlled by the Montreal Protocol, taking
             into account its commitments under relevant international
             environmental agreements; promotion of sustainable forest
             management practices, afforestation and reforestation;
       (iii) Promotion of sustainable forms of agriculture in light of cli-
             mate change considerations;
       (iv) Research on, and promotion, development and increased use
             of, new and renewable forms of energy, of carbon dioxide
             sequestration technologies and of advanced and innovative
             environmentally sound technologies;
       (v)   Progressive reduction or phasing out of market imperfections,
             fiscal incentives, tax and duty exemptions and subsidies in
             all greenhouse gas emitting sectors that run counter to the
             objective of the Convention and application of market in-
             struments;
       (vi) Encouragement of appropriate reforms in relevant sectors
             aimed at promoting policies and measures which limit or
             reduce emissions of greenhouse gases not controlled by the
             Montreal Protocol;
       (vii) Measures to limit and/or reduce emissions of greenhouse

---

The excerpts in this section are reprinted by permission of the Secretariat for
Climate Change, Bonn, Germany.

gases not controlled by the Montreal Protocol in the transport sector;

(viii) Limitation and/or reduction of methane emissions through recovery and use in waste management, as well as in the production, transport and distribution of energy;

(b) Cooperate with other such Parties to enhance the individual and combined effectiveness of their policies and measures adopted under this Article, pursuant to Article 4, paragraph 2(e)(i), of the Convention. To this end, these Parties shall take steps to share their experience and exchange information on such policies and measures, including developing ways of improving their comparability, transparency and effectiveness. The Conference of the Parties serving as the meeting of the Parties to this Protocol shall, at its first session or as soon as practicable thereafter, consider ways to facilitate such cooperation, taking into account all relevant information.

2. The Parties included in Annex I shall pursue limitation or reduction of emissions of greenhouse gases not controlled by the Montreal Protocol from aviation and marine bunker fuels, working through the International Civil Aviation Organization and the International Maritime Organization, respectively.

3. The Parties included in Annex I shall strive to implement policies and measures under this Article in such a way as to minimize adverse effects, including the adverse effects of climate change, effects on international trade, and social, environmental and economic impacts on other Parties, especially developing country Parties and in particular those identified in Article 4, paragraphs 8 and 9, of the Convention, taking into account Article 3 of the Convention. The Conference of the Parties serving as the meeting of the Parties to this Protocol may take further action, as appropriate, to promote the implementation of the provisions of this paragraph.

4. The Conference of the Parties serving as the meeting of the Parties to this Protocol, if it decides that it would be beneficial to coordinate any of the policies and measures in paragraph 1(a) above, taking into account different national circumstances and potential effects, shall consider ways and means to elaborate the coordination of such policies and measures.

Article 3

1. The Parties included in Annex I shall, individually or jointly, ensure that their aggregate anthropogenic carbon dioxide equivalent emissions of the greenhouse gases listed in Annex A do not exceed their assigned amounts, calculated pursuant to their quantified emission limitation

and reduction commitments inscribed in Annex B and in accordance with the provisions of this Article, with a view to reducing their overall emissions of such gases by at least 5 per cent below 1990 levels in the commitment period 2008 to 2012.

2. Each Party included in Annex I shall, by 2005, have made demonstrable progress in achieving its commitments under this Protocol.

3. The net changes in greenhouse gas emissions by sources and removals by sinks resulting from direct human-induced land-use change and forestry activities, limited to afforestation, reforestation and deforestation since 1990, measured as verifiable changes in carbon stocks in each commitment period, shall be used to meet the commitments under this Article of each Party included in Annex I. The greenhouse gas emissions by sources and removals by sinks associated with those activities shall be reported in a transparent and verifiable manner and reviewed in accordance with Articles 7 and 8.

4. Prior to the first session of the Conference of the Parties serving as the meeting of the Parties to this Protocol, each Party included in Annex I shall provide, for consideration by the Subsidiary Body for Scientific and Technological Advice, data to establish its level of carbon stocks in 1990 and to enable an estimate to be made of its changes in carbon stocks in subsequent years. The Conference of the Parties serving as the meeting of the Parties to this Protocol shall, at its first session or as soon as practicable thereafter, decide upon modalities, rules and guidelines as to how, and which, additional human-induced activities related to changes in greenhouse gas emissions by sources and removals by sinks in the agricultural soils and the land-use change and forestry categories shall be added to, or subtracted from, the assigned amounts for Parties included in Annex I, taking into account uncertainties, transparency in reporting, verifiability, the methodological work of the Intergovernmental Panel on Climate Change, the advice provided by the Subsidiary Body for Scientific and Technological Advice in accordance with Article 5 and the decisions of the Conference of the Parties. Such a decision shall apply in the second and subsequent commitment periods. A Party may choose to apply such a decision on these additional human-induced activities for its first commitment period, provided that these activities have taken place since 1990.

5. The Parties included in Annex I undergoing the process of transition to a market economy whose base year or period was established pursuant to decision 9/CP.2 of the Conference of the Parties at its second session shall use that base year or period for the implementation of their commitments under this Article. Any other Party included in Annex I undergoing the process of transition to a market economy which has not yet submitted its first national communication under Article 12 of the

Convention may also notify the Conference of the Parties serving as the meeting of the Parties to this Protocol that it intends to use an historical base year or period other than 1990 for the implementation of its commitments under this Article. The Conference of the Parties serving as the meeting of the Parties to this Protocol shall decide on the acceptance of such notification.

6. Taking into account Article 4, paragraph 6, of the Convention, in the implementation of their commitments under this Protocol other than those under this Article, a certain degree of flexibility shall be allowed by the Conference of the Parties serving as the meeting of the Parties to this Protocol to the Parties included in Annex I undergoing the process of transition to a market economy.

7. In the first quantified emission limitation and reduction commitment period, from 2008 to 2012, the assigned amount for each Party included in Annex I shall be equal to the percentage inscribed for it in Annex B of its aggregate anthropogenic carbon dioxide equivalent emissions of the greenhouse gases listed in Annex A in 1990, or the base year or period determined in accordance with paragraph 5 above, multiplied by five. Those Parties included in Annex I for whom land-use change and forestry constituted a net source of greenhouse gas emissions in 1990 shall include in their 1990 emissions base year or period the aggregate anthropogenic carbon dioxide equivalent emissions by sources minus removals by sinks in 1990 from land-use change for the purposes of calculating their assigned amount.

8. Any Party included in Annex I may use 1995 as its base year for hydrofluorocarbons, perfluorocarbons and sulphur hexafluoride, for the purposes of the calculation referred to in paragraph 7 above.

9. Commitments for subsequent periods for Parties included in Annex I shall be established in amendments to Annex B to this Protocol, which shall be adopted in accordance with the provisions of Article 21, paragraph 7. The Conference of the Parties serving as the meeting of the Parties to this Protocol shall initiate the consideration of such commitments at least seven years before the end of the first commitment period referred to in paragraph 1 above.

10. Any emission reduction units, or any part of an assigned amount, which a Party acquires from another Party in accordance with the provisions of Article 6 or of Article 17 shall be added to the assigned amount for the acquiring Party.

11. Any emission reduction units, or any part of an assigned amount, which a Party transfers to another Party in accordance with the provisions of Article 6 or of Article 17 shall be subtracted from the assigned amount for the transferring Party.

12. Any certified emission reductions which a Party acquires from another Party in accordance with the provisions of Article 12 shall be added to the assigned amount for the acquiring Party.

13. If the emissions of a Party included in Annex I in a commitment period are less than its assigned amount under this Article, this difference shall, on request of that Party, be added to the assigned amount for that Party for subsequent commitment periods.

14. Each Party included in Annex I shall strive to implement the commitments mentioned in paragraph 1 above in such a way as to minimize adverse social, environmental and economic impacts on developing country Parties, particularly those identified in Article 4, paragraphs 8 and 9, of the Convention. In line with relevant decisions of the Conference of the Parties on the implementation of those paragraphs, the Conference of the Parties serving as the meeting of the Parties to this Protocol shall, at its first session, consider what actions are necessary to minimize the adverse effects of climate change and/or the impacts of response measures on Parties referred to in those paragraphs. Among the issues to be considered shall be the establishment of funding, insurance and transfer of technology.

Article 4

1. Any Parties included in Annex I that have reached an agreement to fulfill their commitments under Article 3 jointly, shall be deemed to have met those commitments provided that their total combined aggregate anthropogenic carbon dioxide equivalent emissions of the greenhouse gases listed in Annex A do not exceed their assigned amounts calculated pursuant to their quantified emission limitation and reduction commitments inscribed in Annex B and in accordance with the provisions of Article 3. The respective emission level allocated to each of the Parties to the agreement shall be set out in that agreement.

2. The Parties to any such agreement shall notify the secretariat of the terms of the agreement on the date of deposit of their instruments of ratification, acceptance or approval of this Protocol, or accession thereto. The secretariat shall in turn inform the Parties and signatories to the Convention of the terms of the agreement.

3. Any such agreement shall remain in operation for the duration of the commitment period specified in Article 3, paragraph 7.

4. If Parties acting jointly do so in the framework of, and together with, a regional economic integration organization, any alteration in the composition of the organization after adoption of this Protocol shall not affect existing commitments under this Protocol. Any alteration in the

composition of the organization shall only apply for the purposes of those commitments under Article 3 that are adopted subsequent to that alteration.

5. In the event of failure by the Parties to such an agreement to achieve their total combined level of emission reductions, each Party to that agreement shall be responsible for its own level of emissions set out in the agreement.

6. If Parties acting jointly do so in the framework of, and together with, a regional economic integration organization which is itself a Party to this Protocol, each member State of that regional economic integration organization individually, and together with the regional economic integration organization acting in accordance with Article 24, shall, in the event of failure to achieve the total combined level of emission reductions, be responsible for its level of emissions as notified in accordance with this Article.

Article 10

All Parties, taking into account their common but differentiated responsibilities and their specific national and regional development priorities, objectives and circumstances, without introducing any new commitments for Parties not included in Annex I, but reaffirming existing commitments under Article 4, paragraph 1, of the Convention, and continuing to advance the implementation of these commitments in order to achieve sustainable development, taking into account Article 4, paragraphs 3, 5 and 7, of the Convention, shall:

(a) Formulate, where relevant and to the extent possible, cost-effective national and, where appropriate, regional programmes to improve the quality of local emission factors, activity data and/or models which reflect the socioeconomic conditions of each Party for the preparation and periodic updating of national inventories of anthropogenic emissions by sources and removals by sinks of all greenhouse gases not controlled by the Montreal Protocol, using comparable methodologies to be agreed upon by the Conference of the Parties, and consistent with the guidelines for the preparation of national communications adopted by the Conference of the Parties;

(b) Formulate, implement, publish and regularly update national and, where appropriate, regional programmes containing measures to mitigate climate change and measures to facilitate adequate adaptation to climate change:

(i)   Such programmes would, *inter alia*, concern the energy, transport and industry sectors as well as agriculture, forestry and waste management. Furthermore, adaptation technologies and methods for improving spatial planning would improve adaptation to climate change; and

(ii) Parties included in Annex I shall submit information on action under this Protocol, including national programmes, in accordance with Article 7; and other Parties shall seek to include in their national communications, as appropriate, information on programmes which contain measures that the Party believes contribute to addressing climate change and its adverse impacts, including the abatement of increases in greenhouse gas emissions, and enhancement of and removals by sinks, capacity building and adaptation measures;

(c) Cooperate in the promotion of effective modalities for the development, application and diffusion of, and take all practicable steps to promote, facilitate and finance, as appropriate, the transfer of, or access to, environmentally sound technologies, know-how, practices and processes pertinent to climate change, in particular to developing countries, including the formulation of policies and programmes for the effective transfer of environmentally sound technologies that are publicly owned or in the public domain and the creation of an enabling environment for the private sector, to promote and enhance the transfer of, and access to, environmentally sound technologies;

(d) Cooperate in scientific and technical research and promote the maintenance and the development of systematic observation systems and development of data archives to reduce uncertainties related to the climate system, the adverse impacts of climate change and the economic and social consequences of various response strategies, and promote the development and strengthening of endogenous capacities and capabilities to participate in international and intergovernmental efforts, programmes and networks on research and systematic observation, taking into account Article 5 of the Convention;

(e) Cooperate in and promote at the international level, and, where appropriate, using existing bodies, the development and implementation of education and training programmes, including the strengthening of national capacity building, in particular human and institutional capacities and the exchange or secondment of personnel to train experts in this field, in particular for developing countries, and facilitate at the national level public awareness of, and public access to information on, climate change. Suitable modalities should be developed to implement these activities through the relevant bodies of the Convention, taking into account Article 6 of the Convention;

(f) Include in their national communications information on programmes and activities undertaken pursuant to this Article in accordance with relevant decisions of the Conference of the Parties; and

(g) Give full consideration, in implementing the commitments under this Article, to Article 4, paragraph 8, of the Convention.

Article 18

The Conference of the Parties serving as the meeting of the Parties to this Protocol shall, at its first session, approve appropriate and effective procedures and mechanisms to determine and to address cases of non-compliance with the provisions of this Protocol, including through the development of an indicative list of consequences, taking into account the cause, type, degree and frequency of non-compliance. Any procedures and mechanisms under this Article entailing binding consequences shall be adopted by means of an amendment to this Protocol.

Article 19

The provisions of Article 14 of the Convention on settlement of disputes shall apply *mutatis mutandis* to this Protocol.

Annex A

Greenhouse Gases
Carbon dioxide (CO_2)
Methane (CH_4)
Nitrous oxide (N_2O)
Hydrofluorocarbons (HFCs)
Perfluorocarbons (PFCs)
Sulfur hexafluoride (SF6)

Sector/Source Categories
Energy
Fuel combustion
Energy industries
Manufacturing industries and construction
Transport

Other Sectors
Fugitive emissions from fuels
Solid fuels
Oil and natural gas
Other

Industrial Processes
Mineral products
Chemical industry

Metal production
Other production
Production of halocarbons and sulfur hexafluoride
Consumption of halocarbons and sulfur hexafluoride
Other

Solvent and Other Product Use
Agriculture
Enteric fermentation
Manure management
Rice cultivation
Agricultural soils
Prescribed burning of savannas
Field burning of agricultural residues
Other

Waste
Solid-waste disposal on land
Wastewater handling
Waste incineration
Other

Annex B
Party Quantified Emissions Limitation and Reduction Objectives (QELROs)

(percentage of base year or period)

Australia 108
Austria 92
Belgium 92
Bulgaria* 92
Canada 94
Croatia* 95
Czech Republic* 92
Denmark 92
Estonia* 92
European Economic Community 92
Finland 92
France 92
Germany 92
Greece 92
Hungary* 94

Iceland 110
Ireland 92
Italy 92
Japan 94
Latvia* 92
Liechtenstein 92
Lithuania* 92
Luxembourg 92
Monaco 92
Netherlands 92
New Zealand 100
Norway 101
Poland* 94
Portugal 92
Romania* 92
Russian Federation* 100
Slovakia* 92
Slovenia* 92
Spain 92
Sweden 92
Switzerland 92
Ukraine* 100
United Kingdom of Great Britain and Northern Ireland 92
United States of America 93

---

*Countries that are undergoing the process of transition to a market economy.

Chapter 6

International Institutional Mechanisms

6.1 Introduction

The fact that most environmental problems arise from the existence of externalities, and that these are not necessarily confined to the areas around their origination, require solutions from an institutional vantage. Free markets, lack of properly defined property rights, missing markets, and time-lags in the cause-and-effect relations regarding climate change are some of the underlying factors that tend to perpetuate environmental problems and hence contribute to climate destabilization. The role of coordinating institutions at the international level remains paramount. This chapter is not about a specific set of institutions that are or are not delivering results. Rather, the perspectives on the design and implementation of an institutional framework remains the theme of interest here.

The role of the Intergovernmental Panel on Climate Change (IPCC) is of significance; its Third Assessment Report due by 2001 is expected to add more scientific information to facilitate policy decisions. A number of multilateral institutions and national scientific institutions have significant roles as well. The unprecedented pace at which the relevant scientific and economic information is being generated during the last decade of the twentieth century is an indication of sensitivity of most societies to the global climatic challenges, and this consciousness is likely to be the provider of infrastructure to devise and implement climate-friendly policies.

6.2 Multilateral Institutions

Various institutions have come into existence during the 1980s in response to increasing concerns about global environmental problems. The Intergovernmental Panel on Climate Change (IPCC) was established in 1988 under the coordination of the UN Environment Programme (UNEP) and the World Meteorological Organization (WMO). The IPCC involves about 500 scientists and contributes to analyses and scientific studies. The UN Framework Convention on Climate Change (UNFCCC) was signed in 1992 and entered into force to become operative since 1994. The coordinative role of the UNFCCC Secretariat remains significant. Some of the UNFCCC Articles are given in chapter 5, Appendix 5A. Moreover, various multilateral development finance institutions and organizations like the World Bank and OECD (Organization for Economic Cooperation and Development) also play important roles in this context.

The UNFCCC specifies three categories of commitments: (1) those general commitments that apply to all parties of the Convention; (2) those specifically applicable commitments for parties listed in Annex I (39 industrial countries and economies in transition); and (3) commitments that apply to parties listed in Annex II. The details of these are presented in Appendix 5A of chapter 5. As a continued process of multilateral actions governing global climatic issues, the Conference of Parties (COP) became an institutional arrangement for further activities. The first Conference of Parties (COP-1) was held in Berlin in 1995. It was agreed that the commitments for GHG reductions were inadequate to address the problem of climatic stabilization. This Berlin Mandate was carried through subsequent COPs, and the third one (COP-3) held in Kyoto, Japan, in 1997 proposed a series of rather significant (if not optimal for some) specific targets for GHG reduction; these details are given in Appendix 5B of chapter 5.

The Kyoto Protocol (KP) takes into account the emissions and sequestration potential for carbon from land-use change and forestry (LUCF). The UNFCCC generally requires countries to mitigate climate change by examining "anthropogenic emissions by sources and removals by sinks." Annex I countries are required to provide an accounting of the net changes in LUCF emissions and removals by sinks during the emissions reductions commitment period. Further guidelines are being devised for adoption in future COP deliberations. Regarding compliance with provisions of the Kyoto Protocol, it may be desirable that explicit consequences of noncompliance be introduced in future COP meetings. Some of the consequences of noncompliance are briefly stated in Article 18 of the KP. The UNFCCC dispute-resolution process remains applicable to the KP. Article 16 suggests a multilateral consultative process; the resolution process is ultimately nonbinding and can be initiated by one party to the Convention (as per Article 14) (Breidenich et al. 1998). The KP makes it clear (Article 18) that any procedures or methods that involve binding obligations on parties as a result of non-compliance can take effect only after amending the UNFCCC articles. Whereas this cautious approach is not without its own merits, a "soft law" approach to the global climate change issues can be flawed if it is not in any way linked to emerging GHG problems and impending irreversibilities (or long-term severity of corresponding consequences). It is extremely desirable that the UNFCCC articles be amended to allow for binding obligations on parties with persistent and/or substantial non-compliance. Some of the specific instruments of global climate change mitigation policies, other than emissions trading, are discussed in the following section.

6.3 Joint Implementation and Clean Development Mechanisms

In the UNFCCC, the provision for joint implementation (JI) was made in Article 4.2 (a). This provides that Annex I countries may implement measures jointly with other parties to meet the GHG stabilization objectives. The parties at COP-1 decided to establish a pilot phase of "Activities Implemented Jointly" (AIJ) in order to gain experience and possibly standardize the scheme later. The concept is based on the fact that the capital costs of reducing concentrations of greenhouse gases vary by method of affecting the sources and sinks in different countries. The prevention of these emissions remains a meaningful priority as long as the cost-effectiveness criteria are met. Joint implementation (JI) allows one country to reduce the emissions or enhance the sinks for the GHGs of another country (Party), for example, with afforestation, and obtain accountable credits for the activity. Different forms of the JI activities were envisaged and partly implemented during the past decade, although most are not directly under the UNFCCC supervision. These JIs related to the UN Convention on Desertification, the Montreal Protocol, and the 1994 Sulfur Protocol to the Transboundary Air Pollution Convention. The Kyoto Protocol of the COP-3 permits, under its Article 6, the transfer and acquisition of emission reduction credits accruing as a result of GHG emission reduction projects among Annex B parties. Many JI projects lead to investment schemes in host countries where the investor finds a cost effective alternative to emission reduction with higher incremental costs in the originating country or at the source of emissions.

Kyoto Protocol Article 6—Extract*

1. For the purpose of meeting its commitments under Article 3, any Party included in Annex I may transfer to, or acquire from, any other such Party emission reduction units resulting from projects aimed at reducing anthropogenic emissions by sources or enhancing anthropogenic removals by sinks of greenhouse gases in any sector of the economy, provided that:
   (a) Any such project has the approval of the Parties involved;
   (b) Any such project provides a reduction in emissions by sources, or an enhancement of removals by sinks, that is additional to any that would otherwise occur;
   (c) It does not acquire any emission reduction units if it is not in compliance with its obligations under Articles 5 and 7; and
   (d) The acquisition of emission reduction units shall be supplemental to domestic actions for the purposes of meeting commitments under Article 3.

Kyoto Protocol Article 7—Extract

1. Each Party included in Annex I shall incorporate in its annual inventory of anthropogenic emissions by sources and removals by sinks of greenhouse gases not controlled by the Montreal Protocol, submitted in accordance with the relevant decisions of the Conference of the Parties, the necessary supplementary information for the purposes of ensuring compliance with Article 3, to be determined in accordance with paragraph 4 below.
2. Each Party included in Annex I shall incorporate in its national communication, submitted under Article 12 of the Convention, the supplementary information necessary to demonstrate compliance with its commitments under this Protocol, to be determined in accordance with paragraph 4 below.
3. Each Party included in Annex I shall submit the information required under paragraph 1 above annually, beginning with the first inventory due under the Convention for the first year of the commitment period after this Protocol has entered into force for that Party. Each such Party shall submit the information required under paragraph 2 above as part of the first national communication due under the Convention after this Protocol has entered into force for it and after the adoption of guidelines as provided for in paragraph 4 below. The frequency of subsequent submission of information required under this Article shall be determined by the Conference of the Parties serv-

*The excerpts in this chapter are reprinted by permission of the Secretariat for Climate Change, Bonn, Germany.

ing as the meeting of the Parties to this Protocol, taking into account any timetable for the submission of national communications decided upon by the Conference of the Parties.

4. The Conference of the Parties serving as the meeting of the Parties to this Protocol shall adopt at its first session, and review periodically thereafter, guidelines for the preparation of the information required under this Article, taking into account guidelines for the preparation of national communications by Parties included in Annex I adopted by the Conference of the Parties. The Conference of the Parties serving as the meeting of the Parties to this Protocol shall also, prior to the first commitment period, decide upon modalities for the accounting of assigned amounts.

The AIJ fall broadly into two categories: GHG emission reductions through enhanced energy use efficiency, and the enhancement of GHG sinks with forestry projects. The forestry schemes tend to be among the least costly measures and are popular in the current scenario. However, some critics argue that the schemes are not necessarily durable nor replicable beyond a small limit. Cullet and Kameri-Mbote (1998) argued that the existing claims of net benefits in the GHG reduction seem to be of dubious validity, and the JI does not take fully into account development impacts nor local needs: "JI may discourage technological innovation in environmentally sound technologies in the North . . . and put off necessary adjustments to its development policies."

The need for reducing various ingredients of transaction costs remains a high priority if the JI mechanisms possess a potential net GHG reducing potential. The role of the COP and the UNFCCC remains critical in this phase. Dudek and Wiener (1996) recommended that the COP and national governments act to foster "multiple, non-exclusive, visible clearinghouses for JI information," and for "entrepreneurial investment management vehicles." It was also suggested that the competition mechanisms should be promoted for participants with the creation of contestable market institutions via the participation of public and private institutions in the host countries.

The efficacy of JI schemes can be enhanced partly with verifiable achievement of net carbon offsets at the project level. This requires a well-defined baseline in each specific project setting. Several explorations in defining baselines for different categories of projects can be seen in Michaelowa (1998). In addition, much uncertainty confounds the JI schemes and their net effects. A number of procedural improvements in the implementation are necessary; for some of these details, see Ott (1998).

Article 12 of the Kyoto Protocol established the CDM (clean development mechanism) to help developing countries achieve reduction of the greenhouse gases (GHGs). The CDM seeks to assist developing nations in meeting the objectives of sustainable development, and simultaneously allow the Annex B parties to obtain credit for "certified emission reductions." The details are being deliberated at the national and international levels, including the COP. In principle, the CDM encourages partnerships between the North and South, and also between private and public sectors via technology and resource transfer. If appropriate measures of activity transparency and efficiency are devised to govern the CDM, the mechanism could provide benefits to all participants.

Some of the suggestions proposed by the recent U.S. President's Council on Sustainable Development for more effective CDM include the following (PCSD 1999): Encourage flexible mechanisms that allow the benefits of cost-effective decision making to be realized; create profiles of "clear winner" model projects in all the relevant sectors such as energy, forestry, industry, transportation, and construction; and establish proper methods of accountability.

Kyoto Protocol Article 12

1. A clean development mechanism is hereby defined.
2. The purpose of the clean development mechanism shall be to assist Parties not included in Annex I in achieving sustainable development and in contributing to the ultimate objective of the Convention, and to assist Parties included in Annex I in achieving compliance with their quantified emission limitation and reduction commitments under Article 3.
3. Under the clean development mechanism:
   (a) Parties not included in Annex I will benefit from project activities resulting in certified emission reductions; and
   (b) Parties included in Annex I may use the certified emission reductions accruing from such project activities to contribute to compliance with part of their quantified emission limitation and reduction commitments under Article 3, as determined by the Conference of the Parties serving as the meeting of the Parties to this Protocol.
4. The clean development mechanism shall be subject to the authority

and guidance of the Conference of the Parties serving as the meeting of the Parties to this Protocol and be supervised by an executive board of the clean development mechanism.

5. Emission reductions resulting from each project activity shall be certified by operational entities to be designated by the Conference of the Parties serving as the meeting of the Parties to this Protocol, on the basis of:
   (a) Voluntary participation approved by each Party involved;
   (b) Real, measurable, and long-term benefits related to the mitigation of climate change; and
   (c) Reductions in emissions that are additional to any that would occur in the absence of the certified project activity.

6. The clean development mechanism shall assist in arranging funding of certified project activities as necessary.

7. The Conference of the Parties serving as the meeting of the Parties to this Protocol shall, at its first session, elaborate modalities and procedures with the objective of ensuring transparency, efficiency and accountability through independent auditing and verification of project activities.

8. The Conference of the Parties serving as the meeting of the Parties to this Protocol shall ensure that a share of the proceeds from certified project activities is used to cover administrative expenses as well as to assist developing country Parties that are particularly vulnerable to the adverse effects of climate change to meet the costs of adaptation.

9. Participation under the clean development mechanism, including in activities mentioned in paragraph 3(a) above and in the acquisition of certified emission reductions, may involve private and/or public entities, and is to be subject to whatever guidance may be provided by the executive board of the clean development mechanism.

10. Certified emission reductions obtained during the period from the year 2000 up to the beginning of the first commitment period can be used to assist in achieving compliance in the first commitment period.

Kyoto Protocol Article 11

In the implementation of Article 10, Parties shall take into account the provisions of Article 4, paragraphs 4, 5, 7, 8 and 9, of the Convention.

2. In the context of the implementation of Article 4, paragraph 1, of the Convention, in accordance with the provisions of Article 4, paragraph 3, and Article 11 of the Convention, and through the entity or entities entrusted with the operation of the financial mechanism of the Convention, the developed country Parties and other developed

Parties included in Annex II to the Convention shall:

(a) Provide new and additional financial resources to meet the agreed full costs incurred by developing country Parties in advancing the implementation of existing commitments under Article 4, paragraph 1(a), of the Convention that are covered in Article 10, subparagraph (a); and

(b) Also provide such financial resources, including for the transfer of technology, needed by the developing country Parties to meet the agreed full incremental costs of advancing the implementation of existing commitments under Article 4, paragraph 1, of the Convention that are covered by Article 10 and that are agreed between a developing country Party and the international entity or entities referred to in Article 11 of the Convention, in accordance with that Article. The implementation of these existing commitments shall take into account the need for adequacy and predictability in the flow of funds and the importance of appropriate burden sharing among developed country Parties. The guidance to the entity or entities entrusted with the operation of the financial mechanism of the Convention in relevant decisions of the Conference of the Parties, including those agreed before the adoption of this Protocol, shall apply *mutatis mutandis* to the provisions of this paragraph.

3. The developed country Parties and other developed Parties in Annex II to the Convention may also provide, and developing country Parties avail themselves of, financial resources for the implementation of Article 10, through bilateral, regional and other multilateral channels.

6.4 Political Economy of Global Environmental Policies

A few international agreements are reasonably effective, but most others do not merit such a distinction. In the former category one would consider the 1987 Montreal Protocol on Substances That Deplete the Ozone Layer. This was an historic agreement and a good model for several reasons. It was the first international agreement to set a time-bound reduction of pollution emissions with roles assigned to developed and other countries. Even modifications over subsequent years were more enthusiastic in the implementation than in the original as they tried to accelerate the implementation schedules. The agreement was also the first to apply the "Precautionary Principle" to international policy application. Also, the noncompliance provisions were suggested in the agreement.

The tradition and respect for the rule of law, public support based on informed opinion, and level of socioeconomic development are among the domestic factors affecting compliance regarding international agreements, in the absence of explicit and consequential incentives for compliance, or enforceable disincentives for noncompliance. Also, the effectiveness of mechanisms for monitoring and evaluation of the compliance regimes and verifiability are of significance—unless the provisions can be generally characterized as self-interest sustaining and self-enforcement-inducing.

Institutionalized compliance regulation and control can be classified by a variety of criteria (Lang 1995): composition and size of the control body; regulatory and control powers of the body; investigation triggering origins of control activities, procedural duties of the (potentially) noncompliant state; causes of noncompliance; and consequences of noncompliance.

Three elements related to compliance, essentially the forward and backward linkages in connection with features of compliance itself, can be distinguished (see also Weiss, 1995): implementation, regular compliance, and effectiveness. The first refers to the legislation, the regulations, and other aspects required to *implement* the agreement. *Regular compliance* refers not only to whether countries adhere to the provisions of the agreement and implementing measures, but whether the fixation of the goals and targets induced any undesirable changes in their behavior. Compliance can also be distinguished in terms of *procedural* compliance and *substantive* compliance, and it is the latter that could lead to *effectiveness* of the spirit of the agreement. An agreement may be declared as complied but the objectives may not be attained, a case of ineffectiveness. For example, a treaty that prohibits ivory trade can lead to neglect or near extinction of the animal species when appropriate resources are not deployed for preservation of the species.

6.5 Concluding Observations

The global policies for climate stabilization and sustainable development need to be integrated for their cost-effectiveness and relevance in varied local conditions. Democratic participation, and multistakeholder participation, in addition to transparency and accountability, remain important considerations in any meaningful approach. The design of institutions need not be centrally directed or conditioned by the magic of markets or of bureaucracies. It is a complementary role of each system, private or public, developed or developing economy, market or regulatory, with a short-term and long-term focus, that needs to be recognized for enhanced effectiveness of various policy designs and their practical usefulness. The role of competitiveness or contestable markets also needs to be recognized for achieving dynamic efficiency in various activities aimed at prevention of global climate change and mitigating its effects.

References

Breidenich, C., Magraw, D., Rowley, A., and Rubin, J., 1998. "The Kyoto Protocol to the United Nations Framework Convention on Climate Change." *American Journal of International Law* 92(2):315–331.
Cullet, P., and Kameri-Mbote, A. 1998. "Joint Implementation and Forestry Projects: Conceptual and Operational Fallacies." *International Affairs* 74(2):393–408.
Dudek, D.J., and Wiener, J.B. 1996. "Joint Implementation, Transaction Costs, and Climate Change." OECD Document OECD/GD(96)173. Paris: OECD Secretariat.
Lang, W. 1995. "Compliance-Control in Respect of the Montreal Protocol." In *American Society of International Law Proceedings of the 89th Annual Meeting "Structures of World Order."* New York.
Michaelowa, A. 1998. "Joint Implementation-The Baseline Issue." *Global Environmental Change* 8(1):81–92.
Ott, H.E. 1998. "Operationalizing Joint Implementation." *Global Environmental Change* 8(1):11–47.
PCSD. 1999. *Towards a Sustainable America.* Final report of the U.S. President's Council on Sustainable Development. Washington, DC: U.S. Government Printing Office.
Weiss, E.B. 1995. "Remarks on Compliance-Control in Respect of the Montreal Protocol." In *American Society of International Law Proceedings of the 89th Annual Meeting on "Structures of World Order."* New York.

Chapter 7

The Road (or Air) Ahead

7.1 The Kyoto Protocol and After

The international initiatives on climate stabilization have been in existence for more than a decade in dealing directly with climate change issues, and for several decades in dealing with the ecology and the environment. The science of global climate change has been better understood only during the past five years with a reasonable degree of clarity on various complex interrelationships. To this extent, the emergence of various national and international initiatives to prevent climate change or stabilize the global climate tend to be of very recent origin and still to be evolved. Because most measures aimed at these objectives involve substantial costs, the provision of cost-effective policies and programs remains the most important imperative.

In one of the earliest clear assertions, the Ministerial Declaration of the Second World Climate Conference of November 1990 stated: "Recognizing . . . that the principle of equity and the common but differentiated responsibility of countries should be the basis of any global response to climate change, developed countries must take the lead." The impetus of some of these declarations was felt in different platforms of global policy.

Let us recall two of the relevant Principles of Agenda 21 adopted at the Rio Summit in 1992:

Principle 3. The right to development must be fulfilled so as to equitably meet developmental and environmental needs of present and future generations.

Principle 7. States shall cooperate in a spirit of global partnership to conserve, protect and restore the health and integrity of Earth's ecosystem. In view of the different contributions to global environmental degradation, states have common but differentiated responsibilities. The developed countries acknowledge the responsibility that they bear in the international pursuit of sustainable development in view of the pressures their societies place on the global environment and of the technologies and financial resources they command.

These principles continue to govern a broad range of global environmental policies, international environmental law, and global cooperation. In addition, the role of adaptation and potential contribution of developed countries to other countries in this context was also stated in the Kyoto Protocol (KP) agreement.

Adaptation

An appreciation of the role of adaptation is important in minimizing costs of policies and programs aimed at climate stabilization. A key requirement is enhancement of adaptive capacity via diversification of resources that could otherwise be totally vulnerable to climate changes. Large human settlements along a sea coast vulnerable to damage due to a rise in sea level is an example of such vulnerability; it should be recognized as such, and alternate settlements should be provided for. The UNFCCC charter includes five clauses in its Article 4 that specifically address the features relating to adaptation. These are specified in 4.1(b), (e), (f); 4.3; and 4.4

Article 8 of the KP refers to partial support from developed countries to developing countries in their adoption of relevant adaptation methods: "The Conference of Parties . . . shall ensure that a share of the proceeds from certified project activities is used . . . to assist developing country parties that are particularly vulnerable to the adverse effects of climate change to meet the costs of adaptation." This provision can be made more effective if an incentive mechanism is devised to encourage developing countries to mobilize their resources in this direction and to encourage developed countries to assure augmentation of such resources on a specified basis.

7.2 New Initiatives and Institutional Mechanisms

Various policy measures and institutional interventions are required to achieve climate stabilization and, more specifically, stabilization of the emissions of greenhouse gases (GHGs). Many of these measures are di-

---

Box 7.1 Global Climatic Change—Policy Instruments

Domestic Market-Based Instruments

Emissions trading, permit auctions, research and development (R&D) subsidies, and other incentives to firms, promoting contestable markets for environmental subsidy entitlements, green taxes and green incentives for pollution reduction, differential corporate taxation, and voluntary corporate initiatives.

Domestic Regulatory Instruments

Regulatory standards for energy use efficiency, standards for effluent treatment, recycling regulations, industrywide standards for choice of technology and its regulatory ban in specified categories, application of the Polluter Pays Principle (PPP), application of the Precautionary Principle (PP), periodic licensing and renewal regulations in relation to ex ante and ex post performance features, license fees, monitoring and compliance enforcement mechanisms.

International Market-Based Instruments

Internationally harmonized process and product methods (PPM), harmonized green taxes, tradable emission permits (TEP), joint implementation, clean development mechanisms (CDM), incentives for firms to adopt climate-friendly technologies, differential corporate tax treatment to encourage environmentally efficient companies with global operations, global mechanisms for promoting R&D and technology improvement, and voluntary initiatives of multinational corporate entities.

International Nonmarket Instruments

Application of the PP and PPP, target fulfillment in the emission reduction regimes under multilateral environmental agreements, effective monitoring and compliance in relation to international agreements.

---

rectly or indirectly linked to economic criteria. Cost-effectiveness remains the key to selection of alternative measures, and the costs need not be direct costs only. The role of transaction costs remains very significant in all the instruments and their implementation. Any cost-benefit analysis that assumes transaction costs equal to direct costs or direct costs plus indirect costs is likely to lead to inefficient prescriptions.

Among the economic factors and institutional prerequisites for effective implementation are: the regime of well-defined property rights and liability systems, functioning of competitive markets with features of regulatory compliance, enforceable laws, and fiscal systems capable of implementing tax laws.

Some of the "key findings" on climate change are listed in the recent U.S. President's Council on Sustainable Development (PCSD 1999). These include the following:

1. Climate protection policies should be strongly linked to national agenda for economic growth, environmental protection, and social justice.
2. There exists a need for timely action to reduce the risks of climate change
3. Actions to protect the climate have multiplier effects in benefits.
4. Incentive-based programs such as encouraging learning and innovation are essential.
5. Climate-friendly technologies are critical for sustainable development.

At the global level, the report made the following recommendations, among others:

1. The United States must use its leadership role to help chart a path toward sustainable development both at home and abroad.
2. Multilateral agreements should recognize and address economic, environmental, and equity aspects.
3. New coalitions of broad-based stakeholders at the national and international levels are required to promote relevant changes.

7.3 Improved Effectiveness of Global Initiatives

Global initiatives in the arena of climatic change include policy and administrative measures at various levels of national governments, international institutions and nongovernmental organizations, in addition to those undertaken by various other stakeholders including private industry and the citizenry. Improved effectiveness of these initiatives is dependent on the quality of information and the utilization of the same in each of these decision-making interactive entities. The supply of information, more than its demand, is expected to remain a major driving force in the management of global climatic changes. This information is not only complex but is necessarily based on time lapse (or time-series) of factual observations (in addition to being knowledge-constrained and capital-intensive).

Three Global Observing Systems, called G3OS, have been established in the 1990s by various international organizations: FAO, ICSU, IOC, UNEP, UNESCO, and WMO (see Abbreviations List, p. xiii). These three systems are the Global Climate Observing System (GCOS), the Global Ocean Observing System (GOOS), and the Global Terrestrial Observing System (GTOS). The GTOS focuses on five issues: changes in land quality, freshwater resources availability, pollution and toxicity, loss of biodiversity, and climate change. (Additional details may be seen at the FAO Web site www.fao.org/gtos/pages/obj.htm). The UNEP prepared an Integrated Strategic Plan in 1996 for the three systems and that has been further revised in later years. Continued efforts in these scientific activities are expected to contribute to a better understanding of the complex interrelationships of the climatological phenomena, the role of human influences to some of these, and to help identify the relative roles of different activities—sectoral, geographic, and national contributions to the GHGs—and the compliance of various countries to globally binding and voluntary commitments.

The following major factors influence the effectiveness and pragmatism of climate stabilization policies:

- Information base and quality of scientific and socioeconomic information for initial decision making
- The scope for efficient remedial action based on feedback information
- Flexibility in technical, institutional, and economic mechanisms devised for achieving stated objectives
- Recognition of adaptation mechanisms that can be fruitfully tapped for cost-effective solutions
- Recognition of intergenerational and intragenerational justice requirements in an equitable and efficient sharing of environmental and other resources
- Realization of the role of relatively low (though not equal to zero, but most likely around 2 percent) discount rates in project appraisal and evaluation, since this remains the most critical factor in weighing benefits and costs of alternate intervention policies
- Recognition of the role of transition mechanisms and relative smoothness of solutions to mitigate climate

- Need to avoid excessive costs (including transaction costs) of dislocation or other changes to offset potential disruptions due to climate change
- Higher priority for research, innovation, and development based on such efficiency-enhancing mechanisms
- Fair and equitable sharing by individual countries of the costs of global climate change
- Greater appreciation of the role of feedback mechanisms of different climate change–influencing factors, and focus on the reduction of uncertainties in the dynamics of the climatological system and its consequences
- Integration of behavioral and technical aspects of alternate possibilities for stabilization of the climate

These investigations enable improved management of common-pool resources or global commons. The common-pool resources (CPR) defined as "a natural or man-made system that is sufficiently large as to make it costly (but not impossible) to exclude potential beneficiaries from obtaining benefits from its use" (Ostrom 1990, 30). As Carraro and Siniscalco (1993) argued, the "tragedy of the commons" phenomena are usually founded on a static approach with free riders and null intervention, but in a repeated transaction setting with stakeholder participation, countries tend to cooperate under an expanded set of equilibrium outcomes. This implies, for the purposes of devising pragmatic global strategies, provision of direct and indirect incentives and disincentives for countries to modulate their activities toward climate-friendly directions. Parties to one or more of the climate change conventions and multilateral environmental agreements can offer incentives for nonparties to join the group and also provide disincentives such as limited market access to environmentally harmful products in their respective markets. This framework develops a static noncooperative scenario to one of a dynamic cooperative "game," with potentially beneficial outcomes for all.

Because of the nonexcludability and potential free-riding in the global commons, a series of globally coordinated measures are necessary for the attainment of any desired state of the environment and the climate. This requires, in addition to cooperation between countries and various stakeholders, workable mechanisms for information collation, monitoring and evaluation, and reappraisal for improved policies and their efficient implementation. These activities require the active role of institutions and involve a variety of transaction costs.

Transaction costs arise because of the costs of information, monitoring and enforcement of regimes of resource regulation and management. North (1995) stated: "Information is not only costly but incomplete, and enforcement is not only costly but imperfect. Effective institutions and organizations can reduce the transaction costs per exchange so as to realize more of the potential gains of human interaction."

North also suggested that a well-informed polity tends to reduce misallocation of resources: "It is important that the social benefits (and costs) are clearly known to the polity so that they will be undertaken by governmental organizations."

Let us recognize that one of the best cost-effective mechanisms of "intervention" in global climate change is with an understanding of the environmental ethics. To quote Wapner (1997): "Recognizing the ethical dimension of transnational environmental issues is essential not only to improve our understanding of environmental degradation and aspects of current international agreements but also to fashion higher-quality international agreements in the future."

One of the best routes to prevention of climate change and attainment of climate stabilization is via the process of sustainable development. "Growth and sustainable development cannot be separated from issues of social justice and equity within and between generations; . . . [these] require a social costing which recognizes the impact on 'disadvantages groups' as well as vulnerable ecosystems" (Elliott 1998).

The effectiveness of various global initiatives can be enhanced by reducing both transaction costs and policy uncertainties; by provision of incentives for technical innovations; by integration of environmental policies with economic policies affecting both national and global economies; and the adoption of relevant environmental principles listed below.

The most important guiding principles are the following:

1. The Precautionary Principle (also included in the Articles of the UNFCCC, but greater attention must be directed in practice)
2. The Polluter Pays Principle (largely agreed in international deliberations, but rarely applied in practice)
3. Internalization of Environmental Costs (as a by-product of the application of the Polluter Pays Principle, extended to domestic and international activities, including export-import operations)

4. The Principle of Common but Differentiated Responsibilities (among various countries and blocs of countries, in cost-sharing and responsibility-sharing with other countries categorized by their relative contributions to the global climatic change phenomena and affordability to mitigate the effects)
5. The application of Principles of Sustainable Development (which include additional guiding principles beyond the above four principles)

References

Carraro, C., and Siniscalco, D. 1993. "Strategies for International Protection of the Environment." *Journal of Public Economics* 52:309–328.

Elliott, L. 1998. *The Global Politics of the Environment.* New York: New York University Press.

North, D. 1995. "Constraints on Institutional Innovation: Transaction Costs, Incentive Compatibility, and Historical Considerations." In *Agriculture, Environment, and Health: Sustainable Development in the 21st Century,* ed. W.W. Ruttan. Minneapolis: University of Minnesota Press.

Ostrom, E. 1990. *Governing the Commons.* New York: Cambridge University Press.

PCSD. 1999. *Towards a Sustainable America.* Final report of the President's Council on Sustainable Development. Washington, DC: U.S. Government Printing Office.

Ruttan, V.W., ed. 1995. *Agriculture, Environment, and Health: Sustainable Development in the 21st Century.* Minneapolis: University of Minnesota Press.

Wapner, P. 1997. "Environmental Ethics and Global Governance—Engaging the International Liberal Tradition." *Global Governance* 3(2): 213–231.

Glossary

Part of this glossary is adapted from those developed by the Oak Ridge National Laboratory (U.S.), UNEP, USEPA, and a number of other sources.

Absorption of radiation   The uptake of a solid body, liquid, or gas. The absorbed energy may be transferred or remitted. Also includes the process of conversion into heat of a part of the radiation to which an object is exposed.

Acid rain   Also known as "acid deposition." This is the combination of dry deposition of acidic substances and precipitation; the acidic conversion is usually the result of fossil-fuel burning, which releases sulfur dioxide and nitrogen oxide into the atmosphere. Acidic aerosols in the atmosphere are deposited via rain, snow, fog (wet deposition) or dry particles (dry deposition). The aerosols are present in the atmosphere primarily due to discharges of gaseous sulfur oxides and nitrogen oxides either from anthropogenic sources or natural sources. In the atmosphere these gases combine with water to form acids.

Activated carbon   Carbon that has been treated to remove hydrocarbons, thus enhancing its absorption; it is widely used for controlling odors and in air-freshening types of applications.

Adaptation   A response to potential or actual climate change (or related phenomena) in order to reduce an entity's susceptibility to be damaged in any significant way. Adaptation can be spontaneous or planned or a combination of both.

Adiabatic   Change or exchange occurring without the exchange of heat; it is a change in the volume and pressure of a gas, for example, without an exchange of heat or change in temperature.

Aerosols   Particulate materials, other than water or ice, of fine liquid or dust as gaseous suspensions in the atmosphere. Aerosols are classified as smoke, fumes, mist, and dust. Burning coal, for example, releases sulfur dioxide, which in the atmosphere is transformed into sulfate aerosols. Aerosols participate in various chemical cycles and affect the radiation budget of the Earth–atmosphere system.

Afforestation   Establishing new forests and trees on unforested land. Afforestation of large areas of land can grow trees that will absorb and store carbon from the atmosphere, which could slow carbon dioxide buildup.

Agenda 21   Developed at the United Nations Conference on Environment and Development (UNCED) held in Rio de Janeiro, Brazil, June 1992. This agenda consisted of twenty-seven principles and was adopted by 178 countries.

Airshed   An area within which pollutants or specified gas contents interact and possibly concentrate, unless chemically diffused.

Albedo   The fraction of light that is reflected from a surface or object out of the total light striking the same; an albedo of 100 percent implies complete reflection. Earth's average albedo is about 50 percent.

Aldehydes   A class of chemical compounds that are intermediate between acids and alcohols; they are used in a variety of applications such as production of vitamins, polymer compounds, in perfumes, and in the production of other compounds.

Amazon rain forest   A vast tropical rain forest covering the watersheds and drainage basins of the Amazon River and its tributaries in Brazil, encompassing about an area of about 7 million square kilometers; it is the largest such basin in the world.

Amortization   The periodic repayment of a loan's principal and interest over a prescribed time span.

Annuity   Payment of a constant sum of money for each time period over a number of periods. If the payments are made over an infinite horizon, the annuity is called a "perpetuity" and has a present value s/r, s being the sum in each period, r the discount rate.

Antarctic Treaty   Signed by 25 nations in 1959, this treaty allows scientific research in the antarctic without interference of national sovereignties. Several international agreements arose out of this treaty, such as the Antarctic Protocol on Environmental Protection; Convention on the Conservation of the Antarctic Marine Resources; and a ban on mining exploration in the antarctic.

Anthropocentric The view that human beings are the central feature of planet Earth and that the environment and the ecology should be valued in terms of their utility or lack of it for humans.

Anthropogenic Influences caused or created by human beings.

Anthropogenic climate change Changes in the world's climate system that are a result of human actions and inactions.

Aridity A general term used to describe areas suffering from lack of rain or undergoing drought. More specifically, a condition in which evaporation exceeds precipitation.

Atmosphere The envelope of air surrounding Earth. Earth's atmosphere consists of 79 percent nitrogen (by volume), 20.9 percent oxygen, 0.03 percent carbon dioxide, and trace amounts of other gases. It can be divided into a number of layers according to thermal properties (temperature). The layer nearest Earth's surface is the troposphere (about 10 to 15 km above the surface), next is the stratosphere (up to about 50 km) followed by the mesosphere (up to 80 km), and finally the thermosphere or ionosphere, which extends into space. There is little mixing of gases between layers.

Backstop technology A substitute technology that becomes economically feasible when the price of a nonrenewable natural resource has risen to a particular level (resulting from continued extraction).

Benzene A highly toxic liquid hydrocarbon derived from coal and petroleum; used in the manufacture of plastics.

Berlin Mandate The decision by a 1995 United Nations climate conference in Berlin to seek commitments beyond the 1992 Rio agreement, under which developed nations volunteered to limit greenhouse emissions. Precursor to the 1997 Kyoto talks on these reductions.

Biochemical oxidation The process of transforming organic pollutants into sedimentary organic substances or inert mineral materials.

Biochemical oxygen demand (BOD) An indicator of water pollution; this represents—subject to appropriate accounting of relevant chemical effects within the compounds involved—the extent of biochemically degradable substances in water.

Biodiversity   The number of different types of plant and animal species that live in a particular region. Biodiversity includes (a) genetic variability and (b) the number of species; on land, tropical rain forests have the highest biodiversity.

Biogenic   The effect on the environment of the activities of living organisms.

Biomass   The amount of living matter in a particular region, usually expressed as weight (mass) per unit area (e.g., tons per acre).

Biomass energy   Energy produced by combusting (burning) biomass materials such as wood. The carbon dioxide from burning biomass will not increase total atmosphere carbon dioxide if this consumption is done on a sustainable basis (i.e., if, in a given period of time, regrowth of biomass takes up as much carbon dioxide as is released from combustion). Biomass energy is often suggested as a replacement for fossil fuel combustion, which has large greenhouse gas emissions.

Biome   A characterization of the ecosystem in terms of the nature and composition of its vegetation; a community of plants and animals in a specified region.

Biosphere   The segments of Earth and its atmospheric surroundings that can, in principle, support life. This includes the region on land, in the oceans, and in the atmosphere inhabited by living organisms.

Biota   The collection of all living things, including plants and animals, of a given area.

Biotic element   Any member of the organisms forming the populations and communities in an ecosystem.

British Antarctic Survey (BAS)   A scientific body engaged in all aspect of research within the continent of Antarctica.

Capital consumption allowance (CCA)   The investment allowance for replacing used capital is called depreciation allowance, or CCA.

Capitalized value   The capital value of an asset or liability valued at current market terms.

Carbon budget   The amount of carbon released into the atmosphere by net sources, whether natural factors, like dying plants, or human activities, like burning fossil fuel, minus the amount of carbon absorbed by the ocean, growing green plants, and other carbon "sinks."

Carbon cycle Carbon exchanges from one carbon reservoir to another by various chemical, physical, geological, and biological processes. Alternately, the process by which carbon is cycled through the environment. Carbon, in the form of carbon dioxide, is absorbed from the atmosphere and used by plants in the process of photosynthesis to store energy. Plants and animals then return carbon dioxide to the atmosphere through respiration when they consume this energy. A quarter of the total atmospheric carbon dioxide is cycled each year, approximately half of which is exchanged with land biota.

Carbon dioxide (CO_2) A molecule formed from one atom of carbon and two of oxygen. Carbon dioxide is a greenhouse gas of major concern in the study of global warming. It is estimated that the amount of CO_2 in the air is increasing by 0.25 to 0.5 percent annually. Anthropogenic carbon dioxide is emitted mainly through the burning of fossil fuels and deforestation.

Carbon equivalent (CE) A metric measure used to determine the emissions of the different greenhouse gases based on their global warming potential (GWP). Emissions of greenhouse gases in the United States are most commonly expressed as "million metric tons of carbon equivalents" (MMTCE). Warming potentials are used to convert greenhouse gas carbon dioxide equivalents. Carbon dioxide equivalents then are converted to carbon equivalents by multiplying carbon dioxide equivalents by 12/44 (the ratio of the weight of carbon to carbon dioxide). Thus, the formula to derive carbon equivalents is: MMTCE = (million metric tons of a gas) x (GWP of the 12/44).

Carbon sequestration The uptake and storage of carbon. Trees and plants, for example, absorb carbon dioxide, release the oxygen, and store the carbon. Carbon sinks can serve to partially offset greenhouse gas emissions. Forests and oceans are common carbon sinks.

Catalytic converter A device fitted to automobile exhausts to remove harmful emissions of air pollutants such as hydrocarbons.

Chlorinated hydrocarbons Also known as organochlorines, these include pesticides such as DDT, aldrin, endrin, and PCBs; these compounds are highly toxic and are not biodegradable.

Chlorofluorocarbons (CFCs)   A set of synthetic compounds belonging to the family of greenhouse gases used in air conditioning, as industrial solvents, and in other commercial applications. CFCs destroy ozone in the stratosphere (see ozone), and they are being eliminated under an international agreement negotiated in Montreal in 1987.

Climate   The long-term weather conditions in a particular area. Climatic elements include precipitation, temperature, humidity, sunshine, and wind velocity and phenomena such as fog, frost, and hail storms. Climate deals not only with the atmosphere but also its variations.

Climate feedback   A secondary process resulting from primary climate change that may increase (positive feedback) or diminish (negative feedback) the magnitude of climate change.

Co-generation   A combined heat and power generation method.

Compensated demand curve   A demand curve in which the income effect of price change is excluded so that along the demand curve, real income is held constant; the demand curve exhibits only the substitution effect. In the Marshallian demand curve, both the income and substitution effects are allowed.

Contestable market   A market characterized by free entry and exit for potential entrants using the same technologies as in the case of the incumbent firms or economic entities and having access to the demand and market functions as in the case of the incumbents.

Contingent valuation (CV)   In the absence of market valuation of goods or services (possibly because these are not transacted in the market activities, as in the case of some of the ecological goods), a subjective valuation of these by representative people (usually based on a questionnaire method) is called CV. This presumes the existence of a hypothetical market operation.

Convention on the Control of Transboundary Movement of Hazardous Wastes and Their Disposal (the Basel Convention)   An international convention of 1992 which was held to confront the problem of industrial countries dumping hazardous wastes. A nominal compensation was approved. A complete phasing out of such activities by the end of 1997 was planned as per a follow-up resolution of the convention in 1994.

Copenhagen Amendment   A second amendment to the Montreal Protocol to speed up the phasing out of chemicals that deplete the ozone layer.

Cryosphere That part of Earth's surface consisting of ice masses and snow deposits. Includes the continental ice sheets, mountain glaciers, sea ice, surface snow cover, lake and river ice, Siberia, the Antarctic Ocean, and the Arctic Ocean.

DDT (dichlorodiphenyltrichloroethane) A chlorinated hydrocarbon insecticide with extremely toxic features, supposedly banned worldwide.

Dioxins A class of dangerous chlorinated organic compounds arising from the manufacture of herbicides, bleaches, and a few similar products.

Disembodied technical progress This is technical progress that appears cost free and independent of other economic variables.

Dobson unit (DU) A unit measuring the total amount of ozone in a vertical column above Earth's surface in the stratosphere. Ozone varies with latitude and season, and it ranges typically from 250 to 450 DU. A value of less than 200 DU is associated with the presence of an ozone hole.

Ecology The study of the interactions of organisms with their physical environment and with the other organisms associated with it.

Ecosystem A system of interdependent life-forms and their physical environment; could be described at the local, regional, or other levels; the totality of organisms living in an area, their physical environment, and the interactions among all of these.

El Niño A climate phenomenon occurring at irregular time intervals every 2 to 7 years during the Christmas season (El Niño means "Christ child") in the surface oceans of the southeast Pacific. The phenomenon involves seasonal changes in the direction of Pacific winds and abnormally warm surface ocean temperatures. The changes normally only effect the Pacific region, but major events and global weather patterns are still matters of continued investigations.

Embodied technical progress Technical progress that cannot take place unless it is embodied in new capital.

Endemic A species native to a specific location, occurring naturally in a specific region or a characterization of biogeophysical features; a species or a race native to a particular location.

Enhanced greenhouse effect   The natural greenhouse effect has been enhanced by anthropogenic emission of greenhouse gases. Increased concentrations of carbomethane, and nitrous oxide, CFCs, HFCs, PFCs, SF6, and other photochemically important gases caused by activities such as burning of fossil fuel and adding waste landfills, trap more infrared radiation, thereby exerting a warming influence on Earth's climate.

Environment   The surroundings of an organism or a species; the physical, chemical, and biological traits of the ecosystem in which an organism lives.

Ethnocentrism   Valuation of things and activities in terms of the cultural beliefs of a human population or race.

Exothermic   A reaction that takes place with the release of heat.

Ex situ conservation   The conservation of biological species and their diversity outside their natural habitats; for example, in the germ plasm preservation of some genetic resources.

Externality   Uncompensated effect of economic or physical activity. An externality arises when production or consumption or other activities of an entity provides (a) utility to the latter without paying for costs imposed on other entities, or (b) receives no compensation commensurate with the benefits provided to others.

Factor augmenting technical progress   Technical progress that raises the level of output even when the stocks of capital and labor remain fixed.

Fauna   Animal life, usually specific to a region or time period.

Feedback   A sequence of interactions in which the final interaction leads to influencing the initial one. A positive feedback is one that amplifies the change mechanism; a negative feedback contributes toward the retardation or dampening of the change.

Feedback mechanism   A mechanism connecting one aspect of a system to another. The connection can be amplifying (positive feedback) or moderating (negative feedback).

Flora   Plant life, usually specific to a region or time period.

Fluorocarbons (FCs)   Organic compounds similar to hydrocarbons in which one or more hydrogen atoms are replaced by fluorine. FCs containing chlorine are CFCs (chlorofluorocarbons).

Free rider Deriving benefits without having to pay any costs.

General equilibrium (economy) All markets in an economy that are simultaneously in equilibrium; with balanced demand and supply, prices do not vary.

Genus A group or species with similar characteristics.

Geosphere The soils, sediments, and rock layers of Earth's crust, both continental and beneath the oceans; the mineral abiotic portion of Earth.

Global Environment Monitoring System (GEMS) Administered by the UNEP as a monitoring system overseeing several aspects of the global environment, such as the atmosphere and airborne pollutants; GEMS units are in about four dozen countries worldwide.

Golden rule of accumulation The path of balanced growth where each generation saves for successive generations that constant fraction which was saved for it by the previous generation.

Greenhouse effect (GE) The global warming effect of concentrations of greenhouse gases (mainly CO_2, CFCs, CH_4, and N_2O) that trap heat within Earth's atmosphere; these gases let in solar radiation but retain part of this energy in relation to their increased concentrations in the atmosphere.

Greenhouse gas The gases or trace gases that contribute to the greenhouse effect or to global warming.

Halocarbons Chemicals consisting of carbon, sometimes hydrogen, and one or more of the halogens, namely, chlorine, fluorine, bromine, or idohalons.

Halogen Any of the five highly reactive halocarbon elements: four as above, and (in group VIIB of the periodic table) astatine.

Halons Organic compounds containing chlorine/bromine; these constitute a class of stratospheric ozone-depleting compounds having long atmospheric lifetimes.

Helsinki Agreement The 1989 agreement by 80 countries to cease production of all CFCs by the end of the twentieth century to protect the ozone layer.

Hicksian income The maximum amount of money that an economic entity (for example, an individual) can spend in a given unit time (for example, in a year) and still expect to afford the same amount (adjusted for inflation or similar corrections) in each subsequent time interval of similar units. (Hicks, J.R. 1939. *Value and Capital.* Oxford: Clarendon Press, 175)

Hydrocarbons   Substances containing only hydrogen and carbon. Fossil fuels are made up of hydrocarbons. Hydrocarbon compounds are major air pollutants.

Hydrofluorocarbons (HFCs)   Introduced as alternatives to ozone-depleting substances in serving many industrial, commercial, and personal needs, HFCs are emitted as by-products of industrial processes and are also used in manufacturing. They do not significantly deplete the stratospheric ozone layer, but they are powerful greenhouse gases.

Hydrosphere   That part of Earth consisting of water, including the oceans, seas, ice caps, glaciers, lakes, rivers, and underground water supplies.

Infrared radiation   Electromagnetic radiation of lower frequencies and longer wavelengths than visible light. Solar ultraviolet radiation is absorbed by Earth's surface and re-emitted as infrared radiation.

In situ conservation   A biological conservation method that ensures features to enable genetic resource existence within the ecoystems and natural habitats.

Ionosphere   Also known as the thermosphere, a layer in the atmosphere above the mesosphere extending from about 80 km above Earth's surface. It can be considered a distinct layer owing to a rise in air temperature with increasing height. Atmospheric densities in the atmosphere are very low.

Lifetime (atmospheric)   Also known as residence time. The approximate amount of time a pollutant will spend in the atmosphere before either being converted to another chemical compound or being taken out of the atmosphere via a sink. This time depends on the pollutant's sources and sinks as well as its reactivity. Lifetime affects the mixing of pollutants in the atmosphere; a long lifetime will allow the pollutant to mix well in the atmosphere. Average lifetimes can vary from one day (nitrogen dioxide) to 5,000 years (oxygen) and beyond.

Lithosphere   The outer part of the solid Earth, about 80 km in thickness.

London Amendment A first amendment to the Montreal Protocol to speed up the phasing out of chemicals that deplete the ozone layer.

Marginal physical product The addition to total output with the deployment of an additional unit of labor holding other factors constant.

Marginal product The added output attributable to additional use of a given factor of production.

Market failure This is usually a reference to the feature that, in competitive market situations, the market price of an item differs from its social cost (defined as the private cost plus environmental or other external costs or benefits). When markets are imperfect or noncompetitive, the feature is automatically assumed to prevail.

Mean residence time (MRT) For any chemical gas or biogeochemical reservoir, the MRT is the ratio of its mass Q, to its flux, the time derivative of Q. For example, the MRT of N_2O is about 100 years, and that of water vapor in the atmosphere is about 9.3 days.

Mesosphere The region of the upper atmosphere between 50 and 80 km above the Earth's surface.

Montreal Protocol An international treaty signed in 1987 that limits production of chlorofluorocarbons (CFCs). The discovery of an ozone hole over Antarctica prompted action to control the use of gases that have a destructive effect on the ozone layer. From this concern emerged the Montreal Protocol on substances that deplete the Earth's ozone layer, signed by 24 countries in 1987. It came into force in 1989 and has since been ratified by 120 countries. The original agreement was to control and phase out the production and supply of ozone-depleting chemicals, specifically CFCs and derivatives. A meeting in 1992 was held in Copenhagen to revise the protocol. This meeting agreed to bring forward the phasing out of halons to 1994, and other halocarbons to 1996. At present these targets have either been or are being met.

Multilateral Investment Guarantee Agency (MIGA) Created as an affiliate of the World Bank in 1988, the MIGA provides, at a cost, to its member countries, investment insurance (covering political risks) and marketing services for private or other foreign direct investment.

Nitrification The oxidation of ammonium salts to nitrates, usually via conversion to nitrites.

OECD objectives To formulate, coordinate, and promote policies for economic growth and stability and expand multilateral trade on a non-discriminatory basis; to coordinate Third World aid.

Open-access resource A material resource with no property right held by any individual or entity.

Ozone An unstable gas in which three molecules of oxygen occur together (O_3). Ozone is a greenhouse gas. In the atmosphere, ozone occurs at two different altitudes. Low-altitude tropospheric ozone is a form of air pollution (part of smog) produced by emissions from automobiles and trucks. High in the atmosphere a thin layer of stratospheric ozone is naturally created by sunlight. This ozone layer shields Earth from dangerous (cancer-causing) ultraviolet radiation from the Sun. Chlorine gas from chlorofluorocarbons speeds the breakdown of ozone in the ozone layer. Ozone depletion is the loss or destruction of the stratospheric ozone layer; this is usually done by the catalytic actions of compounds containing chlorine, fluorine, and/or bromine.

Ozone hole The Antarctic ozone hole was first detected in 1985 and is measured by a vertical column of ozone in the atmosphere in *Dobson units*. The hole appears every spring in the Southern Hemisphere (August to October) before disappearing during the summer months (December/January). This decline in total ozone concentration in the atmosphere leads to a consequent rise in the penetration of ultraviolet radiation, which among other effects can increase incidences of skin cancer. It was realized that this hole was being created by manmade substances such as CFCs. This led to a rapid response in the form of the Montreal Protocol. However, owing to the long lifetimes of CFCs the ozone layer is not expected to recover fully for at least half a century.

Ozone layer The ozone in the stratosphere is very diffuse, occupying a region many kilometers in thickness, but is conventionally described as a layer to aid in understanding.

Pareto improvement A reallocation of resources that leads to improving welfare of some without worsening the welfare of others; named after Vilfredo Pareto (1848–1923).

Pareto optimum This is claimed to have been attained by an economy when resources and output cannot be reallocated in a Pareto improvement sense.

Paris Club The forum, mostly comprising some of the OECD (Organization for Economic Cooperation and Development) member countries, where creditor countries negotiate with borrower countries over debt levels and rescheduling aspects.

Perfluorocarbons (PFCs) A group of human-made chlorine composed of carbon and fluorine only: CF_4 and C_2F_6. Chemicals, specifically C_2F_6 (along with hydrofluorocarbons), were introduced as alternatives to ozone-depleting substances. In addition, they emit by-products of industrial processes and are also used in manufacturing. PFCs do not harm the stratospheric ozone layer, but they are powerful greenhouse gases.

Phenology The branch of science dealing with the relationship between climate and periodic biological phenomena related to or influenced by climatic factors, such as bird migration or plant flowering.

Phytoplankton The portion of the plankton community made up of tiny plants like algae and diatoms.

Pigouvian taxes These taxes were devised by Arthur C. Pigou in the 1930s; they refer to taxes or equivalent penalties and charges assessed as required to correct for externalities caused by economic agents or by producers-polluters.

Polluter Pays Principle This was first made official by the OECD in 1975 and represents an allocation of property rights on the environmental assets to consumers, making producer-polluters pay the difference between the social costs and private costs of providing goods and services.

Polychlorinated biphenyls (PCBs) The compounds resulting from the reaction of chlorine with biphenyl; these are generally used as lubricants, in paints and in packaging materials, and have been toxic to marine life—particularly fish.

Prisoner's dilemma This arises out of lack of cooperation or coordination in the confession strategies of the co-partner of two offenders. If both deny their crime, they could be better off. If either of the two denies but the other confesses, both get different punishments, but if both confess, they are much worse off.

Public goods Goods that exhibit both consumption indivisibilities and nonexcludability, combining both features, respectively: once the resource is provided, even those who do not pay for it cannot be excluded from the benefits they confer; one person's consumption of the good does not diminish the amount available for others.

Radiative forcing   This is defined as changes to the energy equilibrium of the atmospheric system of planet Earth following a change, for example, in the concentration of CO_2 or release of solar energy. This is measured as energy in watts per square meter (w/m^2).

Rental   Used to describe profits earned by an asset over a particular time period. Used interchangeably with "(net) receipts."

Sequester   To remove or segregate. Activities, such as planting trees, remove carbon dioxide from the atmosphere, and thus sequester carbon dioxide.

Sink   A reservoir of any medium that assimilates or absorbs pollutants, and thus it takes up or removes a pollutant from a part of the atmospheric cycle. Soil and trees tend to act as natural sinks. For example, the oceans absorb about 50 percent of the carbon dioxide released into the atmosphere. Oceans and forests thus function as carbon dioxide sinks.

Source   Any process or reservoir that supplies a specified greenhouse gas or other environmental goods.

Stratosphere   The upper layer of Earth's atmosphere, above about 7 miles.

Trace gas   A constituent of the atmosphere. Important trace gases contributing to the greenhouse effect include water vapor, CO_2, ozone, and other greenhouse gases.

Transaction costs   The totality of costs (not including market prices of sale/purchase) of exchanging and enforcing property rights or of undertaking market/nonmarket transactions.

Troposphere   The lowest layer of the atmosphere, extending upward to about 7 miles from Earth's surface.

Tropospheric ozone (O_3)   Ozone located in the troposphere that plays a significant role in the greenhouse effect and urban smog.

Tropospheric ozone precursor   Gases that influence how ozone is created and destroyed in the atmosphere gases include carbon monoxide (CO), nitrogen oxides (NO_x), and nonmethane volatile organic compounds (NMVOC).

Ultraviolet (UV) radiation Electromagnetic radiation of higher frequencies and shorter wavelength than visible light. It is divided into three regions based on wavelength: UV-A, UV-B, and UV-C. With the discovery of Earth's ozone hole, it was realized that there would be an increase in the penetration of UV-B radiation with possible adverse effects being an increase in skin cancer or related health problems.

Willingness-to-pay (WTP) This is a subjective assessment of the respondent's preparedness to pay for specific goods or services that are not necessarily transacted in the marketplace.

Web Site Addresses

An Illustrative List

Given below is a sample of the Web sites for exploring more details on various themes; many others can be found on the links provided on several of the major sites. All these addresses are under hypertext transfer protocol (in simple terms this means that they all start with the initial part of the Web site address as http://). Many important nongovernmental organizations are not listed here, but they can be found on links such as the UN or the International Institute of Sustainable Development (IISD). It is possible that some of the listed Web sites undergo transformations from time to time.

Important International Sites

United Nations
  www.un.org

This has several links to the UN organizations involved in development and environment issues. However, a few direct links may also be useful. These are listed below.

Intergovernmental Panel on Climate Change (IPCC)
  ipcc-ddc.cru.uea.ac.uk/

This site serves as the data distribution center for the IPCC, with frequent updates.

United Nations Environment Programme (UNEP)
  www.unep.ch

This site provides a few additional clues to the information bases, as well as a few modeling exercises where the UNEP coordinates some efforts.

UN Department of Policy Coordination and Sustainable Development
   www.un.org/dpcsd

This site of the UN Secretariat office provides a few details of its coordinating activities, especially those of the UN Commission on Sustainable Development, and of a few conventions and conferences. Emerging trends and issues of population can be found at this site.

World Health Organization (WHO)
   www.who.org

This site provides details on activities and public health issues in connection with global climate changes and the role of poverty.

UN Framework Convention on Climate Change
   www.unfccc.de

This Coordinating Secretariat's site includes details of the policies on greenhouse gases and conclusions of the Conference of Parties (COP), including the Kyoto Protocol and other agreements preceding and succeeding the Protocol.

World Trade Organization
   www.wto.org

This site provides details of global trade and its liberalization, with a rather limited role of environmental issues.

World Bank
   www.worldbank.org

This site includes several important features on development focus, poverty, and environmental issues. An important site of the Environmentally Sustainable Development (ESD) Vice Presidency of the World Bank provides more details of the environmental features and operations of the bank. This site is accessible at the address: www-esd.worldbank.org Another site within the World Bank system deals with industrial pollution policy and regulation aspects: www.worldbank.org/nipr

OECD
www.oecd.org

The OECD Secretariat in Paris undertook several significant studies of global warming, and some of the details can be seen on this site.

Important Sites in the United States

U.S. Department of Energy
www.eia.doe.gov/oiaf

This site provides considerable data regarding pollution emissions, with special reference to energy sources.

Oak Ridge National Laboratories (ORNL) Environmental Science Division
www.ornl.gov

Specifically, this site offers current data on the emissions of carbon dioxide from various sources: cdiac.esd.ornl.gov/ndps/ndp030.html

U.S. Environmental Protection Agency (USEPA)
www.epa.gov

This site is useful to gauge the operational activities as well as new proposals like market-based instruments for pollution control, and environmental management. The USEPA also devotes links to global warming issues at www.epa.gov/globalwarming/index.text.html

U.S. Geological Survey (USGS) Global Information Database (GRID)
grid2.cr.usgs.gov

National Aeronautics and Space Administration (NASA)
daac.gsfc.nasa.gov/

This is a very important site of the Distributed Data Archive Center of the Goddard Space Flight Center (NASA) for scientific information, and it has several useful link sites.

National Climatic Data Center
www.ncdc.noaa.gov

Research/Institutional/Media Sites

The Beijer Institute of the Royal Swedish Academy of Sciences
www.beijer.kva.se

This site of an international institute of ecological economics, lists various research programs and documents.

Consortium for International Earth Science Information Network (CIESIN)
Information: www.ciesin.org/kiosk/subindex.htmlv
Ozone updates: sedac.ciesin.org/ozone

These provide a wide array of sources of information, state of the ozone layer, and links on studies and documents on environmental themes.

CNN Earth Main Page
cnn.com/EARTH

Provides current information on several environmental features.

International Environment Resources
www.contact.org/environs.htm

This is useful for various links to other relevant sites on environmental issues.

Second Nature
www.2nature.org

This site has links to several useful sites, including the following one, which provides details of interdisciplinary relevant educational materials: www.2nature.org/programs/starfish/sfhome.nsf

International Institute of Sustainable Development (IISD)
www.iisd.ca/linkages

World Resources Institute
www.wri.org

Carnegie Mellon University
www.envinst.cmu.edu

University of Oregon
gladstne.uoregon.edu/eaglej

This site provides a detailed introduction to the mechanics of global warming and link pages.

Center for Environmentally Responsible Economics (CERES)
www.cerc.wvu.edu/ceres/ceres_index.html

This includes the CERES Global Knowledge Network information.

The Worldwatch Institute
www.worldwatch.org

Known for a few important publications, including the annual State of the World Report; the institute undertakes research work into global warming, among other related issues.

Resources for the Future
www.rff.org

Econet
www.econet.apc.org/econet

This site provides comprehensive information on several environmental upkeep measures and links to several sites of interest.

World Conservation Union/International Union for the Conservation of Nature (IUCN)
www.iucn.ch

This is a vast network of governmental, multilateral, and nongovernmental institutions with considerable influence on global policies and their implementation.

Stockholm Environmental Institute
www.tellus.com

The Stockholm Institute has four locations and a few interesting study programs and publications.

EnviroLink Network

This is a significant environmental database regarding institutions, products, and links.

International Institute for Sustainable Development (IISD)
   iisd1.iisd.ca

This site has much useful information and offers excellent links to other related sites.

International Institute of Applied Systems Analysis
   www.iiasa.ac.at

Sites with Functional Applications

Pollution Prevention

The USEPA Office of Pollution Prevention Program
   www.epa.gov/docs/GCDOAR/OAR-APPD.html

American Institute for Pollution Prevention
   es.inel.gov/aipp

Recycling
   www.grn.com/grn

This site is maintained by the Global Recycling Network.

   www.epa.gov/epaoswer/wastewise.html

This is a USEPA web site dealing with waste management.

Ozone
   www.epa.gov/ozone

This site is a part of the USEPA information and provides links regarding the ozone layer.

Design and Manufacturing
   www.me.berkeley.edu/green/cgdm.html

This is a University of California Center for Green Design and Manufacturing Web site.

Environmental Law
   www.asil.org

This is the site for the American Society of International Law, but it provides other links as well.

The following site has several useful links to environmental law: www.law.indiana.edu/law/v-lib/lawindex.html. This is located on the Indiana University site dealing with international environmental law.

Standards (ISO14000)
   www.ISO14000.com

Environmental Groups and NGOs

The Earth Pledge Foundation
   www.earthpledge.org

Founded to promote the UN Pledge at the Earth Summit; provides references to environmental literature and select activities.

Environmental Defense Fund
   www.edf.org

Natural Resources Defense Council (NRDC)
   www.nrdc.org

World Conservation Monitoring Centre
   www.wcmc.org.uk

Friends of the Earth International
   www.foe.co.uk

Greenpeace International
   www.greenpeace.org

World Wildlife Fund (World Wide Fund for Nature International)
   www.panda.org

Index

Adaptation, 15, 58, 66, 94, 105, 133, 151, 166, 169, 173
Aerosols, 13, 21, 27, 28, 36, 39, 41, 46, 48, 49, 110, 174
Albedo, 7, 48, 174
Anthropogenic, 24, 94, 175
  contributions, 9, 31, 46
  factors, 7, 11, 35
  influences, 4, 7, 13, 29, 125
Anticommons, 33
Arrhenius, Svante, 7, 8, 22

Becker, Gary, 75, 80
Berlin Mandate, 175
Biodiversity, 9, 14, 25, 31, 112, 131, 176
Biogeochemical cycles, 5, 9, 131
Brundtland Report, 59

Carbon cycle 28, 177
Carbon sequestration, 9, 12, 27–29, 36, 131, 132, 177
Chlorofluorocarbons (CFCs), 11, 13, 42–46, 178
Civilization, 5, 6
Clean development mechanism (CDM), 126, 128, 134, 140, 157, 160, 161
Climatic feedback, 13, 15, 16, 178
Coase, Ronald, 130
Commensurability, 70, 76
Common property, 9, 10, 31, 33, 131

Contestable market, 164, 178
Cost-benefit analysis (CBA), 66, 67, 69, 70–73, 76, 80
Cost effective, 18, 40, 50, 51, 52, 56, 92, 95, 102, 125, 129, 133, 134, 143, 160, 163, 165, 167, 169
Cost-effective risk aversion (CERA), 50, 125
Contingent valuation (CV), 68, 70, 71, 178

Deforestation, 6, 12, 29, 30, 32, 35, 49, 131, 132
Desertification, 6
Discount function, 15, 40, 41, 70, 79, 81–85, 95
  rates, 15, 40, 71–73, 75, 76, 78, 80–84, 99, 100, 109, 169
Discounting, 39–41, 52, 57, 72, 73, 75, 77, 79, 80, 81, 84, 85, 95, 109
Discontinuities, 6, 119

Earth Summit, 8, 23, 51
Ecosystem, 14, 15, 24, 25, 27, 29, 58, 60, 65, 67, 69, 72, 77, 94, 104, 131, 165, 171, 179
Ecotaxes, 57, 87, 88, 95, 102
El Niño, 24, 179
Emissions trading, 31, 117, 126, 128–132, 157

Environmental accounting, 65, 92, 93
Externalities, 26, 57, 66, 67, 84, 93,
    101, 111, 130, 133, 135, 155, 180
Existence value, 68, 69

Feedback, 17, 27, 45, 66, 92, 94, 105,
    131, 170, 180
  biogeophysical, 25
Flux, 8, 13, 46
Fourier, Joseph, 7
Free-access resources, 10
Free-rider, 9, 10, 26, 31–33, 181

Geological time, 4, 6
Global commons, 9, 11, 17, 31, 32, 34,
    70, 95, 170
Global warming potential (GWP), 12, 14–
    16, 37–41, 46, 104, 106–110, 115
Greenhouse effect (GE), 7, 15–17, 21,
    22, 24, 26, 28, 35, 37, 41, 45, 103,
    104, 107, 110, 111, 119, 124
  enhanced, 7, 35, 179
Greenhouse gases (GHGs), 4, 9, 11, 13,
    16, 17, 18, 21, 23, 26–29, 35–37,
    41, 49, 52, 57, 76, 81, 87, 94, 103,
    104, 106, 107, 110, 113, 115, 116,
    124–127, 132–134, 137, 139, 140,
    143, 152, 156–160, 166, 181

Human influence, 9, 24, 27

Intergovernmental Panel on Climate
    Change (IPCC), 8, 9, 18, 23, 24,
    27, 30, 50, 81, 83, 155, 156,
Irreversible, 6, 7, 13, 14, 22, 24, 51, 58,
    61, 104, 121, 142

Joint implementation, (JI) 127, 128,
    140, 157, 159

Kyoto Protocol, 30, 126, 127, 132, 145,
    156–158, 160, 165, 166

Land use change, 9, 14, 28, 30, 31, 131,
    148

Land use change and forestry sector
    (LUCF), 156

Marginality principle, 103
Market-based instruments, 18, 167
Marsh, George Perkins, 6
Montreal Protocol, 34, 44, 46, 47, 136–
    138, 145, 162, 183
Morbidity and mortality, 16, 112, 113

Nonlinear
  interactions, 6
  relationships, 42, 113
Net present value (NPV), 71, 109,
New Golden Green Rule, 84, 86, 87
North, Douglass, 171
North-South, 134, 135, 139, 160

Optimal development, 65
Option value, 68, 69, 80
Ozone, 41, 42, 45, 46, 184
  depletion, 44, 47, 112
  factor, 21
  hole, 184
  layer, 9, 31, 41, 43, 47, 184
  problem, 12

Polluter Pays Principle, (PPP) 88, 167,
    171, 185
Population, 7, 63, 64, 79, 111
Precautionary Principle (PP), 50–52, 83,
    102, 162, 167, 171
Property rights, 10, 31, 33, 104, 130,
    155, 168
Public goods, 9, 10, 44, 68, 185

Quantified Emissions Limitation
    Reduction Objectives (QELROs),
    126

Radiative forcing, 27, 29, 30, 37, 39,
    106, 110, 186
Rawls, John, 59
Recursive utility, 73, 74, 80
Regulatory instruments, 167

Resilience, 14, 57, 58, 60, 61, 65, 72, 94, 104, 121

Sequestration of carbon, *see* Carbon sequestration
Shadow prices, 61, 62, 71, 72, 74, 79, 117
Sink, 45, 186
  capacity, 7, 10, 12, 29, 32, 33, 67, 72, 94, 105
Social discount rate (SDR), 78, 79
Social rate of time preference (SRTP), 79–81, 83
Solow, Robert, 62, 77, 79, 80, 116
Source and sink, 7, 9, 28–30, 60, 64, 67, 72, 157
Subsidies, 131
Sustainable development, 6, 11, 34, 57–62, 65, 72, 77, 84, 93, 94, 125, 145, 160, 163, 166, 168, 171, 172

Threshold limits, 25, 33, 121
Time-consistency, 72, 74
Time preference, 75, 79, 80, 82, 104
Total economic value (TEV), 68
"Tragedy of the commons," 10, 11, 32, 33, 170
Transaction costs, 15, 18, 56, 66, 67, 91, 94, 102, 128, 130, 133, 140, 167, 170, 171, 186

UN Framework Convention for Climate Change (UNFCCC), 8, 10, 23, 24, 126, 134–136, 142, 145, 156, 157, 159, 166, 171

Willingness-to-pay (WTP), 68, 70, 187

About the Author

The author has about twenty-seven years of experience in teaching, research, consulting, and top-level management in varied institutional settings. He has worked at Harvard and Rutgers Universities and has published about 40 papers; his other books include *Sustainable Development: Economics and Policy*, *World Trade Organization and the Environment*, and *The Economics of Transaction Costs*. The author can be reached by e-mail at pkrao@att.net.